HOLIDAY-MA
GUIDE T
SOUTH AFRICA

HOLIDAY-MAKER'S GUIDE TO SOUTH AFRICA

TIM O'HAGAN

SOUTHERN
BOOK PUBLISHERS

To Annalé, Suzanne, Anya-Lee, Caitlin
and the moon and the stars

ISBN 1 86812 590 4

First edition, first impression 1995

Published by
Southern Book Publishers (Pty) Ltd
PO Box 3103, Halfway House 1685

While the author and publisher have endeavoured to verify all facts,
they will not be held responsible for any inconvenience that may
result from possible inaccuracies in this book.

Designed by Wim Reinders & Associates, Cape Town
Set in Times 10/12 pt by Wouter Reinders, Cape Town
Reproduction by Hirt & Carter, Cape Town
Printed and bound by National Book Printers,
Drukkery Street, Goodwood, Western Cape

ACKNOWLEDGEMENTS

For the cups of coffee at 2am, the constant encouragement and the endless research I would like to thank my family. To my friends TV Bulpin, Peter Ribton and Kevin Shenton for their help and support, a special thank you.

I would also like to thank:

Petrus and Anelma Bosman, who showed me the secret places of the San and the burial grounds of the dinosaurs;

Franz Rykovitch, who taught me how to sleep with the lions;

The dozens of publicity associations, tourism organisations, game reserve administrators and safari operators from Messina to Matjiesfontein, who contributed to the factual information in this book. Thank you to all of them, but especially to the Captour Visitors' Information Bureau, the South African Tourism Board, Durban Unlimited, the National Parks Board, the Natal Parks Board, the Waterfront Information Centre, the Tourist Rendezvous Travel Centre in Pretoria, the Stellenbosch Wine Route Office and the Paarl Wine Route Publicity Association.

Last but not least, thanks to Kate Rogan of Southern Book Publishers, and to Mary Lennox for preparing the index.

Contents

STELLENBOSCH AND THE WINELANDS 37

THE WEST COAST, NAMAQUALAND AND NORTHERN CAPE 51

THE SOUTHERN CAPE 67

THE GARDEN ROUTE AND LITTLE KAROO 78

THE EASTERN CAPE 96

DURBAN, THE KWAZULU/NATAL COAST AND ZULULAND 114

THE KWAZULU/NATAL INTERIOR AND DRAKENSBERG 135

GAUTENG AND THE NORTH-WEST PROVINCE 153

THE EASTERN AND NORTHERN TRANSVAAL 175

A-Z SUMMARY OF USEFUL HINTS AND PRACTICAL INFORMATION 193

INDEX 202

INTRODUCTION

Like a debutante on the world's stage, South Africa has leapt from the obscurity of her troubled past into the spotlight of world acclaim. Once the outlawed polecat of the community of nations, the country is now a major concourse for princes, presidents and politicians.

Entrepreneurs, industrialists, sportsmen and rock musicians are streaming in, intent on investing in the huge resources and talent the country has to offer.

Perhaps more important, the post-apartheid years are witnessing an unprecedented surge in tourism, as travellers arrive to savour the country's extraordinary natural wonders, scenic delights and huge populations of game.

From the ivory sands of the Cape Peninsula to the rustic bush camps of the Kruger National Park; from the mystic depths of the Tsitsikamma Forests to the cascade-drenched slopes of the southern Drakensberg, new visitors are wondering why it took so long for them to get here.

This guide aims to show you the way – taking the adventurer's route to the places that will make your trip the holiday of a lifetime.

The entire country, its cities, myriad scenic delights, game parks, trails and natural treasures are covered in three sections. South Africa – the Rainbow Nation introduces you to the land, the people, the history, climate and vegetation, the winds of change, the fauna and flora and the new political order.

The main section, starting with Cape Town and the Peninsula, takes you through the entire country, showing you where to go, what to see and do, how to get there and where to stay within each region. Special "At a glance" boxes detail tours and excursions, outdoor adventures, main attractions, shopping opportunities, festivals and important annual events.

Whether you'd like to watch giraffes in silhouette against the setting sun, stroll along the surfline of some distant shore, or sample some of the world's finest cultivars among the vineyards of the Cape's wine routes, this book will show you the way. And if you're unfamiliar with the ins and outs of South African customs, the A-Z Summary of Useful Hints and Practical Information gives you essential tips to make your stay quite unforgettable.

The author

SOUTH AFRICA – THE RAINBOW NATION

On 10 May 1994 Nelson Rolihlahla Mandela stood beneath the imposing towers of the Union Buildings in Pretoria to take the oath of office as the country's first democratically elected president.

It was an emotional moment for hundreds of statesmen and billions of TV viewers around the world, as he announced the birth of a new South Africa – the Rainbow Nation, as it had recently come to be called.

As President Mandela's voice boomed across the public address system, it seemed that South Africa had suddenly taken on a new identity, a new spirit. Indeed, South Africa was free.

Two weeks earlier, Mr Mandela's African National Congress had swept into power, collecting 62,6 per cent of the nearly 20 million votes counted in South Africa's first democratic elections.

To the world witnessing the inauguration on that historic day, the event was nothing short of a miracle. It was the climax of an extraordinary sequence of events that brought South Africa back from the verge of anarchy and ruin to the promise of peace, stability and hope.

As the spectre of apartheid was finally laid to rest, the doors of the world opened wide to South Africa. For the first time since her expulsion from the world body in 1974, the Republic took an honourable seat in the General Assembly of the United Nations. Foreign investment poured in, and some 150 foreign companies set up new businesses around the country. International sports ties were reinstated. South Africa hosted the World Cup rugby tournament in May 1995 and became a leading contender to host the Olympic Games in 2004. Sanctions were ended, air and sea links with the rest of the world were re-established, and the internal conflicts of the past started to wane.

Abroad, in England and America, in Holland, Belgium and France, in Australia, New Zealand and the Pacific, travellers started considering a new destination. Today, with most of the political conflicts of the past behind her, South Africa stands to become one of the world's premier tourist spots. The country's scenic marvels, game reserves, diversity of animal and plant life, natural resources and cosmopolitan community combine to make it an irresistible place for the holiday of a lifetime.

A world in one country

South Africa lies at the southern end of the brooding continent of Africa, flanked by the vast expanse of the Indian and Atlantic oceans.

Crucible of historic events, cradle of man, haven of animal and plant life, treasure-chest of dazzling mineral wealth, this land is quite literally a world in one country – its natural splendour unrivalled anywhere else on earth.

Larger than western Germany, Holland, Belgium, France and Italy combined, South Africa occupies 1 220 430 sq km, its huge land surface stretching 2 000 km, from Cape Agulhas in the south to the Limpopo River in the north, and 1 500 km from Namaqualand in the west to subtropical KwaZulu/Natal in the east.

The coastline, washed by the Atlantic in the west and the Indian Ocean in the east, zigzags some 3 000 km, from Alexander Bay, around Cape Point, and up to South Africa's border with Mozambique.

Along the west coast, from Cape Town to the border of Namibia, fishing hamlets and tiny holiday resorts nestle against the fringes of an icy sea, in a region of stark, isolated beauty. Along the eastern coast, where the warm Agulhas Current pushes 1 760 km southward towards Cape Town, it's holiday time throughout the year as sizzling beaches and bustling resorts such as Durban, Umhlanga Rocks, Margate and Amanzimtoti invite thousands of sun-seekers to their tranquil shores.

Wherever you go in South Africa, you'll be astounded by its rich diversity. From the hectic gaming tables of coastal casino hotels, to the tranquil isolation of the Kalahari's sun-baked dunes, you'll find the world in one country. In the south, along the Garden Route, great forests of giant yellowwood trees surge skyward to form canopies of green as far as the eye can see. In the Eastern Transvaal, near old prospecting towns built on gold, the jagged peaks of the Drakensberg plummet precipitously to the lowveld – that part of wild Africa that entranced men like Hemingway and Sir Percy Fitzpatrick. Here, in the isolation of the bushveld, are some of the world's most diverse and exciting game parks and nature reserves, the largest of which is the Kruger National Park, home of hundreds of species of animal. Along the KwaZulu/Natal coast, and the Eastern Cape's Wild Coast, vervet monkeys dart beneath the cover of ilala palms and tangled subtropical bush. And in the southwestern corner of the subcontinent, the graceful monolith of Table Mountain towers serenely above what Sir Francis Drake described as "the Fairest Cape in the whole circumference of the earth". At its heart is the exciting, beautiful city of Cape Town – South Africa's own Tavern of the Seas.

The new South Africa

There has been a radical transformation of the geographic boundaries of the old apartheid-style South Africa. South Africa formerly consisted of four provinces, the Transvaal, Natal, Orange Free State and the Cape Province. In addition, under National Party rule, the country was fragmented into numerous parcels of land, known as black independent states or homelands. The concept of homelands came from the grand masters of apartheid to enforce their racist doctrine, and it involved the forced removal of millions of people.

These states, which included Transkei, Ciskei, Venda and Bophuthatswana, were "granted independence" under apartheid rule, but no country in the world recognised them as independent nations.

Under the new constitution all the homelands have been scrapped, and the maps have been redrawn. Instead of four provinces, there are now nine, incorporating all the areas previously set aside as "homelands". The new provinces are the Western Cape, the Northern Cape, the Eastern Cape, North-West, Free State, KwaZulu/Natal, Eastern Transvaal, Northern Transvaal and Gauteng. Gauteng was known previously as PWV Province, PWV being an acronym for Pretoria, Witwatersrand and Vereeniging. The province includes South Africa's largest and wealthiest city, Johannesburg.

The land

Most of South Africa's interior rests on a vast, semicircular plateau – an extension of the Great African Plateau that starts in the Sahara Desert, some 5 000 km to the north. This plateau rises abruptly from the coastal terrace around it, so that if you're driving inland from the coast for more than 250 km, you'll most certainly find yourself ascending one of the country's many beautiful mountain passes. The plateau's height, which varies from a relatively low 900 m in the Kalahari to nearly 3,5 km in parts of Lesotho, has a distinct effect on climate and vegetation.

On the high ground the air is crisper, thinner and colder in winter than at the coast; the rain falls mainly in summer, and the vegetation changes dramatically – from the forested hills and valleys of the coast to undulating grassy plains, scattered with low ridges.

The strip of land between the plateau and the sea, known as the marginal zone, is fairly narrow – 80-240 km wide in the east and south, and 60-80 km wide in the west, but it contains a variety of different landscapes, from the floral splendour of the Cape Fold Mountains to the vast open spaces of the Little and Great Karoo, and the rolling hills of the eastern midlands.

On the plateau, the most conspicuous regions are the southern Kalahari, whose gravel plains and ochre sands span a large section of the Northern Cape, and the plains of the Upper Karoo and the highveld, which together form large parts of the Eastern Cape, Free State, North-West Province and Gauteng.

Towards the east, on the edge of the Eastern Transvaal lowveld, the jagged peaks of the Drakensberg form a massive and majestic rim to the Great Escarpment. In places more than 3 km from foot to crest, this chain of mountains runs southward in an unbroken necklace through KwaZulu/Natal, tapering off eventually to the south. The great wall of the KwaZulu/Natal Drakensberg, which reaches its highest points at the 3 299-m Mont-aux-Sources (the Mountain of Springs), Champagne

Castle (3 376 m) and Giant's Castle (3 313 m), is one of the enduring scenic wonders of the world.

This range – Drakensberg means literally "Dragons' Mountain" – was formed 150 million years ago, when South Africa was a great swampland, inhabited by monstrous land creatures. At this time, volcanic eruptions resulted in the greatest outpouring of basaltic lava the world has experienced.

When the eruptions ended, a sea of lava up to 1 500 m thick lay over a large portion of southern Africa. Over millions of years, the action of wind and water has carved deeply into the basalt roof, creating soaring pinnacles and peaks, deep valleys, ravines and gorges along the entire length of the Drakensberg.

Other, much older, imposing mountain ranges make up the rim of the Great Escarpment along the subcontinental divide. These include the Roggeveld and Nuweveld mountains of the Karoo and the Kamiesberg of Namaqualand. Along the Western and Eastern Cape coast, from the Hottentots-Holland Mountains through to the hinterland of the Tsitsikamma Forests, runs the Cape Fold Mountains, whose sister ranges survive today in the Argentine and in Antarctica. Born 300 million years ago, these magnificent mountains were thrust up through the earth's crust by the violent stretch and pull of its surface, when the supercontinent, Pangaea, started breaking up into the continents as we know them.

Today, the cobalt-blue peaks of the Cape Fold series, which include the western ranges of the Cederberg, Olifants River, Drakenstein and Groot Winterhoek mountains, and the more compacted hills of the Langeberg, Tsitsikamma and Swartberg in the east, form a majestic divide between the pristine wilderness of the Garden Route and the sun-baked, seemingly endless plains of the Great Karoo.

Imposing as the Cape Fold mountain massifs are, they do not match the age of the hard granite rocks (known as Sand River Gneiss) of the Northern Transvaal which, at more than 4 000 million years, are among the oldest rocks on earth.

Rivers of life
Only 25 per cent of South Africa's surface is nurtured by perennial rivers, and their total runoff amounts to just half that of the Zambezi, further north. The country's largest river, the Orange, runs almost the entire length of the interior plateau, and together with its main tributary, the Vaal, meets a large percentage of the country's domestic, industrial and agricultural water needs.

The Orange starts in the KwaZulu/Natal Drakensberg, and runs westwards for 2 250 km, disgorging itself in the Atlantic at Alexander Bay. On the way it feeds two of the largest of South Africa's storage dams, Lake Gariep in the Northern Cape and the Vanderkloof Dam, 140 km away. Later the Orange cascades over the scenically beautiful Augrabies Falls, near South Africa's border with Namibia, and then proceeds westward, flanked in places by an incongruous belt of green, through the desolate wasteland of the Northern Cape. The Vaal is actually longer than the Orange, but carries less water.

Apart from these two rivers, another dozen or so major rivers flow from the interior to the sea, some plummeting in a series of graceful waterfalls over the rim of the Drakensberg or slicing through breathtaking ravines in the Cape Fold Mountains.

History

About 250 million years ago, the interior plains of South Africa were one vast swampland, inhabited by grotesque mammal-like reptiles – among them *Rubidgea,* a short, flesh-eating animal, and the 6-m-long Red Bed dinosaur *Massospondylus.* For 50 million years these mammal-like reptiles flourished on the plains of the Karoo until, about 190 million years ago, great volcanic eruptions spilled lava across a large section of the subcontinent and put an end to their rapid evolution.

For nearly 200 million years southern Africa was unknown and uninhabited, a vast subcontinent that sheltered the surviving species of primitive animal life. Then, about one-and-a-half million years ago, a strange, man-like creature (*Australopithecus*), capable of using crude pointed tools, worked his way southwards from East Africa and became the first inhabitant of southern Africa who bore any resemblance to modern man. Through the aeons *Australopithecus* was succeeded by more developed ancestors of man such as *Homo habilis* and *Homo erectus*, who by one million years ago had learned how to make tools and hunt with them.

The later Stone Age, 40 000 years ago, saw the emergence of a brown-skinned nation of small, wiry people called the San or Bushmen, whose few remaining descendants survive today in the vast wilderness of the Kalahari.

The San, and a similar Later Stone Age group called the Khoikhoi, were probably the sole human inhabitants of South Africa when a more advanced group of Bantu pastoralists and cultivators moved into the region about 2 000 years ago.

It was only at the end of the 15th century that Portuguese navigators in flimsy caravels pioneered a sea route round the Cape, and in 1503, a Portuguese admiral named Antonio de Saldanha became the first European to climb to the top of Table Mountain.

In 1652, the first mate of the Dutch ship *Drommedaris,* three and a half months out of Texel, in Holland, sighted land at today's Cape Town. On board was Jan van Riebeeck. His mission was to establish a refreshment station at the Cape of Good Hope for the ships of the Dutch East India Company on their trade route to the East.

Van Riebeeck arrived with about 100 souls, built a fort near the sea, mounted exploratory expeditions into the interior, and established farms in the Paarl and Stellenbosch areas of the southwestern Cape. The Dutch occupation lasted nearly 150 years – until four British warships sailed into Simon's Bay near Cape Town and crushed the tiny Dutch garrison. The British occupation was to have a decisive effect on southern African politics until 1910, when South Africa became a single state by the Act of Union.

By the turn of the 19th century the Cape was populated by about 26 000 whites, 30 000 slaves and 20 000 Khoikhoi. The growing population resulted in a rapid expansion eastwards along the coast and into the interior. This was bolstered in 1820 when Britain shipped hundreds of immigrants into the Eastern Cape, to act as a buffer between the Xhosa tribes in the north and the colony in the south, and to give the Cape Colony a more "English" flavour. The eastward movement of these settlers and Cape Dutch frontiersmen came to a halt near the Great Fish River, where the Xhosa met them head-on in nine brutal frontier wars between 1779 and 1878.

While the frontier wars were raging in the east, a new group of itinerant adventurers, the Voortrekkers, was emerging further south. Disillusioned by the bureaucracy of British rule in the Cape, a group of Afrikaners set out in a series of dangerous – and tragic – journeys of exploration into the interior. Known collectively as the Great Trek, these journeys became pivotal events in South African history, and strongly influenced the culture and thinking of the Afrikaner nation.

The Great Trek started in 1834 at a time when the legendary Zulu king, Shaka, had given impetus to the *difaquane* – a series of bloody tribal conflicts that started in KwaZulu/Natal, and spread north and westwards as far as Zimbabwe, leaving the plains of South Africa's interior littered with the bones of victims.

It was ultimately Shaka's successor, Dingane, who wrought devastation among the ranks of the trekkers moving eastwards into KwaZulu/Natal. In February 1838, Piet Retief and his party of 100 men were massacred at Dingane's kraal, Umgungundlovu, in the Valley of a Thousand Hills. Another group of trekkers, led by Hans van Rensburg, was killed in the Limpopo Valley east of the Soutpansberg.

The Boers finally avenged their losses on 16 December 1838 by routing the Zulus at the Battle of Blood River. They then set up their first republic, which they named Natalia. When this state fell to the British four years later, it became the Crown Colony of Natal.

Disenchanted Boers moved back across the Drakensberg, while the British entrenched their position in Natal. Four decades later the British, fearing a resurrection of the Zulu nation, invaded their kingdom. In the ensuing conflict, the British lost 1 200 soldiers. The Zulus were also heavy losers: their territory was sliced up into 13 different chiefdoms. Today, the impact of British culture is very much evident in KwaZulu/Natal, more so than in any other province in South Africa.

Meanwhile, the Boers found a home for themselves in the grassy plains of the north, and formed two independent Afrikaans republics: the Republic of the Transvaal (later to become the South African Republic) in 1852, and the Republic of the Orange Free State two years later. When South Africa's provincial boundaries were redrawn in 1994, the Transvaal was officially scrapped and subdivided into what is now Gauteng, Northern Transvaal, Eastern Transvaal and North-West.

The discovery of gold and diamonds

Up until the middle of the 19th century, the subcontinent was thinly populated, with few roads, no railways and a handful of small towns separated by huge tracts of grassland, forest, semi-desert and bushveld, inhabited by elephants, lions, rhinoceroses and a variety of other animals.

Predictably, the discoveries of gold and diamonds were followed by a stampede of fortune seekers, speculators, traders and entrepreneurs, and a retinue of well-heeled immigrants and low-paid African workers. In the scramble for diamonds and gold, thousands of small claims diggers found the going rough, and formed partnerships to consolidate their claims. From these partnerships emerged the names of men who would change the course of South African history: Cecil John Rhodes, Barney Barnato and Alfred Beit. Suddenly, Kimberley and Johannesburg were among the world's fastest growing towns.

The huge influx of foreigners (known to the Afrikaners as *uitlanders*) and the increasing British interest in the region dismayed the president of the South African Republic, Paul Kruger. But he needed the money being generated by the *uitlanders*, so he tolerated their presence, but denied most of them and all their black workers political rights.

However, mounting pressure for more political rights by the *uitlanders*, imperial expansion and Britain's desire to avenge an earlier defeat by the Boers at Majuba Hill, led to the outbreak of the Anglo-Boer War (also known as the South African War) in 1899.

After two-and-a-half years of savage fighting, the Boers surrendered, and at the Peace of Vereeniging the republics which they had held so dear became British colonies.

For a variety of reasons, the Boer War was to have an indelible effect on the attitudes of the Afrikaner nation in the ensuing years.

There was – and still is in some quarters – outrage at the huge toll the war took on Boer lives: 28 000 Boers, most of them women and children, died from illness and unsanitary conditions during the war, many of them in British concentration camps.

Lord Kitchener's scorched earth policy saw to the devastation of hundreds of farms and the summary evacuation of their inhabitants.

Innocently caught up in the struggle between white nations, 14 000 black people became victims of the war.

In 1910, unification of the Cape, Transvaal, Orange Free State and Natal colonies came about through the South Africa Act (the Act of Union). An outstanding guerilla general of the Boer War, Louis Botha, became the country's first Prime Minister. The Westminster system of government was adopted, but significantly, black people were excluded from the democratic process.

The birth of black resistance

The years between the establishment of union in 1910 and the present day have been epochal for South Africa, witnessing first the rise of white dominance over blacks, and the entrenchment of this dominance through apartheid, and then the emergence of black resistance, international outrage and finally the dismantling of apartheid, and the election of an ANC government in 1994.

Black people did not believe the constitution of the Union gave them a meaningful say in running the country, so, in 1912, the South African Native National Congress, later named the African National Congress, was formed to work for African unity and the furtherance of political rights.

But in spite of this new body, conditions for black people deteriorated, and in 1923 legislation was passed limiting the movement of blacks within the country, and empowering local authorities to move or "resettle" them from one area to another. The crunch came in 1936, when the government withdrew the franchise from blacks in the Cape Province.

Although the ANC had started out as an organisation dedicated to achieving its ends through peaceful means, many within the ANC started realising that conciliatory gestures were having no impact on the ongoing repression and hardships handed out in the name of apartheid.

A Youth League was formed by a new generation of hardliners – men such as Oliver Tambo, Walter Sisulu, Govan Mbeki and Nelson Mandela – and they started campaigning vociferously for a better deal for blacks.

When the National Party came to power in 1948, the scene was set for an era of repression, black militancy and counter repression. During this time discriminatory laws were introduced, scores of black people were banned under the Suppression of Communism Act, and between 1956-59 the ANC vented its anger in a series of countrywide riots. On 21 March 1960, a nationwide campaign against the compulsory carrying of passes culminated in the tragedy of Sharpeville, in which 69 people were killed and 178 wounded in a confrontation between civilians and police.

The same year the African National Congress was banned, and black resistance went underground.

Late in 1960 the white electorate voted to cut its ties with the British Commonwealth, and the following year South Africa became a republic.

On 3 December 1963, Nelson Mandela, commander-in-chief of the African National Congress' military wing, Umkhonto we Sizwe (Spear of the Nation), stood in the dock in Pretoria's Palace of Justice, charged with sabotage. Pleading not guilty to the charge, Mandela told the court, "The government should be in the dock, not me."

As Mandela was being sentenced to life imprisonment in what was widely known as the Rivonia Trial, the grand architect of apartheid, Dr Hendrik Verwoerd, held on tightly to the reins of government.

Just three years later, on 6 September 1966, he was killed by an assassin's knife

8

in the Houses of Parliament in Cape Town. The assassin was a Greek national, Dmitri Tsafendas, who himself was sentenced to death (later commuted to life imprisonment). Ironically, just two months after Mandela's inauguration as President in May 1994, Tsafendas was released into the care of a mental institution.

After Verwoerd's death, South Africa's isolation by the rest of the world continued to be enforced. Sanctions were introduced, economic and cultural boycotts were enacted and sporting ties were cut.

At home, black discontent surfaced publicly in 1976, in a spate of civil unrest that saw buildings, schools, shops and houses go up in flames in black townships across the country.

Winds of change

In 1983 the new Prime Minister, PW Botha, instead of trying to remove apartheid, actually reinforced it. But the winds of change had already gathered momentum. Several large black trade unions came into being, a broad, multiracial democratic front was formed across South Africa, and the ANC was mobilising solid international support. Then, in 1989, a National Party ministerial rebellion put Botha out of power and brought in a man regarded as one of the prime movers in dismantling apartheid – FW de Klerk, Transvaal leader of the National Party.

In 1990 De Klerk undertook to abolish apartheid, and promised sweeping reforms. One of his early moves as the new State President was to release Mandela from his long incarceration. After Mandela's release, negotiations between the two leaders led to an itinerary of reform pending the establishment of an interim government. De Klerk's programme of reform was endorsed by 70 per cent of South Africa's whites in a whites-only referendum held in March 1992.

In 1993 Mandela and De Klerk were joint recipients of the Nobel Peace Prize, and shared *Time* magazine's nomination as Men of the Year.

South Africa was clearly set on an irreversible road to democracy. Largely through the joint efforts of Mandela and De Klerk, and ably assisted by their constitutional negotiators at the multi-party negotiating process at Kempton Park, Cyril Ramaphosa and Roelf Meyer, gradual consensus emerged and a date, 27 April 1994, was set for the country's first democratic elections.

More than 20 million people went to the polls on the three days allocated to the general election. The African National Congress received 62,6 per cent of the vote, FW de Klerk's National Party 20,4 per cent, Mangosuthu Buthelezi's Inkatha Freedom Party 10,5 per cent, the conservative Freedom Front 2,2 per cent, the Democratic Party 1,7 per cent, the Pan Africanist Congress 1,2 per cent and other parties 1,4 per cent. Elected as Deputy Presidents to President Mandela's Government of National Unity were FW de Klerk and Thabo Mbeki, a rising star within the ranks of the African National Congress.

On that day many people recalled the words Mandela had spoken 30 years before at the Rivonia trial:

"During my lifetime I have dedicated myself to this struggle of the African people. I have fought against white domination, and I have fought against black domination. I have cherished the ideal of a democratic and free society in which all persons live together in harmony and with equal opportunities. It is an ideal which I hope to live for and to achieve. But if needs be, it is an ideal for which I am prepared to die."

The people
South Africa is a multi-ethnic melting pot of vastly differing cultures, brought together over hundreds and thousands of years by the spirit of exploration and discovery in man. Archaeological discoveries suggest that a hardy, nomadic community of hunter-gatherers known as the San (Bushmen), a race of yellow-skinned pastoralists called the Khoikhoi and various black tribes were well established in South Africa over 2 000 years ago – more than 15 centuries before the first whites arrived on the subcontinent.

After the Portuguese arrived in South Africa in 1488, the stage was set for a rapid influx of immigrants. Within four centuries – in addition to the indigenous black communities – the country was inhabited by British, Dutch, French, Malay, Indian, German, Spanish, Chinese, Japanese and Portuguese people. Today, more nations are represented in South Africa than in the Balkan Peninsula or the former Soviet Union.

In 1991, the total population of South Africa was estimated at 37 962 000, of whom 28 622 000 were African, 5 068 000 whites, 3 286 000 were people of mixed race descent (coloured) and 987 000 Asian.

The Zulus and Xhosas, descendants of the Nguni tribes that are believed to have come to South Africa from central Africa, form the majority of blacks in South Africa. The North Sothos, South Sothos, Tswanas, Shangaan-Tsongas and Swazis comprise most of the balance of the black community.

The whites in South Africa are descended mainly from the Dutch, British, French and German settlers who came to the country in the 17th and 19th centuries. More recently, immigrants have included the above nationalities, as well as Namibians, Zimbabweans, Mozambicans, Chinese and Portuguese. About half-a-million people of Portuguese descent have chosen South Africa as their home. Some 120 000 Jewish people reside here, of whom 70 000 live in Johannesburg. In language terms, Afrikaans-speaking South Africans outnumber their English-speaking counterparts 60-40.

Most of the 3,25 million coloured people in South Africa live in the Western Cape. A subgroup, the Cape Malays, numbering about 200 000, have chosen the Cape Peninsula as their home. Most of them live in Cape Town's Malay Quarter.

The Asian community's forebears arrived in 1860 to work in KwaZulu/Natal's sugar cane fields, and has since grown to become the fourth largest Asian community in the world, after India, Pakistan and Sri Lanka.

```
┌─── INFORMAL SETTLEMENTS ─────────────────────────────────────┐
```

INFORMAL SETTLEMENTS

The rapid urbanisation of South Africa has led to the emergence of large, informal residential areas on the perimeters of the major cities. These areas – usually large concentrations of makeshift houses or shacks – house an estimated seven million informal settlers or "squatters".

In an attempt to meet the needs of this growing army of squatters, the government of national unity is trying to allocate suitable sites and, where possible, provide basic services to meet domestic needs. If you are unfamiliar with South Africa, it is not advisable to enter squatter townships at all.

About 85 per cent of the country's Indians live in KwaZulu/Natal – mainly in and around Durban, and along KwaZulu/Natal's north coast.

The most densely populated part of South Africa is Gauteng, home to more than half the population. More than two million people live in the sprawling black township of Soweto, making it easily the largest human residential area in the country. Of the urban population, 80 per cent live in Gauteng and the other major urban areas around Durban, Pinetown and Pietermaritzburg, Port Elizabeth and Uitenhage, and Cape Town.

Climate

The tag "sunny South Africa" is well deserved, but "arid South Africa" would probably be more appropriate: the country's average annual rainfall is just 502 mm, against a world mean of 857 mm. One fifth of the country receives less than 200 mm, and it's so hot and dry in some areas – such as the northwestern Cape and the Kalahari – that several months often pass without one cloud appearing in the sky.

The average number of cloud-free hours a day varies throughout the country, from 7,5 to 9,4, compared with New York's 6,9, Rome's 6,4 and London's 3,8.

The cold Benguela Current, flowing northwards up the west coast, and the warm Agulhas Current, flowing down the east coast, have a considerable influence on the country's climate, causing the hot, arid conditions which prevail on the west coast and its interior, and the lush, well-watered and humid conditions that characterise the east in summer.

If you travel westwards from Durban, following an imaginary line to Alexander Bay on the west coast, the amount of rain that falls annually diminishes in relation to the distance travelled. While the KwaZulu/ Natal coastline and its hinterland gets 1 000 mm of rain a year, only 200 mm falls far to the west, and some areas are lucky to get more than 50 mm. And although Durban in the east, and Port Nolloth in the west lie on the same latitude, they differ by at least 6 °C in their mean annual temperatures.

Down in the southern coastal regions, the picture is quite different. Here northwest winter storms, with interludes of soaking drizzle, lash Cape Town, the Cape Peninsula and the southern Cape coast in winter, and snow often falls on the peaks of the mountain ranges, sending night-time temperatures plummeting to below zero.

The chilly, wet spells are sometimes broken by isolated days of hot, warm weather, ushered in by the northeast or "berg" winds of the interior.

The benign effect of the Cape's Mediterranean climate comes to the fore in summer with hot, often cloudless days that send people scurrying to the beach. With summer comes the most notorious of the Cape's climatic influences, the southeast wind, which varies from a gentle breeze cooling the scorching midsummer temperatures on Muizenberg beach, to a howling gale that hurls itself across the Cape Peninsula, from the Hottentots-Holland Mountains to Cape Point.

If you drive along the eastern seaboard from Cape Town to the KwaZulu/Natal north coast in summer, you will find the climate changing in stages from Mediterranean to subtropical, with a blend of the two climates along the Eastern Cape coast. The further north you travel, the wetter and more humid it gets.

In the interior, from the Northern and Eastern Transvaal through to Johannesburg, Pretoria, the North-West Province, and down to Beaufort West, the summers are also hot and wet, with frequent torrential downpours – and sometimes thunder, lightning, sudden squalls and hail – in the late afternoons. Winters, on the other hand, are virtually rainless, with crisp, sunny and clear days, and cool to cold nights. Many people prefer to visit the lowveld and its game parks, such as the Kruger National Park, in winter (May, June, July and August) because it is not so hot, and more animals tend to converge on the waterholes in the dry season.

The national parks and game reserves
There are at least 300 wildlife sanctuaries in South Africa, ranging from national and provincial parks to small private game reserves and marine reserves. The largest and most visited reserve is the Kruger National Park. Roughly the size of Wales, or comparable in area to the American state of Massachusetts, the park occupies nearly two million hectares of the northeastern Transvaal (known as the lowveld or bushveld).

This is big-game country, with more species of wildlife than are found in any other game sanctuary on the African continent (see *Fauna, p. 13*).

Natal's major game parks – and South Africa's oldest – are Umfolozi and Hluhluwe (recently combined to form one reserve, the Umfolozi-Hluhluwe Park) and St Lucia game reserves, all of which have a variety of large and small mammals. Umfolozi-Hluhluwe, which lies about 270 km north of Durban, has impressive populations of elephant, lion, black rhino, white rhino, blue wildebeest, leopard, giraffe and a variety of antelope and birds (for detailed descriptions of the reserves see the regional sections).

When to visit the reserves: The lush vegetation of summer provides thick cover for many species of game, making them very difficult to spot. With this in mind, the winter months (when the grass is short and the absence of rain brings animals to waterholes in large numbers) are the most favourable for game-viewing. The best times of day for spotting animals are early morning and late afternoon, when the animals leave their shady spots to forage or visit a waterhole.

Contacting the reserves: To reserve accommodation in any of the national parks, contact the National Parks Board, PO Box 787, Pretoria 0001, tel. (012) 3431991; or PO Box 7400, Roggebaai 8012 (Cape Town), tel. (021) 222810.

For information on KwaZulu/Natal's game reserves, contact the Natal Parks Board, PO Box 1750, Pietermaritzburg 3200, tel. (0331) 471981, or any South African Tourism Board Office listed in the *At a glance* sections in this book.

Fauna

Southern Africa has a huge variety of wild animals. From the Big Five – lion, elephant, rhinoceros, hippopotamus and buffalo – to the tiniest birds, insects and marine organisms, this variety is unmatched anywhere else in Africa. No less than 273 species of mammal, 718 species of bird, 120 species of amphibian (including five families of frogs) and 145 species of reptile, inhabit the bushveld, forest, semi-desert, savannah plains, waterways and oceans of South Africa.

Most of the land mammals (130 species) and more than half the birds (512 species) are found in the Kruger National Park, making it one of the world's greatest animal and birdwatching paradises. More than 8 100 elephant – you'll encounter some of them crossing the road – and 120 000 impala are found in the park alone.

Springbok, wildebeest, zebra and buffalo form vast herds in their natural habitats, particularly in the Kalahari Gemsbok and Kruger National Parks, while dozens of other antelope species flourish in small groups throughout the parks of KwaZulu/Natal, the Eastern Transvaal and the interior.

In the wake of these herds come the carnivores: lions, leopards, cheetahs, wild dogs, hyaenas, jackals and a host of smaller scavengers and cats, most of which you're likely to see on game drives through the reserves.

Many visitors describe their first encounter with a rhino as the highlight of their trip: if you're lucky – and brave – you may see a white (square-lipped) or black (hook-lipped) rhino from very close quarters on one of the reserve's wilderness trails.

A favourite with tourists are the five species of primate scattered throughout the reserves: chacma baboon, vervet monkey, samango monkey, lesser-tailed bushbaby and thick-tailed bushbaby.

Dozens of other, less conspicuous mammal species play their part in the wildlife community, and the longer you stay in a reserve, the more conspicuous they will become.

If you're a birdwatcher, South Africa offers some of the most spectacular birds of prey in the world – from the regal martial and tawny eagles to the elegant fish eagle and bateleur. The community of winged scavengers is just as awesome, and includes such carrion hunters as the lappetfaced, whitebacked and Cape vultures.

Vegetation

The huge differences in climate create ideal conditions for a profusion of vastly different species of plants and trees throughout South Africa, from the tiny ericas and heaths of the Western Cape's floral kingdom to the huge baobabs of the far Northern Transvaal.

The grasslands and bushveld

The eastern interior of the country, including large parts of the North-West Province, Free State and Gauteng, is covered by what South Africans call "veld" – short and tall grasslands, conspicuous in the central parts for their lack of trees.

To the north and east of these rolling, grassy plains is the bushveld, or savannah, that part of South Africa where grassland, scattered trees and drought resistant undergrowth – such as that of the Kruger National Park – support a huge variety of animals. This is a land of acacias (such as the camel thorn), euphorbias and tree aloes.

To the far north are the mopane, marula and baobab trees, whose monstrous girth and ghostly branches inspired legends among the San (Bushmen).

The arid west

The further west you travel into the interior of South Africa, the sparser the grasslands become until, in the vast plains of the Great (or Nama) Karoo – an area almost the size of France – the vegetation gives way to low-growing, hardy shrubs and bushes such as camelia, kapok and quassia, with very few trees.

In the far west, between the Orange River Mouth and Doring Bay in the south, in the region known as the Succulent Karoo, semi-desert-loving plants such as mesembryanthemums, pebble plants (*Lithops*), aloes and quiver trees flourish in a rocky environment with little rain.

The Cape Floral Kingdom

Further south, in the Mediterranean zone of the Western Cape, is the world's richest plant kingdom. More than 8 600 species of flowering plants – one tenth of the world's total – are to be found here. Known collectively as fynbos, these plants are represented by 2 256 species in the mountains and valleys of the Cape Peninsula alone, an area 5 000 times smaller than Britain. The plants include South Africa's famous orchid, known as "the pride of Table Mountain" (*Disa uniflora*), the beautiful king protea (*Protea cynaroides*) and the elegant silver tree (*Leucadendron argenteum*).

The profusion of heathers, proteas, leucadendrons, leucospermums and other low-growing shrubs that flourish here – there are more than 600 species of heather alone – continues along the slopes and valleys of the Cape Fold Mountains right up the east coast to Cape St Francis.

The forests

Although there are relatively few forests in South Africa, there are nearly 1 000 species of tree. The high rain forests of the southern Cape, notably the Knysna and Tsitsikamma forests, are the most spectacular and densely wooded in the country. Here giant yellowwood trees, black ironwood and stinkwood, boekenhout and Cape chestnut form canopies of green as far as the eye can see. Along the eastern coastline of southern Africa you will find isolated coastal forests and riverine woods, and along the KwaZulu/Natal north coast patches of mangrove forest flourish in subtropical seclusion. Some milkwood forests have survived the expansion of human settlement along the coast, and in KwaZulu/Natal there are still remnants of evergreen forests of ebony and ilala palms.

In the gorges and ravines of the KwaZulu/Natal and Eastern Transvaal Drakensberg mountains there are still many tracts of yellowwood and stinkwood trees and members of the olive family, where you will find an abundance of birdlife and small animals.

Getting around

South Africa maintains an excellent network of roads, and travel between the cities – by air, road or rail – is safe, reliable and quite comparable to travel in Western nations. There are also first-class travel links with all South Africa's neighbouring countries: Zimbabwe, Botswana, Namibia, Lesotho and Swaziland, and their game reserves and tourist destinations. More recently, Mozambique and its islands have again become holiday destinations for South Africans.

The abolition of apartheid and the evolution of a democratic government in South Africa have resulted in the re-establishment of direct air and sea links with countries worldwide. The South African Tourism Board (Satour) will provide details of all-inclusive round-trip package tours available to South Africa from North America, Britain, Europe and other parts of the world by such airlines as British Airways, KLM, Air France, Swissair, Lufthansa, Sabena, Cathay Pacific and Varig. Satour also has comprehensive details of tour packages available within the country (contact Satour, tel. (012) 3231430/2 or at the Tourist Rendezvous Travel Centre, Sammy Marks Complex, corner Prinsloo and Vermeulen streets, Pretoria 0002, tel. (012) 3231222).

Routes for all seasons

A recent trend in southern Africa has been the emergence of dozens of routes, specifically designed for people who want to see as much as possible of the country in the limited time available to them. There are culture routes, heritage, wine, whale, crayfish, craft, battle sites routes and even flower routes.

If you would like to know more about specific routes, contact Routes for all Seasons, Coast to Coast Tourism Bureau, PO Box 7327, Stellenbosch 7600, tel. (021) 8864669 or 8879157.

Inter-city travel

Bus: Travelling between cities and towns on luxury buses or coaches is a popular, reasonably inexpensive way of getting around South Africa. The coaches are airconditioned, comfortable and well-equipped, and run regular, scheduled inter-city trips between the larger urban areas.

The luxury Greyhound Citiliner links Johannesburg, Pretoria, Nelspruit, Cape Town, Bloemfontein, Kimberley, Durban, East London and Port Elizabeth. Translux is another reliable coach service that covers the major routes in South Africa on a daily basis. To contact these services, consult your telephone directory, nearest publicity association or the South African Tourism Board.

Smaller operators are Intercape, which runs two trips daily between Cape Town and Port Elizabeth (with refreshment stops during the day); the Garden Route Inter-City, which operates between George, Mossel Bay and Johannesburg and Transcity, which operates daily between Johannesburg, Pretoria and Cape Town, stopping at Kimberley or Bloemfontein.

Car rental: International car-hire firms, such as Budget, Avis and Imperial, are established in major towns and cities throughout the country, as well as at the main airports and in the bigger game parks and nature reserves (Skukuza, in the Kruger National Park, has a car-hiring facility). For details see *A-Z summary* starting on p. 193.

Air: South African Airways, the country's national airline, offers regular daily flights between the major centres. The airline also runs midnight flights between Johannesburg, Durban, Cape Town, East London and Port Elizabeth at a 40 per cent reduction on the fare, but advance booking is essential. Bookings can be made at South African Airways offices in Bloemfontein, Cape Town, Durban, Johannesburg, Port Elizabeth and Pretoria.

Rail: A comprehensive, electrified rail network extends over most of the country, and reservations for inter-city travel can be made through Connex Travel, the travel bureau of Transnet in Johannesburg, Cape Town and Durban.

The Blue Train, one of three luxury expresses in the world, takes passengers from Pretoria and Johannesburg to Cape Town in 26 hours. The train offers five-star cuisine and amenities, including baths, showers, a lounge bar and a cocktail bar (contact Satour or your nearest publicity association for phone numbers of these train services, and those listed below).

Other popular inter-city rail services are: The Orange Express (once a week between Cape Town and Durban, via Kimberley and Bloemfontein); the Trans-Natal Night Express (daily between Durban and Johannesburg) and the Trans-Karoo Express, a daily service between Cape Town and Johannesburg.

Tours and touring

South Africa's four major cities, Johannesburg, Pretoria, Durban and Cape Town, are particularly well-geared to handle tourists' needs, and a variety of tour operators provide first-class transport to, and tours of, the game reserves, beaches, mountain resorts, African villages, historical sights, casino complexes and other attractions. Most operators offer attractive tour packages, ranging from a few hours to a few weeks, and provide accommodation en route to tourist destinations at quality hotels, country inns or game lodges.

The principal means of touring is by luxury coach, and recommended tour operators covering most of South Africa are Connex Travel, Springbok Atlas, Grosvenor Tours, Impala Tours and Welcome Tours.

Specialist safari and adventure tours, concentrating on the wild places of southern Africa (including Namibia, Botswana, Zimbabwe, Swaziland and Lesotho) operate mainly out of Johannesburg, Pretoria, Cape Town and Durban, and usually offer personalised service in luxury minibuses for small groups of people. Destinations include the national game parks and private game reserves of southern Africa, the Drakensberg escarpment and the game reserves of northern KwaZulu/Natal. Possibly the most comprehensive and adventurous safaris are organised by Wilderness Safaris, which runs tours of South Africa, Botswana, Namibia and Zimbabwe, tel. (011) 8844633.

Other recommended tour operators are: Bonaventure Tour Operators, Reservations Africa, Holidays for Africa, Prestige Travel, Drifters Adventours, Safari Lodge Tours, Safari Escape Tour, Wild Adventure Expeditions, Swann Tours, TWS Tours, Specialised Tours and Zululand Safaris. Satour will supply addresses and phone numbers of these operators.

Fly-in tours: Some tour operators offer fly-in safaris to landing strips in southern Africa's game reserves. There are regular scheduled flights from Johannesburg to Nelspruit, Phalaborwa and the Kruger National Park (some will take you there and back the same day) as well as flights to Pietersburg and Tzaneen in the Northern Transvaal. Comair offers flights to several private game parks in the lowveld, and group flights to the Kruger National Park from Durban.

Helicopter tours: See Gold Reef City and the mine dumps of Johannesburg, Durban's Golden Mile, Cape Town's beautiful peninsula or the Cape winelands from a helicopter. Court Helicopters runs special helicopter tours on a daily basis over the festive season, and special tours can be arranged out of season (contact Satour for details).

Regular pleasure flights over Johannesburg and Soweto take place from the Heliport, Gold Reef City, on weekends and public holidays.

Dragonfly Helicopter Adventures at White River offers a rotary-winged safari over a private game reserve and a view over the scenic parts of the Eastern Transvaal.

Hot air balloon: This novel way of seeing the country is becoming very popular in South Africa. Airtrack Adventures offers champagne flights north of Johannesburg (contact Satour). Zulu Lifestyle and Balloon Safari includes a night stopover at a traditional Zulu village, next to a game reserve, north of Johannesburg.

Balloon companies to contact are Bill Harrop's Original Balloon Safaris in Randburg and the Hot Air Ballooning Company, which also organises flights in the Pilanesberg National Park and the Eastern Transvaal.

If you're in KwaZulu/Natal, the KwaZulu/Natal Midlands Balloon Safari is a four-day adventure with overnight accommodation in a country hotel; in the Cape, Wineland Ballooning in Paarl offers a leisurely glide over the green vineyards of the southwestern Cape (your local Satour office or publicity association will provide addresses of these and other touring facilities).

Cruises and boat trips: Scheduled or chartered pleasure cruises are run by dozens of companies the length and breadth of the South African coast. The *At a glance* sections of this guide, Satour or the local publicity associations supply full details of such cruises at coastal resorts. Some of the more popular are: *Waterfront:* Alabama 2000, which offers cruises with cabaret shows and dinner, and Sealink Tours which offers cruises to Clifton; *Cape Town:* the *Circe* pleasure cruise to Seal Island in Hout Bay; sunset cruises between Cape Town and Hout Bay; a cruise to Duiker Island in False Bay. *Port Elizabeth:* bay cruises (including a sunset cruise), and a shipwreck cruise to Thunderbolt Reef on the tug *Blue Jay;* weekend daytime cruises on the *Nauticat,* a pink pleasure cruiser. *East London:* bay cruises. *Durban:* harbour and bay cruises on the *Sarie Marais.*

Steam trains: In an age of electrification and computer-driven transport, steam trains have survived as highly popular, alternative ways to tour parts of South Africa. The Transnet Museum in Johannesburg offers 14-day steam safaris to various parts of the country, during which linking bus tours are laid on to give you maximum exposure to scenic delights and tourist attractions. The Union Limited runs regular day tours, such as the Heidelberg Express and the Magalies Valley Steamer which take you on a fun-filled jaunt through the highveld.

A delightful steam adventure is a ride on Port Elizabeth's green Apple Express, which chugs through beautiful mountain scenery on one of the few remaining narrow gauge railways in the world.

Other popular steam rides are the Outeniqua Choo Choo (George-Knysna), the Jacaranda Express (Johannesburg-Cullinan), the Banana Express (Port Shepstone-Harding) and the Strelitzia Steam Train (Durban-Kelso).

Parasailing: This is a novel way to see the Golden Mile from the air (daily on the hour in front of Addington Hospital).

For more details on touring, see *Tourist information* in the last chapter, or Satour's information headquarters at the Tourist Rendezvous Travel Centre, Sammy Marks Complex, corner of Prinsloo and Vermeulen streets, Pretoria 0002, tel. (012) 3231222.

1. The rugged edges of Cape Point jut into the sea where the Indian and Atlantic oceans meet.

▲ 2

▼ 3

▼ 4

2. The Orange River near Noordoewer flows along the border between Namibia and South Africa.

3. A sailing ship cruises into a calm Table Bay with Table Mountain in the background.

4. A mother cheetah and her cub investigate a road sign in the Kruger National Park.

5. The protea is part of the unique floral kingdom of the Western Cape.
6. The strange form of the "halfmens" or half-human tree in the Richtersveld.
7. A farm stall near Citrusdal celebrates the new South Africa.
8. A gaily painted South Sotho mud home in the Free State.

▲ 9   ▼ 10

9. A twilight view of Cape Town with Table Mountain in the background.
10. The picturesque Malay Quarter on the slopes of Signal Hill in Cape Town, also known as the Bo-Kaap.

11. Llandudno on the Cape Peninsula has one of Cape Town's most popular beaches.
12. The imposing entrance gate to the Cape Town Castle, South Africa's oldest building.
13. An aerial view of Robben Island, where Nelson Mandela was imprisoned for most of his 27-year incarceration.

▲ 14 ▼ 15 ▼ 16

14. A tranquil view of the popular Victoria and
Alfred Waterfront development in Cape Town's
harbour.
15. A sunset view of Hout Bay from the heights
of Chapman's Peak.
16. The Greenmarket Square flea market in
Cape Town's city centre is a popular meeting
place of different cultures.

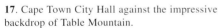

17. Cape Town City Hall against the impressive backdrop of Table Mountain.
18. The graceful façade of the Houses of Parliament in Government Avenue, Cape Town.
19. The Gardens near the parliament buildings in Cape Town.

▲ 20 ▼ 21

▼ 22 ▲ 23

20. Mouille Point lighthouse, a well-known landmark near Sea Point.
21. An early morning view of the Sea Point promenade.
22. The yachts in Hout Bay harbour make a pretty picture on a calm day.
23. The picturesque main street of Simon's Town on the False Bay coast.

▲ 24

▲ 26 ▼ 27

▼ 25

▼ 28

24. The start of Chapman's Peak Drive, coming from Kommetjie towards Hout Bay.

25. Kalk Bay harbour, looking towards Simon's Town in False Bay.

26. The Twelve Apostles dominate the coastline of Clifton.

27. The colourful changing booths at St James beach on False Bay.

28. A magnificent view of the uninterrupted white stretch of Long Beach, Noordhoek.

▲ 29

▼ 30   ▼ 31

29. The famous Kirstenbosch Botanical Gardens on the slopes of Table Mountain.

30. Rhodes Memorial, the impressive monument to Cecil John Rhodes, overlooks the suburbs of Cape Town.

31. Lively performers at the annual Cape Minstrel Carnival in Cape Town.

32. The warm winter colours of the vineyards in the Hex River Valley, with snowcapped peaks in the background.

33. Mist rolling over Lion's Head and into the city of Cape Town.

▲ 32

▼ 33

34. This house, in Dorp Street, Stellenbosch, is a national monument.
35. A graceful Cape homestead, typical of the winelands.
36. Boschendal wine estate at the foot of the Groot Drakenstein Mountains.
37. Oom Samie se Winkel in Stellenbosch is a treasure trove of collectables.
38. Wine tasting on the Franschhoek Wine Route.

▼ 38

▲ 39

39. The monument to the Afrikaans language commemorates the birth of Afrikaans in 1875.
40. De Oude Woning, next door to the Paarl Publicity Association.

▼ 40

41. A typical rural cottage near Franschhoek.
42. The Huguenot Memorial in Franschhoek.

▲ 41   ▼ 42

▲ 43

▲ 44

▼ 45

43. The flower carpet in springtime covers vast areas of Namaqualand.
44. A rural farm scene in Namaqualand.
45. Doringbaai fishing harbour up the Cape west coast.

CAPE TOWN AND THE PENINSULA

In the southern corner of the African continent, straddling a peninsula of sandy beaches and scenic bays, a massive sandstone monument rises from the icy waters of the Atlantic Ocean to form a flat-topped mountain more than 1 km high. To the world, this awesome, nearly vertical column of rock is known as Table Mountain. To South Africans it is the matriarch and guardian of one of the world's most beautiful cities – Cape Town.

Sir Francis Drake, rounding the Cape in the *Golden Hind* in 1580, was so awed by what he saw that he called the mountain and the peninsula on which it stands "the Fairest Cape in the whole circumference of the earth". To generations of explorers and adventurers who followed, Cape Town became known as the "Tavern of the Seas" – a place of scenic wonder, where seafarers could rest, replenish their stocks and marvel at the luxuriant beauty around them.

Today, more than 400 years after Drake's odyssey through the southern seas, Cape Town – the Mother City – is one of the world's great holiday destinations.

Once a huddle of huts assembled around a mud-walled fort, Cape Town has grown into the second largest city in South Africa, with a population of more than 1,5 million people. Founded by Dutch commander Jan van Riebeeck in 1652 as a replenishment station for the Dutch East India Company, it is one year older than New York, and 130 years older than Sydney. Its fusion of vastly different cultures – Malay, Dutch, Asian, English, Xhosa, Khoisan – has resulted in a cheerful, cosmopolitan capital where ancient traditions of the east live cheek by jowl with the west; where monuments of the past stand firm with the modern architecture of the present.

The mother city is a fascinating blend of the old and the new. Within the city the 17th century pentagonal Castle rubs shoulders with towering skyscrapers and subterranean shopping centres; in the Malay quarter, known as the Bo-Kaap (literally meaning "above Cape"), bulbous minarets rise up above buildings festooned with cast-iron adornments from another age. Cobblestoned streets lead into cosy squares and long pedestrian malls, where street vendors peddle antiques, clothing, handcrafts, African art and an endless selection of bric-a-brac. Near the Grand Parade, also in the city centre, flower sellers offer a dazzling array of indigenous blooms at ridiculously cheap prices, while along the pavements roving salesmen tout all sorts of goods, from umbrellas and avocado pears to tape cassettes and ties. In the arcades and alleyways buskers bring music and melodies to passers-by. Guitarists,

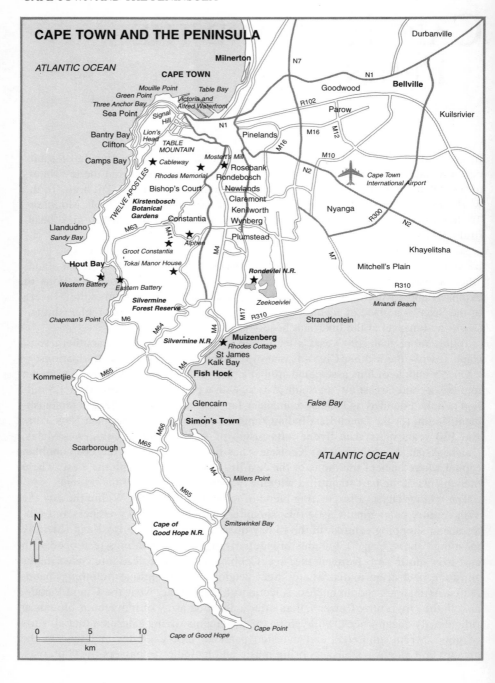

CLIMATE

Cape Town enjoys a temperate, Mediterranean climate, although extremes of temperature can range from 40 °C in summer to 0 °C in winter. The summers are generally warm and dry, the winters cool and wet – and sometimes miserably cold. In summer, the gale-force southeasterly wind spreads its famous "tablecloth" of billowing cloud across the top of Table Mountain, then hangs to the edges, just below the giant sandstone rim. Locals call this wind the "Cape Doctor" because it brings coolness to searing summer temperatures, and cleans the city up. If the southeaster is blowing hard, and you want to spend the day on the beach, head for the Atlantic suburbs of Llandudno, Clifton, Bantry Bay, Bakoven, Sea Point, Three Anchor Bay or Mouille Point – the beaches there are generally protected from the wind because they lie in the lee of Table Mountain. If there's a northwester blowing, luxuriate on the quiet beaches, or in the slightly warmer waters of False Bay.

Cape Town is notorious for its changeable weather, and often experiences great temperature extremes, so always take warm clothes with you when you're out and about – even in summer.

---

flutists, harmonica players, tribal singers, drummers and dancers ... you name it, Cape Town's got it all.

Down at the Waterfront there's a carnival atmosphere as the Atlantic laps at the feet of lunchtime strollers and musicians, and seafood sizzles in the pans of dockside bistros and restaurants. For those nautically minded, there are boat cruises and yacht trips; for sightseers there are helicopter and bus rides to all corners of the peninsula. And for shoppers, there is an unrivalled assortment of shops, craft markets and seaside stalls selling anything you can imagine.

To the west and south of the city centre, the coastline curves round to reveal bikini beaches and scenic mountain drives where sandstone cliffs plummet vertically to the shore. For an incomparable overview of all this, of city and peninsula, bustling harbour and golden beaches, there is the cableway to the summit of Table Mountain.

WHAT TO SEE

■■■■ CAPE TOWN
Table Mountain
Capetonians are very proud of their mountain, and not without good reason. The slab-like summit, extending nearly 3 km in length, commands some of the finest views in the world. To the north, you can see the deep blue well of the Atlantic rolling off to a distant horizon; 7 km from shore, white breakers form a ragged ring around Robben Island, one-time leper colony, and now a popular tourist destination. Below you the mountain's ramparts give way to the city of Cape Town, beyond which to the north are the seaside suburbs of Bloubergstrand and Milnerton. Far off to the east, the Hottentots-Holland Mountains form an imposing backdrop to the Cape Flats and its huge carpet of shanty towns.

Looking west from the summit of Table Mountain you will see the stately peaks of the Twelve Apostles brooding high above the ragged shore, and below, the wave-beaten wrecks of the *Antipolis* and *Romelia,* casualties of Cape Town's vicious winter storms. To the south, the Cape Peninsula snakes out into the southern seas, then shears off into the Atlantic Ocean at Cape Point.

But it isn't just the view that makes Table Mountain a special place. Its immediate slopes, together with the other mountains of the Cape Peninsula, are the natural home of a dazzling array of plants and flowers: 2 256 different plant species grow here, and together they constitute one of the six floral kingdoms of the world.

You can reach Table Mountain's summit the hard way – by walking or climbing – or by taking the cable car, which gets you to the top in about seven minutes. The cableway operates daily throughout the year, weather permitting, from 08h00 to 22h00 in summer, and from 08h30 to 18h00 in winter. If the weather looks doubtful, call the Table Mountain Aerial Cableway Company at (021) 248409.

The cable car departure point is at the top of Kloof Nek. Either drive there, take a taxi, or catch the Kloof Nek bus in Adderley Street (outside OK Bazaars). To avoid waiting in long queues for hours, advance bookings for the cableway can be made in December and January only, by phoning Captour at (021) 4185214.

Until 1891, there were only six known routes to the top of the mountain. Today there are more than 300. Some, like the climb up Skeleton Gorge and Nursery Ravine (access is from Kirstenbosch Botanical Gardens), the route up Platteklip Gorge (on the city side of the mountain), or the walk from the Constantia Nek parking area on the southern back of Table Mountain, are within the capabilities of most reasonably fit people. Other scenic walks offering grand views of Cape Town, the Atlantic and the mountains are the Pipe Track, which starts at Kloof Nek near the lower cableway station and runs above the western seaboard beneath the Twelve Apostles, and the main contour path across the western face of Table Mountain, above the lower cableway station. For more information on available routes get the Mountain Club of South Africa's *Table Mountain guide: walks and easy climbs,* or Shirley Brossy's *A walking guide for Table Mountain.*

If you do decide to walk up the mountain, take a good map and a rucksack stocked with liquid nourishment, food and some warm clothing. Also check on the weather forecast. And be careful: 94 people died on Table Mountain in the 96 years preceding 1987. In winter, cold fronts sweep across the Peninsula very suddenly, and daytime temperatures can plummet precipitously. Do not undertake unknown or hazardous routes – they could be fatal.

At the top cable station is a souvenir shop and a restaurant, from where you can walk to Maclear's Beacon – at 1 113 m the highest point of the mountain. This is an ideal place for a picnic on a summer's evening. You can walk for kilometres on the top of Table Mountain, and there are many routes to choose from.

Looking down from Table Mountain you will see the towering sugarloaf called Lion's Head on the left. There's a fairly easy track which takes you round the western and northern flanks of Lion's Head to the top. You'll find this track about 800 m after the turn-off to Signal Hill (at the summit of Kloof Nek Road). Drive 3 km further on to reach the smaller rump of Signal Hill, where there's a spacious parking area and picnic sites. Both vantage points offer spectacular views over the Atlantic seaboard. Signal Hill is the perfect place to watch the sun sink over the western horizon in summer or winter. Take along a picnic hamper and a pair of binoculars.

The Victoria and Alfred Waterfront

A charming blend of the old world and the new, Victoria and Alfred Waterfront has become one of South Africa's premier tourist destinations, with an estimated 765 000 tourists visiting it every year. Just a stone's throw from the central business district, the Waterfront is a bustling but scenic retreat from the clamour of the city. Here, the sounds of seals and gulls, harbour and sea mingle with the music of promenade buskers and roadside vendors selling crafts and curios.

There are about 25 seaside restaurants (with cuisine ranging from Greek to American, Italian to Portuguese), half a dozen coffee shops, and about 15 takeaway outlets at the Waterfront. There's little in South Africa to match the variety of shops and craft stalls. Victoria Wharf, the Waterfront's shopping complex, has more than 100 fashion and speciality stores. Here, there's a range of just about every commodity you can think of, from biltong (strips of dried meat) and baked bread to the finest lines in ladies and men's wear. At the Red Shed and Blue Shed craft markets you'll find pottery and pencils, seaweed art and township craft. And, unique perhaps to the Waterfront, a quaint little rocking horse shop.

For entertainment, there's a fine selection of cinemas and theatres, the most notable of which are the Dock Road Theatre complex, which runs regular local productions and the BMW Imax Theatre which opened its doors in late 1994. Nearby, the colourful dockside pubs of Quay Four and Mortons reflect a festive mood.

Leisure attractions include a Great White Shark exhibition, a state-of-the-art brewery, the South African Maritime Museum, a visit to the naval ship, SAS *Somerset,* and the South African Fisheries Museum.

The New Scratch Patch, in an old Victorian building on the Waterfront, offers children and adults fun-filled hours hunting for gems and other semiprecious stones. Upstairs there's a new jewellery shop offering souvenirs and investment gems.

The half dozen pubs and taverns offer good food, and generally excellent views of the harbour and sea basking in the Mediterranean sunshine.

Special shows for children are held at the open-air theatre in front of Victoria Wharf, and for the more energetic, there are a variety of harbour cruises and deep-sea sailing charters. Particularly recommended are the Robben Island and champagne sunset cruises (see *Cape Town at a glance,* p. 34).

Regular helicopter charters are run by Court Helicopters and Civair. Both companies offer short flips over the harbour, and more distant trips along the Atlantic seaboard to Cape Point.

For excellent service and five-star quayside comfort, there's little to beat the Waterfront hotels, and they provide a convenient base for leisure and shopping expeditions.

A shuttle-bus service operates between the Waterfront, Cape Town's railway station and the city centre and Sea Point, and departs at 15-minute intervals from 06h30 to 23h00.

Old buildings, such as the Clock Tower, on the South Quay of Alfred Basin, with its collection of nautical relics, revive memories of the days it was first used as the port captain's office in 1883. You can reach the Clock Tower by crossing from the Pier Head on the Penny Ferry.

Near the north gate of the Waterfront, the old Breakwater Prison, now housing the University of Cape Town's Graduate School of Business, is a grim reminder of the days when convicts walked the treadmill or laboured on rock piles.

One of the Waterfront's most ambitious projects is the construction of Sea World, a huge oceanarium built with a special submarine spectators' tunnel. It is expected to attract 500 000 visitors a year.

For more information on this vibrant dockside entertainment and shopping complex, contact the Waterfront Information Centre, tel. (021) 4182369.

The Castle

This 17th century pentagonal fortress is the oldest occupied building in South Africa. Once Jan van Riebeeck's refuge from marauding lions, it was built as the headquarters of the Dutch East India Company, which ruled the Cape between 1652 and 1795. The Castle's construction started in 1666, and it became the defensive headquarters of the various governors of the Cape. Although no shot was fired at the enemy in the 300 years of its existence, the Castle became a focal point for coaches carrying criminals and commanders, and a centre of Cape Town's aristocratic social life. The original entrance was so close to the sea that it was often swamped by waves.

Ancient rooms within the Castle house the William Fehr Collection, a fascinating assembly of paintings and decorative arts reflecting the early history of the Cape.

In 1993 the Castle opened its Good Hope Collection of 17th, 18th and 19th century furniture and paintings to the public – so this is the place to walk through the early history of South Africa.

Guided tours take you through torture chambers, parapets and cells with ancient graffiti carved on their thick wooden doors. At noon on Fridays, as the noonday gun booms across the city from Signal Hill, a colourful Castle Guard corps, dressed in 17th-century-style uniforms, performs a ceremonial changing of the guard, complete with band. You'll find the Castle just south of the Grand Parade, about a 10-minute walk from Adderley Street.

City Hall and Grand Parade

The Grand Parade, which fronts the imposing entrance to the City Hall, is really a massive central parking area, flanked by dozens of flea market street stalls. You'll pick up bargains in clothes and bric-a-brac on Wednesday and Saturday mornings here – and a basketful of fresh fruit or flowers, if you like.

The City Hall, an old Victorian structure built in 1905, is the venue for symphony concerts on Thursday and Sunday nights. The City Hall building also houses the Cape Town public library, where visitors are welcome to browse. (For more details contact the Captour Information Bureau, tel. (021) 4185214.)

Bo-Kaap

Known by Capetonians as the Malay Quarter, this village of tightly packed traditional dwellings and tiny streets on the slopes of Signal Hill is one of the older, quainter sections of Cape Town (many of the buildings are more than a century old). A highlight here is a visit to the Bo-Kaap Museum, a house built in the 18th century that portrays the lifestyle and home comforts (including a prayer room) of a Malay family in the 19th century. There are guided tours of the Bo-Kaap (for details contact Captour, tel. (021) 4185214).

Greenmarket Square

Dubbed "the marketplace of Africa", this intriguing cobblestoned square in the middle of the city is a colourful, lively complex of streetside stalls peddling everything from bangles and beadwork to cotton dresses and carved goods. There are plenty of bargains to be had here, so feel free to haggle over the prices. The square gets its name from market gardeners who once sold their goods here. Greenmarket Square is a good starting point for any walking tour of the city – it is within a 10-minute stroll of most of the major city hotels, the Golden Acre shopping complex, the Houses of Parliament, the Gardens, Bo-Kaap and St George's Cathedral.

Station flea market

All kinds of wares, ranging from curios, bric-a-brac, jewellery and books, to records, toys and diverse handcrafts are on sale here. Fronting one of the most beautiful gardens in Cape Town, and right next to the departure point for buses touring the peninsula (and trains bound for southern suburbs such as Muizenberg, Fish Hoek and Simon's Town), this flea market is particularly well situated. The Station flea market is just a few hundred metres from the Golden Acre shopping complex.

The Gardens

Formerly the vegetable gardens laid out by the Dutch East India Company at the Cape, the Gardens at the northern end of Adderley Street, flanking St George's Cathedral, are one of South Africa's most attractive and botanically fascinating city parks. Covering about 6 ha, the gardens are home to more than 8 000 species of plants and trees, flanked by stately avenues of oaks in an atmosphere of secluded charm and tranquility.

Squirrels scamper between avenues of oaks along the sun-dappled walkway known as Government Avenue, which cuts right through the gardens. Just off Government Avenue, the Houses of Parliament are open to the public, but if you're a foreigner, you may be required to show your passport. Nearby is the State President's city residence, Tuynhuys.

Also in the Gardens area is the South African National Gallery, which houses more than 6 500 works of art. The European collection here includes Gainsborough's *Lavinia,* and notable works by Raeburn, Reynolds, Romney and Morland. The gallery's Dutch pictures include works by Van der Kessel, Vijtmens, Heremans and other 17th and 18th century artists.

The South African Library in the Gardens houses a massive collection of reference books dealing with Africa, including the Grey Collection, donated by Sir George Grey, a former governor of the Cape Colony. A first folio Shakespeare (1623) is the library's most valuable book, while other treasured titles are a 14th century copy of Mandeville's *Travels* (in Flemish) and a 15th century copy of Dante's *Divine comedy.*

The planetarium, attached to the South African Museum, has projectors that can reproduce the day or night sky over Cape Town at any stage over a 26 000 year period.

Just outside the Gardens, on the corner of Adderley and Bureau streets, is the Groote Kerk, an historic Dutch church rebuilt in 1841, after it had been demolished in 1836. Referred to by its early members as "die moeder van ons almal" ("the mother of us all"), it was first consecrated in January 1704, but the first stone of the original church was laid in 1678. Today the church houses a treasure trove of memorabilia, including rare and almost priceless collections of Cape silver and old family crests, as well as a delicately handcarved wooden pulpit, regarded as one of sculptor Anton Anreith's finest pieces of work.

Museums

The South African Museum, which is the country's oldest, has fascinating showcases of fossil reptiles dating back 200 million years, a vast array of artefacts and implements left by Stone Age humans and the early San (Bushmen) of southern Africa, and a whale well with the skeleton of a blue whale on display. Of special interest are the plaster casts of a San community made by the artist James Drury early in the 20th century. A shop at the museum offers books and African art for sale.

The Cultural History Museum in upper Adderley Street was originally the Dutch East India Company's slave lodge – and an unofficial brothel. It was converted into government offices during the second British Occupation early in the 19th century.

Subsequently it became a supreme court building and a debating chamber of the Cape Legislative Council until 1885, when the Houses of Parliament were opened. The museum has an interesting archaeological section, and exhibits various collections of coins, glassware, silver, furniture, weapons and other relics of bygone ages.

Robben Island

Nelson Mandela, who became the first democratically elected president of South Africa in May 1994, spent more than a quarter of his life with other political prisoners in the bleak maximum-security prison on this island. In February 1995 President Mandela and a retinue of state officials returned to the island to celebrate the fifth anniversary of the president's release from prison. Today the island is becoming increasingly popular as a tourist destination. You can join one of the island tours organised by the Department of Correctional Services, which leave Cape Town harbour on Tuesdays, Wednesdays and Saturdays in summer. The half-day tour starts with a 45-minute boat trip, followed by a two-hour bus tour of the island, during which you can see the dismal prison complex, and the quarries where maximum-security prisoners used to break up rocks. For details telephone (021) 4111006.

■■■■ THE CAPE PENINSULA

Behind Table Mountain a jagged promontory of land snakes southwards into the blue wilderness of the Atlantic Ocean. On both sides of this emerald peninsula, the sea meets the land in a melding of extraordinary beauty. To the east, ivory sands unfold to the surf at Simon's Town, Fish Hoek, Kalk Bay and Muizenberg. Further inland is the Kirstenbosch Botanical Garden. On the western side, the suburban holiday areas of Noordhoek, Hout Bay, Llandudno, Camps Bay, Clifton and Sea Point all offer panoramic views of the Atlantic and the mountains. At Llandudno you can have a champagne picnic on the beach as you watch the sun go down; or stroll to nearby Sandy Bay, South Africa's scenic naturist resort.

At the southern end of the Peninsula, the Cape of Good Hope Nature Reserve peers out over what the Portuguese explorers of the 15th century called Cabo Tormentoso – "the Cape of Storms".

Sea Point

Restaurants, night clubs and upmarket shops line Main Road, in this the most densely populated suburb of Cape Town. Between Beach Road and the sea, an attractive 3-km-long promenade takes you past beautiful lawns, rocky coves and, at the Sea Point Pavilion, a huge seawater swimming pool catering for children and adults. There's a fine restaurant overlooking the sea at the pavilion, within quick access of some beautiful beaches.

The promenade links Sea Point to Three Anchor Bay and Mouille Point in the east. This part of the coastline has snatched several ships to its rocky depths, including the *Seafarer,* whose rusted remains can still be seen off Mouille Point. Three Anchor Bay is the site of the Maze, the first complex of hedges, lawns and paths of its kind on the African continent. Further on, at Mouille Point, there's a children's amusement park, with a steam train, putt-putt course, dodgem cars and paddle boats. Another few hundred metres on is the Mouille Point Lighthouse – one of South Africa's oldest.

Clifton beaches

Four dazzling white beaches, separated by granite boulders, have made Clifton one of the most popular places in Cape Town and a mecca for the body beautiful crowd from all over the world. Lying in the lee of Table Mountain, they are usually well protected from the summer southeaster and are therefore ideal for sun-seekers and strollers looking for a wind-free haven. But watch out – the water is extremely cold here, and only the brave venture into the sea for long.

Clifton's beaches are ideal for picnics or sundowners on a summer evening. Parking can be a problem here in December and January, so arrive early if you intend spending a day at the beach. There are resident lifeguards, change rooms and a shop.

Camps Bay

Table Mountain, the cableway and the Twelve Apostles chain of mountains form a dramatic backdrop to this beach fringed by palm trees and terraced lawns. There are barbecuing facilities, picnic spots and a tidal pool here, but the water is cold and swimming is not safe. The beach is not patrolled by lifeguards. In December and January, the beaches here are packed, so get there early.

Llandudno

Just before you crest the hill that descends into Hout Bay from Cape Town, the coastline shears westwards to create a beautiful turquoise bay fringed by a ribbon of ivory sand. This is Llandudno, a tiny village perched on the slopes of a hill over the Atlantic, which is one of Cape Town's most sought after residential areas.

The huge granite boulders, the tranquil wash of surf on an isolated shore, and the beach's exposure to late afternoon sun (until 20h30 in midsummer) make Llandudno a favourite spot for picnics or sundowners during summer. Added attractions are the wreck of the *Romelia*, just 200 m offshore near Sunset Rocks, and the 1-km walk to the nudist beach of Sandy Bay. While you're at Sandy Bay, take the half hour walk eastwards to the Oude Schip Peninsula, where you'll have a clear view of a huge barge, *Boss*, wrecked on the rocks across the bay in June 1994.

If you're going to Llandudno or Sandy Bay for the day, a sunscreen is essential (in midsummer the sun sets after 20h00). The water is extremely cold, bathing at

Llandudno is unpredictable (there are strong cross-currents on the eastern side), but there is a resident lifesaving club. Again get there early, as parking spots near the beach are at a premium.

Hout Bay

Take your bathing costume and hiking boots if you visit Hout Bay. Jan van Riebeeck named this emerald seaside hamlet t'Houtbaaijen (wood bay) – a reference to the majestic forests of pine, yellowwood, ironwood and blackwood that carpet the slopes of its surrounding mountains.

You can explore the mountains via a number of scenic walks around Hout Bay and off Chapman's Peak Drive (for details of walks read Mike Lundy's *Twenty walks around Hout Bay* or contact Captour Information Bureau, tel. (021) 4185214). The Hout Bay Museum also organises interesting walks (see *Cape Town at a glance,* on p. 34).

The main beach, which stretches for 1 km between the harbour in the west and the foot of Chapman's Peak Drive, is favoured by tourists and Capetonians alike, but the water here can be very cold, even in summer.

Popular attractions in Hout Bay are sea cruises to Duiker Island, (enquire at Circe Launches in the harbour), and a visit to Mariner's Wharf, an emporium modelled on its namesake in San Francisco, where you can buy live rock lobsters, prawns and a variety of fresh seafood. Mariner's Wharf Restaurant is one of several local eateries that serve excellent fresh seafood and a tantalising array of good wines.

No visit to Hout Bay is complete, however, without stopping over at the World of Birds, the largest bird park in Africa. Here you'll see more than 3 000 birds, representing 450 species, including parrots and parakeets, eagles, vultures and hawks, and even owls and ostriches. There are over 100 spacious, landscaped, walk-through aviaries, which bring you face to face with many of the species. You'll also see meerkats and samango monkeys.

Chapman's Peak Drive

Without a doubt one of the world's most scenic coastal drives, this route enables you to drive on the fringe of the Atlantic seaboard for some 15 km, from where the beach ends at Hout Bay, up and through ragged mountain folds of sandstone and granite. At its apex, the drive skirts cliffs that fall precipitously 600 m to the thundering surf below. At the end of Chapman's Peak Drive, you descend into the lush, lowland plain of Noordhoek, with its tidy cottages, smallholdings and paddocks.

To savour the stillness and beauty of the surrounding mountains, park at any of several picnic spots on the way up to Chapman's Peak. These offer stunning views of Hout Bay, the craggy mountain called The Sentinel, which hangs over the sea, and the open blue vistas of the Atlantic. There are a number of footpaths and tracks that take you up the mountain to its summit, and down to the Noordhoek Valley on the other side.

Noordhoek to Cape Point

For an extension of the beautiful drive down to Noordhoek, head west to the tiny village of Kommetjie, a skin-diver's paradise, where you can swim in a tidal pool, stroll down to the Slangkop lighthouse or watch the boats pulling crayfish from the kelp beds. The road continues around the coast to Scarborough, where it's well worth stopping at the Camel Rock Restaurant.

Cape Point and Cape of Good Hope Nature Reserve

Set aside a full day to visit this beautiful reserve. About 70 km from the centre of Cape Town, the reserve and the scenic coastal drive towards it via Chapman's Peak and Scarborough are usually regarded as the highlights of a visit to Cape Town. Covering 40 km of coastline, the 7 750-ha reserve is a floral wonderland, with over 1 200 indigenous plant species, 160 species of birds (including ostrich) and a quiet community of wildlife, ranging from Cape mountain zebra, springbok, steenbok, grysbok and grey rhebok to baboon, caracal and Cape fox.

A network of good, tarred roads will take you to beautiful, terraced picnic spots at the water's edge, such as Buffels Bay on the eastern side, where there are open barbecue spots and a tidal pool, or to Olifantsboschbaai, where a small beach gives way to a rocky coastline. Here lie the wrecked remains of the *Thomas T Tucker,* which broke up on the rocks in 1942.

Take your own picnic, but don't feed the baboons, they can be very aggressive. If you are picnicking, close your car windows and lock the doors as a further precaution against baboons raiding your vehicle.

The reserve converges in the south at Cape Point, a great pinnacle of rock which falls almost sheer to the Atlantic. You can climb the steps or ride a shuttle-bus – the Flying Dutchman – to the top, from where you may see southern right whales in spring and early summer, dolphins and a variety of seabirds.

The original lighthouse at Cape Point was built in 1860. The present lighthouse, the most powerful in the southern hemisphere, is closer to the point itself than the original. The lighthouse was relocated after 1911, when the ship, the *Lusitania,* failed to see the light, struck Bellows Reef and sank. You can see the Bellows, mostly covered by a surging mass of foam, about 3 km offshore from Cape Point.

At Kanonkop you can stand alongside an old cannon that once belonged to the Dutch East India Company, and enjoy a panoramic view of the whole of the reserve. The cannon was used as a signal to inform Simon's Town of the arrival of ships in False Bay.

Another interesting monument is the Vasco da Gama cross, above Bordjiesrif, which honours the Portuguese navigator who rounded the Cape in 1497 with a small fleet of seven ships. The monument serves as a warning beacon to ships.

A few kilometres into the reserve, on the left, is a neat little tea room and restaurant, where you can stop for lunch or buy souvenirs.

Cape Point to Muizenberg

Travelling eastwards from the rocky buttresses of Cape Point, the coastal road bypasses some of the most beautiful beaches in the world – tiny secluded places such as Smitswinkel Bay, Miller's Point and Boulders, where the water is warm and wind-protected. The road then enters Simon's Town, named after the Dutch governor of the Cape, Simon van der Stel, who explored the bay in 1687. Within the dockyard is a cylindrical stone fort called the Martello Tower. Built in 1796, it is thought to be the oldest of its kind in the world. The Simon's Town Museum features fascinating naval and local history displays. The road to Muizenberg continues through Fish Hoek, where a small beach offers safe bathing, to Kalk Bay and St James, where stately homes designed by the English architect, Sir Herbert Baker, tower over the ocean. Kalk Bay Harbour, with its colourful fleet of fishing boats, and hectic fish trading on weekends, is a fascinating stop. A seaside restaurant and pub nearby, the Brass Bell, has a tantalising menu of fish fresh from the sea, cooked on an open fire. You can sit on the Brass Bell's deck with a drink, and watch waves crashing against the building's forefront a stone's throw away.

Muizenberg

This is one of the Peninsula's popular playgrounds and premier bathing beaches. Here gentle breakers sweep up to white sands against a backdrop of colourful bathing boxes lining the beach. Dominating the beachfront is the red-and-white striped pavilion, with restaurants overlooking the sea, and a recreation area which has bathing and paddling pools, a playground and water slides, putt-putt and a miniature train. During the peak holiday season in December and January, it may be difficult to find parking here, so many people prefer to travel by train from the city. There are change rooms and toilets in the car park.

Bathing is safe along the entire beach, and the gradual slope of the beach seawards makes this a popular surfing spot. Sunrise Beach, just 2 km east of Muizenberg, is ideal for bathing and boardsailing, and has wonderful views of the Peninsula's mountains. There are toilets and change rooms at Sunrise Beach, and a refreshment kiosk which operates at weekends and during the holiday season.

Rondevlei Nature Reserve

Just a few minutes' drive from the beaches of Muizenberg is a tranquil, reed-lined lake that serves as a sanctuary to more than 200 species of bird and an assortment of reptiles and mammals. Lying on the eastern side of the Muizenberg mountains, the reserve is a birder's paradise, and entices nature lovers with its mellow ambience of birdsong, relaxation and lapping water.

Observation towers and thatched hides overlook the 12 070-ha reserve (50 ha of which is water), and mounted telescopes enable you to zoom onto the animal or bird of your choice. If you're patient, there's plenty to see: hippopotamuses, steenbok, clawless otters, grysbok, tortoises, porcupines and several species of snake.

The 215 species of bird seen at Rondevlei include herons, darters, cormorants, flamingoes and pelicans, as well as spurwing geese, spoonbills, storks, plovers and gulls.

While you're at Rondevlei, drop in to the Leonard Gill Field Museum to see various mounted specimens of birds and mammals in the park. Don't forget to take along a camera and binoculars – and a picnic hamper for lunch.

Groot Constantia

This, one of the Peninsula's most magnificent old Cape Dutch homes, lies in a tranquil setting of rolling vineyards and fields south of Kirstenbosch. It was designed and built by the Dutch Governor of the Cape, Simon van der Stel, who lived there until 1712. Wines of legendary quality and flavour were produced here at the turn of the 18th century by Hendrik Cloete, and today part of the old cellars has been turned into a wine museum. The Groot Constantia homestead, magnificently restored in 1925, is a national monument and museum, notable for its period furniture, Chinese, Japanese and Rhenish porcelain, and for its two-storeyed cellar, designed by French architect Louis Thibault.

You can buy Constantia wines on the estate, or enjoy them with a meal in one of the two restaurants. Informative cellar tours take place daily on the hour. For details of tours contact the Captour Information Bureau, tel. (021) 4185214.

Kirstenbosch National Botanical Gardens

Lying on the eastern slopes of Table Mountain, this natural and cultivated reserve, established in 1913 on an estate bequeathed to the nation by Cecil John Rhodes, has 9 000 of the country's 18 000 indigenous flowering plant species. The beautiful terraced lawns, landscaped gardens and scenic walks along the back of Table Mountain are breathtaking. Recommended trails at Kirstenbosch are the 6-km, three-hour Silvertree Trail, the 45-minute Stinkwood Trail (1,2 km) and the one-and-a-half hour Yellowwood Trail (2,5 km).

The variety of plants, flowers and indigenous trees is quite staggering. They include mesembryanthemums, pelargoniums, ferns, cycads, proteas, ericas and watsonias, and such beautiful trees as yellowwoods, ironwoods, rooi els, keurboom and white stinkwood. Perhaps the most outstanding floral specimens are the silver tree (*Leucadendron argenteum*) and the red disa (*Disa uniflora*), a member of the orchid family, also known as "Pride of Table Mountain", which flowers along streams and in cool ravines between January and March. Many of the indigenous plants here are exclusive to the area and grow nowhere else in the world.

Attracted to this Eden of flowering plants is a multicoloured bird population, including Cape sugarbirds, bulbuls, white-eyes, Cape robins and various species of sunbird.

The magic of the Cape's floral kingdom

The mountains and valleys of the Cape Peninsula are home to the Cape floral kingdom, not only the smallest of the world's six floral kingdoms, but also the richest, with the highest known concentration of plants on earth.

This region, including Table Mountain, has more plant species (2 256) than the whole of Great Britain, which is 5 000 times bigger.

When the early Dutch naturalists arrived at the Cape in the 17th century they were amazed at the extraordinary wealth of the local vegetation. They called it "fynbos", meaning, literally, "fine bush", because of the gracious, narrow leaves of many of the plants, notably the proteas and the heaths.

Today there are no less than 7 300 different species of fynbos, including more than 1 000 daisies, 600 irises and 400 lilies. The Western and Eastern Cape have 69 of South Africa's proteas. Among the better known plant species are the king protea (*Protea cynaroides*), the delicate red disa (*Disa uniflora*), which is the symbol of the Cape, and the graceful silver tree (*Leucadendron argenteum*).

The fynbos belt is not confined to the Cape Peninsula, but extends north to beyond the Cederberg range and eastwards along the slopes of the Cape Fold Mountains, which include the Hottentots-Holland, the coastal Langeberg range and the Tsitsikamma and Outeniqua mountain ranges.

Although there are always various species of fynbos in flower, the best time of the year to see flowering fynbos on the mountains of the Peninsula is in spring (September and October).

Among the more prominent flowering plants are sugar bush proteas (*Protea repens*) candelabra flowers (*Brunsvigia* spp.), watsonias, wild hyacinth (*Lachenalia contaminata*), chincherinchee (*Ornithogalum thyrasoides*), common everlastings (*Helichrysum vestitum*), wild dagga (*Lobostemom glaucophyllus*) and a profusion of ericas.

The Cape's floral kingdom also nurtures some rare species of plants, such as the marsh rose (*Orothamnus zeyheri*), the snow protea (*Protea cryophila*) and the beautiful blushing bride (*Serruria florida*), which came close to extinction.

There are hundreds of walks and trails, from easy rambles to tough climbs, that will take you into this floral wonderland. For details, contact the National Botanical Institute, tel. (021) 7621166 or Captour (see *Tourist information*, p. 35). Alternatively, a visit to the Kirstenbosch Botanical Gardens (see p. 32) will reveal a fynbos wonderland of magical proportions.

Open daily, the gardens have a restaurant with souvenirs, information kiosk and bookshop. You can buy indigenous plants throughout the year, but try to visit Kirstenbosch in springtime, when the flowers are at their best. For more information contact the National Botanical Institute at Kirstenbosch, tel. (021) 7621166.

Rhodes Memorial

Set among towering pines on the eastern slopes of Devil's Peak, Rhodes Memorial stands as a tribute to Cecil John Rhodes, former Prime Minister of the Cape, whose life had a lasting impact on the future direction of South Africa. The focal point of the neo-classical granite memorial is a bronze statue designed by Sir Herbert Baker and Francis Masey entitled *Physical Energy*. The drive to Rhodes Memorial passes by European fallow deer browsing under the trees. There's a tearoom near the memorial, where you can look east across the Cape Flats to the unfolding panorama of the Hottentots-Holland Mountains in the distance. Access to Rhodes Memorial is off Rhodes Drive, just past the University of Cape Town campus, as you head out of town.

CAPE TOWN AND THE PENINSULA AT A GLANCE

When to go: The warm dry summers are best. Winters can be cold, with heavy rains, and temperatures plummeting to zero, but these discomforts can be remedied with a blazing log fire in a cosy room. Temperatures start climbing in September when the early spring flowers surge from the ground in a profusion of colour. Summer heralds the onset of the southeasterly winds, which blow through December, January, February and early March. Autumn (late March, April) with its windless, temperate days and cool nights is regarded by many as the best time of the year in Cape Town.

Getting around: The suburban train system is the best in South Africa, connecting the city centre with the southern suburbs, the False Bay coast and the Peninsula as far as Simon's Town. Buses, minibus taxis and saloon car taxis serve the city and its suburbs, but these are not always reliable (particularly on weekends). A better option would be to hire a car (contact Captour, tel. (021) 4185214, or the Waterfront Information Centre, tel. (021) 4182369).

Main attractions: Table Mountain; the Waterfront; Clifton, Hout Bay, Llandudno and Muizenberg beaches; tours to the winelands (see p. 47); Kirstenbosch National Botanical Gardens; Groot Constantia; Chapman's Peak Drive; Cape of Good Hope Nature Reserve.

Tours and excursions: Captour's Visitors' Information Bureau, 3 Adderley Street (outside the station, next to the Translux Building), tel. (021) 4185214, handles tour bookings (coach, sea and air) and car hire reservations. It also has booklets and brochures listing available tours in and around Cape Town. Private tour operators include Springbok Atlas Tours, Hylton Ross Tours and Holidays, Goldtravel (Pty) Ltd and Gamespotter Safaris. Their telephone numbers are listed in the local directory. Transnet luxury coach services (day tours or longer) arrive/depart daily from the Cape Town railway station. Major international car hire operators offer cars in the city.

Walking tours: A two-hour "City on Foot" tour starts at the top of Adderley

Street from the Cultural History Museum. For guided walking tours in the Peninsula call Captour, tel. (021) 4185214 for more information.

Launch trips: There are several harbour tours departing from the Waterfront daily (including a trip to Robben Island and back), and floating restaurants where you can drink and dine on the sea. Sunset cruises depart from Hout Bay regularly (for details of all launch trips contact Captour, tel. (021) 4185214, or the Waterfront Information Centre, tel. (021) 4182369).

Beaches and bathing: For bathing, the warmer waters of the False Bay coast-line (Muizenberg, Sunrise Beach, Strandfontein, Fish Hoek, Kalk Bay, Simon's Town) are preferred. Summer sea temperatures here range from 19 °C down-wards, while the sea temperature on the Atlantic side is often lower than 15 °C. There are public swimming pools in Sea Point, Muizenberg and Newlands (which are very cold in winter), and numerous tidal pools along the coastline, including Camps Bay, Saunders' Rocks, Kommetjie, Buffels Bay and Kalk Bay. There is a heated indoor public pool in upper Long Street where you can also have a Turkish steam bath and sauna.

Tourist information: Captour, 3 Adderley Street (outside the station, next to the Translux Building), Cape Town 8001, tel. (021) 4185214. Satour (SA Tourism Board), 3 Adderley Street, Cape Town 8001, tel. (021) 216274. National Parks Board, PO Box 7400, Roggebaai 8012, tel. (021) 222810.

Shopping: The Golden Acre and its adjacent Strand concourse network, togeth-er with the Victoria Wharf complex at the Waterfront, are the major retail shop-ping centres in Cape Town. For casual, fun shopping, you will find open-air markets at Greenmarket Square, the railway station and the Parade packed with a range of curiosity items, crafts and souvenirs. Speciality shopping is at its best at Cavendish Square in Claremont and at the Tyger Valley Centre between Durbanville and Bellville. Long Street has several antique shops, but beware of tourist traps. Arts, crafts and curio shops abound on the Foreshore and in Strand, Adderley and St George's streets. For a different shopping experience try Access Park, a complex of 60 factory shops in Kenilworth, just off the M5.

Festivals and annual events: The Cape Minstrel Carnival (January); J & B Metropolitan Horse Race (January); the Cape Festival (March); Community Chest Carnival (March); flower shows (August); Rothmans Week Regatta in Table Bay (December).

ACCOMMODATION GUIDE

Visitors have a wide choice of excellent hotels, ranging from the Victoria and Alfred Hotel on the Waterfront, to less sophisticated one-star hotels in the suburbs. There are also guesthouses, holiday apartments and private accommodation advertised in the local news-papers. Book well in advance for the peak holiday season in December and January.

*The Bay***** New hotel overlooking sea at Camps Bay. 65 rooms, 5 suites with bal-conies. PO Box 32021, Camps Bay 8040, tel. (021) 4384444.

The Cape Sun***** City centre. 330 rooms, 20 suites; conference facilities for 750. PO Box 4532, Cape Town 8000, tel. (021) 238844.

The Cellars-Hohenhort Country House Hotel***** Elegant country hotel on landscaped gardens in the Constantia Valley. 38 rooms; 15 suites. PO Box 270, Constantia 7848, tel (021) 7942137.

Mount Nelson***** In the Gardens area. 131 rooms; 28 suites; conference facilities. PO Box 2608, Cape Town 8000, tel. (021) 231000.

The Alphen**** Beautiful Constantia homestead on wine estate. 29 suites and rooms. PO Box 35, Constantia 7848, tel. (021) 7945011.

Capetonian Protea**** Close to harbour and city. 162 rooms; 7 suites; conference facilities for 100. PO Box 6856, Roggebaai 8012, tel. (021) 211150.

Karos Arthur's Seat**** Sea Point near beachfront. 117 rooms, 6 suites; conference facilities. Arthur's Road, Sea Point, Cape Town 8001, tel. (021) 4349768.

Town House**** Near city centre. 104 rooms. PO Box 5053, Cape Town 8000, tel. (021) 457050.

Victoria and Alfred Hotel**** Excellent dockside position in the heart of the Waterfront. 68 rooms. PO Box 50050, Waterfront 8002, tel. (021) 4196677.

The Vineyard**** Historic Newlands house, built in 1799. Beautiful grounds, excellent cuisine. 113 rooms; 9 suites. PO Box 151, Newlands 7725, tel. (021) 642107.

Holiday Inn Garden Court – De Waal*** In the Gardens area. 127 rooms, 3 suites; conference facilities for 150. PO Box 2793, Cape Town 8000, tel. (021) 451311.

Holiday Inn Garden Court – Newlands*** Luxury hotel in southern suburbs, near racecourse and cricket grounds. 139 rooms, 5 suites. Main Road, Newlands 7700, tel. (021) 611105.

Holiday Inn Garden Court – Woodstock*** In Woodstock, five minutes from city. 290 rooms, 2 suites; conference facilities for 900. PO Box 2979, Cape Town 8000, tel. (021) 4484123.

Inn on the Square*** Central Cape Town. 168 rooms. PO Box 3775, Cape Town 8000, tel. (021) 232040.

The Ritz Protea*** Sea Point. 222 rooms; conference facilities for 400. PO Box 2744, Rhine Road, Sea Point 8060, tel. (021) 4396010.

STELLENBOSCH AND THE WINELANDS

Whitewashed homesteads nestling under avenues of oaks, rolling green hills covered with wild flowers, fertile valleys alive with the sounds of surging streams, restaurants with French names and Dutch flavours ... such is the setting of the Cape winelands, home of some of the world's finest wines.

At the epicentre of the winelands, just 45 minutes' drive from Cape Town, is South Africa's oldest town, Stellenbosch. Although Stellenbosch's fame has been driven by viticulture, its enormous wealth of cultural, historic, architectural and scenic options combine to make it the Cape's second-biggest tourist attraction after Table Mountain.

Within a 12 km radius of Stellenbosch are five co-operative wineries and 18 wine farms, lying on four main roads.

Whether you're a connoisseur of fine wines, a lover of Cape Dutch, Georgian and Victorian architecture, or simply a nature-lover seeking magical trails through the mountains, the drowsy university town of Stellenbosch is the place to start your tour of the country's wine routes. You'll get a good overview of the history of the Dutch and French Huguenots in southern Africa, and you'll discover some of the oldest towns in the country.

Most of these colourful towns were established by the first European settlers in South Africa in the 17th and 18th centuries. They reveal old homes that have been beautifully restored and converted to exhibit the craftsmanship of the early settlers.

Old homes, such as De Volkskombuis in Stellenbosch, and farmhouses and cellars, such as those at Boschendal, near Franschhoek, are living museums of a rich cultural heritage.

Cape Dutch yellowwood and stinkwood tables and chairs, antique china, Cape copper, silver, glassware and other period pieces adorn the interiors of these old homes with their atmosphere of tranquillity. Cosy estate restaurants along the wine route offer alfresco meals next to sparkling rivers, in the shade of vine pergolas or towering oaks. The mouth-watering cuisine includes traditional dishes such as bobotie (spicy mince dish), bredies and casseroles, one of which is made with "waterblommetjies" (water hawthorn) and smoorsnoek (salted snoek).

Most estates allow you to taste their vintage wines; a few offer cellar or vineyard tours where you can peek at the secrets of the country's viticulture, developed over a period of three centuries. Others offer donkey rides, picnic sites and pleasant country walks.

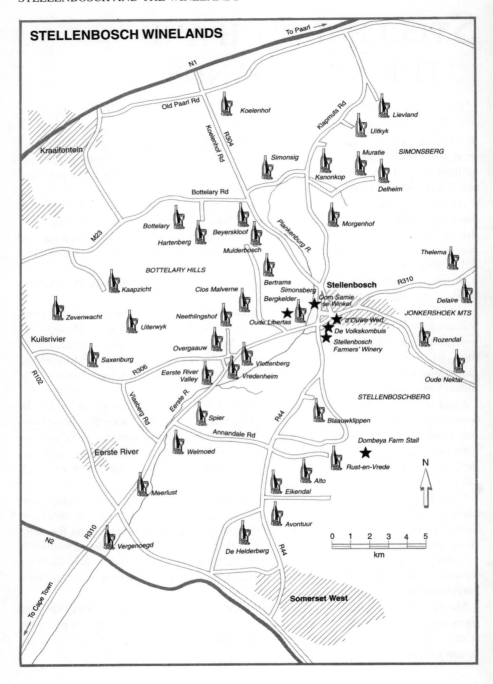

CLIMATE

Summer in the winelands is warm to hot, with temperatures of up to 35 °C in January and February, so dress lightly if you're travelling the wine routes. If you're going hiking in the mountains, wear a hat, and take along a sunscreen and plenty of water. The summer heat subsides in March and April, and many consider this the best time to visit the winelands. Winters are cold, with heavy rains, so take along a raincoat.

Apart from the Stellenbosch Wine Route, there are 11 others winding through the hills and valleys of the southwestern Cape. They include a route through Constantia, the oldest estate, in the southern suburbs of Cape Town; the Paarl and Franschhoek wine routes, which are really extensions of the Stellenbosch route, and the Swartland and Olifants River wine routes, about two hours' drive up the west coast from Cape Town. These last two are covered under the west coast and Namaqualand, p. 60.

All the wine routes are easily accessible from Cape Town, and each one carries an easily recognisable symbol on roadsigns identifying the route. You can visit many of them, sample their top wines and have a meal in one of the estate's restaurants, in one day. For detailed guides to all the wine routes, contact the Captour Visitors' Information Bureau, 3 Adderley Street (outside the station, next to the Translux Building), Cape Town, tel. (021) 4185214. For the Stellenbosch Route, contact the Tourist Information Bureau, 36 Market Street, Stellenbosch, tel. (021) 8833584, or the Stellenbosch Wine Route office, 36 Market Street, Stellenbosch 7600, tel. (021) 8864310.

You can tour the winelands in a luxury, airconditioned bus or a private car, glide over the vineyards in a hot-air balloon, or take a helicopter or aeroplane flip (for details, see *Tours and excursions,* p. 47). To tour the historic sites in and around Stellenbosch, hire a bicycle from Budget Rent-a-Car at 98 Dorp Street, tel. (021) 8839103.

WHAT TO SEE

▆▆ STELLENBOSCH

Just 50 km from Cape Town, Stellenbosch was named after its founder, the Dutch Governor Simon van der Stel, who was convinced that this spot in the fertile valley of the Eerste River was the perfect place to produce wine. Van der Stel planted vines, and the first avenue of oaks in 1679. Some of the oaks still stand today and have been declared national monuments.

The first buildings went up around Die Braak (the village square) – now a grassy place to snooze in the sun – and along Dorp Street, the town's earliest main thoroughfare.

> ┌──── **TIPS FOR TRAVELLERS** ────
> A popular place to start your tour is at the Stellenbosch Farmers' Winery complex where there is an underground cellar-restaurant and open-air amphitheatre. The SFW has wine tasting (but no sales) from Monday to Friday.
>
> Most wine estates on the Stellenbosch Wine Route are open Monday to Friday between 08h30 and 17h00, and offer tasting and wine sales. Some, but not all, open on Saturdays from 08h30 to 13h00.
>
> A few estates offer wine tasting without selling wine; others offer sales without wine tasting. For opening times of specific estates and services offered, see *Tourist information*, p. 48.

Historical buildings

Stellenbosch has more beautiful old buildings and museums than any other town in South Africa. A walk down Dorp Street will introduce you to the longest row of historic buildings in the country. These gracious monuments include the old Lutheran Church built in 1851, and today used as the University Art Gallery; the Town House, at No. 116 Voorgelegen, and La Gratitude, a private dwelling erected in 1798 which carries an "all-seeing eye of God" above a gabled window.

Also in Dorp Street is the Libertas Parva, an H-shaped home built by Lambertus Fick in 1783. Today it houses the Rembrandt van Rijn Art Gallery (artists include Irma Stern, Van Wouw and Pierneef) and, in its cellar, the Stellenryck Wine Museum where you can admire the old vats, Cape furniture and brassware.

Another historic old house is d'Ouwe Werf, in Church Street. Reputed to be the oldest boarding house in South Africa, d'Ouwe Werf stands on the site of the first church building erected in South Africa (1687). It offered lodgings to paying guests in 1802, and serves today as a quaint, irresistible little hotel and coffee shop. Priceless antiques adorn the entrance. d'Ouwe Werf staff can suggest wineland tours you can make, with the hotel as the base (brochures and maps are supplied).

Museums

There are five museums and 76 national monuments in Stellenbosch. For pure historical value, the Stellenbosch Village Museum, consisting of about 5 000 sq metres of the oldest part of town, is way ahead of the rest. The museum is actually a collection of historic houses (restored and furnished in line with their period), whose main entrance provides access to the whole village. This village includes the Schreuderhuis (1709), the country's oldest standing town house; the Blettermanhuis, a typical Cape home, with six gables and an H-shaped ground plan, built in 1788; Grosvenor House (1781), the only perfectly intact example of an early double-storey townhouse with a flat roof and the Mother Church, built in neo-Gothic style by Carl Otto Hager in 1734.

At Die Braak is the VOC Kruithuis, which was built in 1777 and houses a military museum.

Another museum is the Oude Meester Brandy Museum which shows the entire process of brandy-making, from distillation to final blending. It has a fine collection of old labels, stills, bottles and glassware.

Oom Samie se Winkel

One of Stellenbosch's really colourful characters, Oom Samie, was the first general dealer in town. His old shop, a national monument, has been trading since 1904, and is filled with jugs and jars, bags and bushels and the aroma of tobacco, lavender, dried fish and soap. Home-made preserves, curios and other traditional wares are sold here. Nearby is the well-known pub and wine library, De Akker.

Volkskombuis Restaurant

The full title of this restaurant is "De Volkskombuis aan de wagenweg" which literally means "the people's kitchen on the wagon road" (to Cape Town). This is a beautifully restored, Herbert Baker-designed home on the oak-lined banks of the Eerste River that specialises in traditional Cape dishes, based on the early French, German and Dutch cuisines. A beautiful walk, the Eerste River Trail, starts here and ends at the Lanzerac Restaurant.

The Lanzerac Hotel

A visit to Stellenbosch would be incomplete without dropping in to the Lanzerac, a beautiful Cape Dutch estate and mansion built in 1830, which houses an excellent restaurant and a tantalising wine cellar. The architecture here includes pilaster gables and Batavian tiles.

Jonkershoek Valley

Just 10 minutes from the centre of town, the Jonkershoek Valley is an ideal setting in which to capture the full scenic beauty of the Stellenbosch countryside, with its cool crisp air, mountain landscape and tumbling rivers. The Eerste River ploughs through this valley beneath the towering peaks known as the Twins, Haelkop and Stellenboschberg. Lush indigenous forests and wild flowers flourish in this setting, home of the famed Lanzerac and Oude Nektar estates.

The 204-ha Assegaaibosch Nature Reserve within the valley offers short walks, wild flower gardens and picnic sites, with barbecue places near the entrance gate. For details contact the Tourist Information Bureau, tel. (021) 8833584. The neighbouring Jonkershoek State Forest is open between May and September, but a permit is required.

Helshoogte Pass

One of the great scenic routes of the Cape, this pass forms part of what is known as the Four Passes drive from Cape Town. From the summit (7,5 km from Stellenbosch) there are magnificent views of Simonsberg, the Berg River Valley

The Stellenbosch Wine Route

This route was the brainchild of three winemakers from Stellenbosch, who were inspired by France's Routes du Vin and the Weinstrassen in Germany. It was officially opened in April 1971, and introduced the world of wine to the public on a large scale. On a visit to this wine route you have a choice of more than 280 wines (many estates offer cheese or picnic lunches as well), in what is generally accepted as the finest wine region of them all. The 50 or so wine producers and 25 estates rank among the best when it comes to champion wines and winning awards.

Among the highly recommended estates on the Stellenbosch Wine Route are:

Blaauklippen (4 km from Stellenbosch along the Strand Road): View a rare collection of artefacts, have a coachman's lunch and taste some glorious wines at this estate, founded in 1789. Horse-drawn carriage tours of the vineyards are available in summer.

Delaire: Enjoy stunning views of the Boland's mountains and valleys from this estate on top of the Helshoogte Pass. Light lunches and picnic baskets are available.

Delheim: This beautiful estate on the slopes of Simonsberg offers a cold lunch in summer, or soup in the cellar in winter, as you sample its noble wines. The views are stunning, so take a camera along.

Hartenberg: Eat a vintner's lunch on this tranquil estate in the scenic Devon Valley. Wines include Chatillon (dry white), Weisser Riesling, Sauvignon Blanc and Chardonnay.

Eikendal: This estate offers a rural Swiss-style lunch in summer, with a playground for children next to the tasting room. Wines include Merlot, Pinot Noir, Sauvignon Blanc and Chenin Blanc.

Neethlingshof: First farmed in 1692, this estate, nestling behind a long avenue of pines, offers a superb range of quality wines and an excellent meal at the Lord Neethling Restaurant.

Oude Nektar: Lying in the beautiful Jonkershoek Valley, Oude Nektar offers picnic lunches with its delicious wines.

Simonsig: Tour the cellars or stroll through the vineyards of this estate – the first in South Africa to make sparkling wine by the *méthode champenoise*. There's a play area for children, a curio shop, wine tasting and sales.

Spier: This picturesque farm, named after Speyer in Germany, and restored by its owner, has two excellent restaurants – one a former slave house. The wine cellar has been converted into the Ou Kelder Art Gallery.

Van Ryn Brandy Cellar: This is one of the country's largest distilleries, a proud landmark with a chateau character that looks as it did when it was built in 1904. There are weekly tours (Monday to Thursday at 10h30 and 14h30, and on Fridays at 10h30), to show you the fine art of brandy making, musical evenings and a "brandy breakfast", a train journey from Cape Town to the distillery three times a year. To book a seat on the tour (the dates vary from year to year) telephone the cellar (021) 8813875.

and the Groot Drakenstein mountains. It's a perfect place for a picnic, but take along a jersey – it can get cold here.

Farm and craft stalls
No tour of the wine routes is complete without stopping off at a farm stall. Here are some well worth visiting: Blue Jay Farm Stall (on the Klapmuts Road, 2 km from Stellenbosch) – fruits in season; Mooiberge Farm Stall (R44 at intersection of Annandale/Lyndoch roads) – nuts, dried fruit, homemade jams; Polkadraai Farm Stall (near Stellenbosch) – pick your own strawberries; Dombeya Farm (Annandale Road) – handwoven and knitted crafts.

PAARL
Folded mountain ranges of reddish sandstone reach for the sky in this peaceful land of vineyards, valleys and streams. At the heart of this region is Paarl, the largest inland town in the Western Cape and one of the three oldest in South Africa. Flanked by the muddy waters of the Berg River, Paarl lies at the foot of a cluster of giant granite domes. In October 1657, an explorer named Abraham Gabbema called these domes the *paarl* and *diamandt* mountains because, moistened by rain, they looked like giant pearls and diamonds.

The area to the east of these domes later became known as the Paarlvallei (pearl valley), whose first vineyards were planted by the French Huguenots in 1688 and which today represent one of the richest farming areas in the Western Cape.

Paarl itself, 10 km long from end to end, is a quiet former wagon-making town of oak-lined avenues and gabled Cape Dutch, Georgian and Victorian homesteads. It is the headquarters of the Co-operative Wine-growers Association (KWV) – at La Concorde – and has its own wine route.

Oude Pastorie
Beautiful old Cape Dutch furniture, silver, brass and copper are on display in this architectural masterpiece, built in 1786.

Strooidakkerk (Thatched-roof church)
Designed by French architect Louis Thibault, this is one of the oldest churches in South Africa still in use. It was consecrated in 1805 and stands as a national monument.

The Paarl Wine Route

Full-bodied white and red wines, tingling sherries and glowing ports can be tasted on this route, where 17 cellars and estates are open to the public. Among the more classy wines are delicate Sauvignon Blancs and Rieslings, and noble red cultivars, such as Cabernet Sauvignon, Shiraz and Merlot.

Backsberg: This lovely estate lies on the slopes of the Simonsberg near Paarl. Enjoy a guided tour of the wine cellars, and wander at leisure through the small museum of early wine-making equipment.

Laborie: At the foot of Paarl Mountain is the historic manor house and wine cellar of Laborie. Although the wine cellar is not open to the public, a restaurant offers an à la carte menu, traditional dishes such as waterblommetjiebredie (water hawthorn ragout) and the finest Cape wines.

Nederberg: This estate, which has the biggest-selling range of quality wines in South Africa (and more than 900 gold medals to its name), is the venue for the annual Nederberg Wine Auction. The original H-shaped house, built in 1792, and its stately gables, have been perfectly preserved. The estate offers wine tasting and sales, but cellar tours are by appointment only, and picnic lunches must be booked in advance.

Paarl Rock Brandy Cellar: Founded in 1856, this small family cellar offers a brandy-tasting room with a view of Paarl, tours, an audiovisual presentation and a museum.

Rhebokskloof: You can tour the vineyards of Rhebokskloof in a four-wheel drive vehicle, then wine and dine in the estate's traditional Cape restaurant.

Simonsvlei: Year after year, Simonsvlei wins gold medals for its outstanding collection of wines. You can find out why by tasting their wines and touring their cellars.

Keurfontein Wine Tasting Centre: Here you can buy wine from top estates and co-operatives, sample a cheese platter, enjoy a bar lunch in the ladies' bar, or a leisurely meal in the restaurant. In summer you can relax on the pool deck.

For more information on the Paarl Wine Route, the location of the cellars and when you can visit them, write to the Paarl Publicity Association, PO Box 74, Paarl 7620, tel. (02211) 23829.

The Paarl Mountain Nature Reserve

Sugarbirds, sunbirds, Cape buntings and robins flourish in Paarl Mountain's indigenous fynbos (heath) reserve, which has about 200 indigenous flower species. The reserve is well known for its grand displays of flowering proteas and disas, wild aloes, olive and silver trees (*Leucadendron argenteum*). It's an ideal place to picnic under the trees, walk a short trail or fish for bass in one of the several dams.

The early Khoikhoi (Hottentots) called Paarl Mountain "Tortoise Mountain" because of its hard, tortoiseshell appearance. Comprising three granite outcrops –

Britannia Rock, Gordon Rock and Paarl Rock, the mountain provides a stately setting for the Afrikaans Language Monument. Built of concrete made from local granite, this monument towers above the Groot Drakenstein Valley.

Three linked columns, a 57-m-high spire and a fountain symbolise the debt Afrikaans owes to the western world, to the Cape people of eastern origin and to Africa. The scenic Jan Philips Mountain Drive to the top of the mountain includes pleasant picnic spots and the Mill Stream Wild Flower Garden.

Safariland Holiday Resort and Game Park

Just 15 minutes' drive from Paarl you can see elephant, giraffe, eland, wildebeest, springbok and other animals in this 200-ha game park. Self-catering accommodation in bungalows, swimming pools, a curio shop and 10 km of game-viewing drives are the main attractions here. Contact the park at PO Box 595, Suider-Paarl 7624, tel. (02211) 640064.

■■■ FRANSCHHOEK

Named after the Huguenot settlers who discovered the valley in 1688, this cosy little town (Franschhoek means "French glen") is known mainly for its graceful Huguenot Memorial and museum complex, which includes Saasveld, a Cape Dutch home rebuilt here during the 1960s. Make a detour west of Franschhoek to visit the Franschhoek Mountain Manor, which has great food and excellent accommodation in one of the finest country settings in South Africa. It is also the site of Die Binnehof Wine House, which has a selection of all the Franschhoek Valley wines, plus a selection of top wines from the other three wine routes.

The Fruit Route

About one hour's drive from Cape Town, just west of the Du Toitskloof and Bain's Kloof mountains, a deep green valley extends north and west past country towns such as Wellington, Wolseley, Ceres, Tulbagh, Prince Alfred Hamlet, Malmesbury and Riebeeck-Kasteel.

Here the dark, rich soils, well watered by rivers that run off the surrounding mountain ranges, nurture the fruit that makes the area the centre of the dried fruit industry in South Africa, and a major contributor to the annual grape harvest. Wellington, on the banks of the Berg River, is the heart of the Fruit Route, and, on the farm Versailles, houses an old blockhouse – one of 8 000 small forts built by General Sir Horatio Kitchener during the South African War of 1899-1902.

An interesting national monument in Wellington is Twistniet, the original homestead on which Wellington was built.

Bain's Kloof

Just southeast of Wellington, this tarred pass is an outstanding monument to the

Restaurants of Franschhoek

The Franschhoek Wine Route is known not only for its fine wines – some excellent restaurants are to be found in the area. They include:

Boschendal: One of the finest country estates on any of the wine routes, Boschendal was bought by Cecil John Rhodes from Paul de Villiers, the man who built it in 1812. You can dine outside in sumptuous rustic surroundings or in the magnificent restaurant. The estate, declared a national monument in 1976, displays gracious period furniture and delicate friezes, and offers a variety of excellent wines.

The estate features a "waenhuis" (coach house), now a gift shop, and at the neighbouring homestead of La Rhône there is a taphouse where you can taste and buy wines.

Le Petite Ferme: Cosy and unpretentious, this restaurant on the Franschhoek Pass – acclaimed as one of the best in South Africa – offers excellent country-style food and spectacular views of the mountains and valley. The restaurant also serves morning and afternoon teas, tel. (02212) 3016.

Le Quartier Français: This restaurant in Main Road, Franschhoek, serves elegantly prepared French dishes and Cape-style cooking, tel. (02212) 2248.

Clos Cabrière: This famous old Huguenot farm is the home of the Pierre Jourdan range of *méthode champenoise* wines. It is the only farm in the country specialising exclusively in *méthode champenoise,* tel. (02212) 3484.

La Maison de Chamonix: This magnificent restaurant in Uitkyk Road has been voted one of the top three restaurants in the country, tel. (02212) 2393.

skill of the roadbuilder Andrew Geddes Bain, who built it without dynamite or cement in 1850. The ascent provides beautiful views of the valley, Groenberg Mountain and the distant Swartland. At the top is a shady picnic area from where you can walk down to a tumbling river on the southern side (for permits telephone (021) 4833592).

The Franschhoek Wine Route

Officially known as the Vignerons de Franschhoek, this route runs through a valley under the towering peaks of the Franschhoek, Klein Drakenstein and Groot Drakenstein mountains. Of the 14 producers here, 12 are open to the public and specialise in Chardonnay, Sémillon, Sauvignon Blanc, Cabernet Sauvignon, Shiraz and Pinot Noir. Wines produced on the Vignerons de Franschhoek may be tasted and bought at La Cotte Inn, Le Quartier Français, Franschhoek Vineyards Wine Centre, Die Binnehof Wine House at Franschhoek Mountain Manor, Dieu Donné Winery, Boschendal, Bellingham, La Bri and La Motte.

The other wine routes

Perhaps lesser-travelled, but no less appealing, are the Worcester and Robertson wine routes, both of which are a couple of hours' drive northwest of Cape Town (Worcester is on the N1; Robertson is reached by branching off at Worcester).

The Worcester region accounts for 25 per cent of South Africa's grapes, making it the largest producer in the country. The wine route comprises 22 co-operative wineries, producing a large variety of wines, ranging from very dry to the uncompromisingly sweet, but delectable, hanepoots and muscadels.

Recommended stops on this route are Bergsig, Slanghoek and Nuy co-operatives. For more details of this route, contact the Worcester Publicity Association, 23 Baring Street, tel. (0231) 71408.

The Robertson route boasts some 11 co-operatives and seven private producers. Ones to watch for are Rooiberg Co-operative and Roodezandt. While you're in Robertson stop in at Branewynsdraai, a superb restaurant that serves good food and a variety of local wines, tel. (02351) 3202. Further details are available from the Robertson Wine Trust, tel. (02351) 4406.

THE WINELANDS AT A GLANCE

When to go: The summer months (November through March) are ideal for visiting the winelands. At this time, the lush green vines are heavy with grapes in season. The indigenous flowering plants of the winelands, however, are at their best in late winter (July, August), and early spring.

Getting around: A network of well-signposted, excellent roads traverses the winelands and their wine routes, and all of them are easily accessible from Cape Town. The distances and driving times of the major towns from Cape Town are: Stellenbosch: 41 km (35 minutes); Paarl 60 km (45 minutes) and Franschhoek 57 km (45 minutes).

Main attractions: Magnificent scenery. Historical wine estates. Wine tasting and fine restaurants. Picnicking. Walks and hikes. Mountain climbing. Freshwater angling. Hot-air ballooning.

Tours and excursions: *Coach tours:* Specialised wine tours for small or large groups in airconditioned, luxury coaches are offered by most Cape Town tour operators. Particularly recommended are Springbok Atlas Safaris, PO Box 819, Cape Town 8000, tel. (021) 4486545 (Neethlingshof, Stellenbosch, Paarl, Franschhoek route: 8-9 hours); Hylton Ross Travel, PO Box 32154, Camps Bay, Cape Town 8000, tel. (021) 4381500 (Stellenbosch, Du Toitskloof, Huguenot Tunnel, Wellington, Paarl route: 9 hours) and Vineyard Ventures, PO Box 5345, Helderberg 7135, tel. (024) 551658, which offers a variety of vineyard tours.

For information on the Stellenbosch Wine Route call in at the route's offices at 36 Market Street, Stellenbosch, tel. (021) 8864310 (open Monday to Friday) or the Stellenbosch Tourist Information Bureau, also 36 Market Street, Stellenbosch, tel. (021) 8833584. To go on the Ceres Fruit Route, tel. (0223) 61287.

Walking tours: Hundreds of hikes, trails, walks and rambles are available in the winelands. For details contact Stellenbosch Vineyard Hiking Trails, tel. (021) 8833584, or Satour or Captour (see *Tourist information* below).

Day drives: All the wine routes have scenic day drives. For detailed maps of individual routes contact Captour or Satour (below); or Wine Route Rent a Car (Paarl), tel. (02211) 632306.

River adventures: Breede River Adventures offers canoeing trips, hiking, horse-cart trails and abseiling on the mountains, tel. (021) 4610033.

Ballooning: For a hot-air balloon trip over the winelands, contact Wineland Ballooning, tel. (02211) 633192.

Helicopter flips: Court Helicopters, tel. (021) 215900 or 9340560.

Tourist information: For tours of the winelands contact the SA Tourism Board (Satour), 3 Adderley Street (outside the station, next to the Translux Building), Cape Town 8001, tel. (021) 216274 or Captour Visitors' Information Bureau, 3 Adderley Street, Cape Town, tel. (021) 4185214.

Shopping: Try any one of these six shopping centres in Stellenbosch: De Wet, Drostdy, Stellmark, Vallerida, Trust Bank and Admar.

Festivals and annual events: Stellenbosch – University of Stellenbosch Carnival (March); Nederberg Wine Auction (April); Van der Stel Festival (October); Food and Wine Festival (October). Paarl: Vineyard Festival (March). Worcester: Wine and Food Festival (August).

ACCOMMODATION GUIDE

Visitors have a wide choice of excellent guesthouses, country inns and hotels, ranging from Stellenbosch's d'Ouwe Werf Country Inn (one of the oldest in South Africa) to the Swiss-style Franschhoek Mountain Manor. Book well in advance for the peak holiday season in December and January.

STELLENBOSCH

Lanzerac**** Five minutes from town. Historic setting. Excellent restaurant.
  30 en-suite rooms. Conference facilities. PO Box 4, Stellenbosch 7599, tel.
  (021) 8871132.
d'Ouwe Werf*** Historic, quaint setting in town. 25 en-suite rooms. Conference
  facilities. 30 Church Street, Stellenbosch 7600, tel. (021) 8874608.
Devon Valley Protea*** Cosy country hotel. 21 en-suite rooms. Conference facilities.
  PO Box 68, Stellenbosch 7599, tel. (021) 8822012.
Stellenbosch Hotel*** Classy hotel in town. 20 en-suite rooms and suites.
  PO Box 500 Stellenbosch 7599, tel. (021) 8873644.
Wine Route Hotel** Klapmuts Road. 47 en-suite rooms. Conference facilities.
  PO Box 431, Stellenbosch 7599, tel. (021) 8895522.
Bonne Esperance Charming new Victorian guest lodge in Stellenbosch. 15 rooms. Bonne
  Esperance, 17 Van Riebeeck Street, Stellenbosch 7600, tel. (021) 8870225.

L'Auberge Rozendal Excellent new wine estate, guest lodge near Stellenbosch. 16 rooms with scenic views. PO Box 160, Stellenbosch 7599, tel. (021) 8838737.

PAARL

Grande Roche Hotel***** Beautiful country hotel in the heart of the winelands. 5 rooms, 24 family suites. Conference facilities. PO Box 6038, Paarl 7620, tel. (02211) 632727.

Belcher Wine Farm In Paarl itself. Self-catering cottage among vineyards. 6-8 guests. PO Box 541, Suider-Paarl 7624, tel. (02211) 631458.

Mountain Shadows Near Paarl. Cape Dutch manor house in beautiful surroundings. 14 rooms. Tours arranged. PO Box 2501, Paarl 7620, tel. (02211) 623192.

Roggeland Country House Charming country house hotel. Located at crossroads of three wine routes near Paarl. 8 bedrooms. Conference facilities. PO Box 7210, Noorder-Paarl, 7623, tel. (02211) 682501.

Safariland Holiday Resort and Game Park 20 minutes from Paarl. Fully furnished, self-contained luxury and family bungalows. PO Box 595, Suider-Paarl 7624, tel. (02211) 640064.

FRANSCHHOEK

Franschhoek Mountain Manor*** Unbeatable, tranquil country setting. 40 en-suite rooms. Conference facilities. PO Box 54 Franschhoek 7690, tel. (02212) 2071.

La Cotte Inn* Charming country hotel. Huguenot Road, Franschhoek 7690, tel. (02212) 2081.

SOMERSET WEST AREA

Lord Charles***** Five minutes from town. Excellent hotel. 188 rooms. 8 suites. Conference facilities. PO Box 5151, Helderberg 7135, tel. (024) 551040.

Van Riebeeck*** Highly rated, Gordon's Bay. 78 rooms. Conference facilities. PO Box 10, Gordon's Bay 7150, tel. (024) 561441.

Arksey Guesthouse 30 minutes from Cape Town. 12 en-suite bedrooms, courtyard and pool. Popular pub, great hospitality and good food. PO Box 1212, Somerset West 7130, tel. (024) 24913.

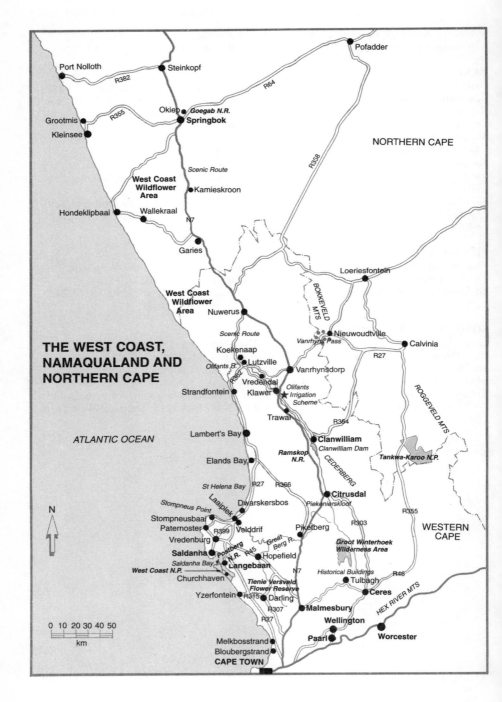

THE WEST COAST, NAMAQUALAND AND NORTHERN CAPE

NORTHERN CAPE

WESTERN CAPE

ATLANTIC OCEAN

Port Nolloth
Steinkopf
R382
Pofadder
R64
Okiep
Goegab N.R.
Springbok
Grootmis
R355
Kleinsee
R358
Scenic Route
West Coast Wildflower Area
Kamieskroon
Hondeklipbaai
Wallekraal
N7
Garies
Loeriesfontein
West Coast Wildflower Area
Nuwerus
BOKKEVELD MTS
Scenic Route
Nieuwoudtville
Koekenaap
Vanrhyns Pass
Calvinia
Lutzville
Olifants R.
Vanrhynsdorp
R27
Vredendal
R362
Olifants Irrigation Scheme
Strandfontein
Klawer
Trawal
ROGGEVELD MTS
R364
Clanwilliam
Lambert's Bay
Clanwilliam Dam
Ramskop N.R.
Tankwa-Karoo N.P.
Elands Bay
CEDERBERG
St Helena Bay
R27
R366
Citrusdal
Laaiplek
Dwarskersbos
Piekenierskloof
Stompneus Point
Stompneusbaai
Velddrif
Pikelberg
R303
R355
Paternoster
R399
Great Berg R.
Groot Winterhoek Wilderness Area
Vredenburg
R45
Saldanha
Postberg N.R.
Hopefield
Langebaan
Historical Buildings
R46
West Coast N.P.
Saldanha Bay
N7
Tulbagh
Churchhaven
Tienie Versveld Flower Reserve
Ceres
Yzerfontein
R315
Darling
HEX RIVER MTS
R307
Malmesbury
R27
Wellington
Melkbosstrand
Paarl
Worcester
Bloubergstrand
CAPE TOWN

N

0 10 20 30 40 50
km

THE WEST COAST, NAMAQUALAND AND NORTHERN CAPE

This Cinderella coastline of South Africa, stretching from Cape Town in the south to the Orange River mouth in the north, is a land of extraordinary contrasts. Scorchingly hot, bone dry and arid along most of its 50 km hinterland for most of the year, the region undergoes a brilliant metamorphosis in late winter, when rain suddenly transforms it into the most extravagantly beautiful flower garden.

In Namaqualand, the land of the Nama Hottentots, this springtime surge of botanical delights creates an enduring spectacle that brings people flocking to it from all parts of the country.

But the Namaqualand flower show is just one of the delights of this unforgettable coastline. As you head north from Cape Town, look back and you will see the famous full-frontal view of Table Mountain, its purple battlements surging up into a layer of billowing cloud. Ahead lies the breadbasket of South Africa, the dark green wheatlands of the Swartland, whose shores are washed by the ice-blue waters of the Atlantic Ocean; the citrus country of Citrusdal and Clanwilliam, whose eastern skyline is dominated by the rugged peaks of the Winterhoekberge, the Cederberge and the Koue Bokkeveld; north of the Olifants River, the Namaqualand countryside stretches out in a seemingly endless plain for 48 000 sq km. In the far north, wind-sculpted pillars of rock of the Richtersveld stand shoulder to shoulder with ghoulish quiver trees and bizarre, human-looking plants, known to the locals as "halfmens" (half-person).

At the coast, the Saldanha-Langebaan area offers sandy white beaches and a natural lagoon which is the focal point of a magnificent wetland wilderness area. This is a peaceful region, blessed with peaceful names such as Schrywershoek, Churchhaven and Darling.

To the north, past Paternoster, Elands Bay and the provincial boundary that separates the Northern Cape from the Western Cape, tiny coastal hamlets hide between low coastal dunes, eking out an existence from the crayfish and pelagic shoals that swarm along these shores. Off the coast seabirds and seals swarm to tiny islands, seeking refuge against the northwest gales of winter.

The west coast has a very special charm. It is a land of frontier posts and fishing ports; of wide open spaces and unending vistas. For weary travellers seeking refuge from the rat race, it is one of the quiet places of Africa.

CLIMATE

Most of the west coast bakes in the summer sun, and gets little relief from sparse winter rains. The northern parts get a meagre 150 mm of rain a year. Winter days are cool to warm; the nights and early mornings bitterly cold.
   The southeasterly wind blows strongly along the coast in summer, and the southern parts of the west coast are lashed by northwesterly storms in winter.

There are several specialised touring routes of the west coast available, the principal ones being the Wine Route, the Wild Flower Route, the Rooibos Tea Route and the Crayfish Route. There's even a Birdwatching Route. See *West coast at a glance* p. 64 for tour operators and contact numbers. A special five-day Flower Safari, organised by the Coast to Coast Tourism Bureau, takes visitors from Cape Town to Namaqualand, the Olifants River Valley and the west coast, then back to the Waterfront in Cape Town. For details telephone (021) 8864669.

WHAT TO SEE

■■■ THE WEST COAST AND NAMAQUALAND

Bloubergstrand

This coastal hamlet on the fringe of the Atlantic commands one of the Cape Peninsula's finest views of Table Mountain and the bay over which it towers. Just 25 minutes' drive from Cape Town, Bloubergstrand (meaning literally "blue mountain beach") has a gently sloping beach, popular with surfers and boardsailors. The water is very cold throughout the year.
   Bloubergstrand is probably at its best at sunset. Drive out from Cape Town for a stroll and sundowner on the beach in summer, and then savour some excellent seafood at Onse Huisie, a restored fisherman's cottage and national monument that has been converted into a restaurant.

Melkbosstrand

The gently sloping beaches of Melkbosstrand (beach of milkwood trees) are popular picnic spots for Cape Town residents looking for a quiet day away from the city. Be sure not to go there when the southeasterly wind is blowing strongly, as the beaches are very exposed, and it can be unpleasant. Just north of the main Melkbos beach is Kapteinsbaai, a good place to collect shells.

The Saldanha-Langebaan area

About two hours' drive north of Cape Town, the Atlantic surges into a massive, magnificent bay of clear blue water that narrows at its southern end to form a lagoon 16 km long and 4,5 km at its widest point. The bay, named after the Castilian navigator, Antonio de Saldanha, who entered Table Bay in 1503, and Langebaan Lagoon, which abuts it, have become focal points of the South African tourist industry – and for good reason: the lagoon, the islands around it, and about 20 000 ha of the coastal zone form the newly proclaimed West Coast National Park, one of the great wetlands of the world, and one of the best birdwatching areas for coastal species in southern Africa.

West Coast National Park

Ornithologists boast that the briny water of this wilderness is home to some 60 million bacteria. Algae, molluscs, crustaceans and other organisms thrive in such abundance that they provide easy pickings for the 100 000 marine birds that fly in (many from the Arctic) in summer.

Squadrons of swift terns (50 per cent of the world's population live here), flamingoes, crowned cormorants, curlew sandpipers, herons, gannets, gulls, plovers, pelicans, sanderlings, knots and turnstones fly in to feast among the shallow waters and on the mud and sand banks for shrimps, prawns, snails and crabs.

The park includes the islands of Marcus, Malgas, Jutten and Skaap, which are also rich in bird life, including thousands of jackass penguins and gannets. Skaapeiland is home to the largest breeding colony of kelp gulls in southern Africa. Boat trips can be arranged to Malgas Island and other boat trips are on offer too. Contact the National Parks Board in Cape Town, tel. (021) 222810.

The park also encompasses the pretty Postberg Nature Reserve, and the tiny lagoon-side hamlets of Stofbergsfontein, Churchhaven and Schrywershoek (named after Ensign Isaq Schrijver, a 17th-century explorer employed by the Dutch East India Company).

Much of the area of the West Coast National Park is restricted, but it is well worth driving along the western peninsula to Churchhaven and Postberg Nature Reserve (take a picnic and a full day for this trip). For park enquiries contact the Park Warden, West Coast National Park, PO Box 25, Langebaan 7537, tel. (02287) 22144.

Headquarters and information centre of the West Coast National Park is Langebaan Lodge, which offers guided birdwatching walks to the salt marsh and driftsands areas. Horseback and hiking trails can be organised, with an overnight stop at an old farmstead called Geelbek. For alternative accommodation you can stay at the Langebaan Herberg, which will give you details of the Crayfish Route.

Langebaan

The little village of Langebaan, which lies at the point where Saldanha Bay joins Langebaan Lagoon, peers out over Skaapeiland and Meeueiland. In spring flowers such as vygies, gazanias and forget-me-nots create a carpet of colour between the cottages which dot the shoreline, and the lagoon is a hive of activity, with boardsailors and catamaran enthusiasts skimming across the surface. The water is very cold here, and swimming is only for the brave.

While you're in Langebaan, try a seaside supper with a difference: Die

Namaqualand's extravagant flower show

Lying between the fertile winelands and wheatlands of the south, and the desert dunes of the Namib Desert in the north, is one of the world's most prolific natural flower gardens – Namaqualand. South Africans know it as the Cinderella part of southern Africa, because of the miraculous change it undergoes every year when winter rains transform it into a fairyland of extravagant floral beauty.

Sterile, sun-scorched and drought-stricken throughout most of the year, it changes dramatically at the end of July when meagre rains, coming in off the icy Atlantic, stir the soil with new life and the promise of spring.

Suddenly, a great rush of growth sweeps across Namaqualand as flowers spring from the ground in an extraordinary symphony of colour. Daisies carpet the countryside in delicate seas of white, followed by purple sheets of wild cineraria and everlastings. These are soon joined by the red and orange mantles of Namaqualand daisies, and the subtle fluorescence of mesembryanthemums. In all, 4 000 floral species put in an appearance along this coast. They include aloes, lilies and a host of other plants.

Namaqualand becomes a mecca for nature lovers from all over South Africa. The N7 highway from Cape Town runs right through Namaqualand. The highway, and smaller roads branching off it along the coast, afford good views of this botanical feast.

The best time to see the flowers is from late August to mid-September. During this time, you can phone Satour's Flower Hotline at (021) 9491489/90, which will advise you of specific flower viewing areas, and the phone numbers of people to contact in these areas. Try to see the flowers on clear sunny days. The best viewing times are between 11h00 and 15h00.

If you want to go it alone, here are some popular routes that take you through the heart of Namaqualand's flower displays:
Kamieskroon – Leliefontein – Gariesfontein – Kamieskroon;
Springbok – Hondeklipbaai – Wallekraal – Kamieskroon – Springbok;
Springbok – Steinkopf – Port Nolloth – Grootmis – Springbok;
Nuwerus – Koekenaap – Strandfontein – Vredendal – Vanrhynsdorp – Vanrhyn's Pass.

Be sure to set aside at least one day for each of these routes. If you want to visit most of them, set aside a week, and phone the tourism information centres listed in *West Coast at a Glance*, p. 64.

Recommended reading: *Namaqualand – South African wildflower guide*, by A le Roux and E Schelpe; *Garden of the gods*, by Freeman Patterson.

Strandloper is a seafood restaurant on the beach, and serves just about anything marine you can think of, from mussels to crayfish, tel. (02287) 22490.

Club Mykonos
North of Langebaan Lagoon is a Greek-style hotel, time-share and resort complex of spacious whitewashed apartments, where you can stay in furnished luxury on the edge of the Atlantic. Among the many attractions are a gymnasium and sports complex (with heated pools, squash and tennis courts), restaurants, coffee shops and delicatessens.

There's also a waterfront cluster of shops and a 140-berth marina, and beyond that a beautiful, isolated stretch of beach where you can have a picnic.

Saldanha Bay
The smell of fish hangs heavy in Saldanha Bay, for this safe harbour – one of the great natural harbours of the world – is a major concourse for the ships that harvest the pelagic riches of the west coast. There are factories manufacturing fishmeal, fish canning factories, and factories that process west coast rock lobsters for export. The port is also a terminal point for huge, international iron-ore carriers and is geared to handle up to 33 million tons of ore a year.

While the countryside around Saldanha is dull and flat, a walk to the top of Hoedjieskop above the town reveals the beautiful expanse of the Atlantic stretching north and south along the coastline. To the left, the iron ore jetty snakes out into the bay, enclosing the attractive Hoedjiesbaai, where there is safe swimming and waterskiing.

Every Wednesday the town offers guided tours of the harbour and loading terminal (enquire at the harbour or contact the Vredenburg-Saldanha Publicity Association).

In the last 10 years, a new industry, called sea farming or aquaculture, has made significant strides in Saldanha Bay, with the artificial cultivation of marine fauna such as blue Mediterranean mussel, South African clam and Japanese oyster.

Halfway between Saldanha Bay and Vredenburg, a road leads down to an isolated part of the coast called Jacobsbaai. Here, and at the nearby farm of Swartriet, you can hire cottages that are just a stone's throw from the beach.

Paternoster
This fascinating west coast fishing village, with its quaint, whitewashed fishermen's cottages, is a must on any traveller's itinerary – if only to sample the excellent seafood (including a snoek barbecue) at the Paternoster Hotel, and walk along the tranquil beach in front of it. Traditionally a sport diver's paradise, this hamlet yields quotas of large rock lobster from its cool waters. Today, tiny fishing boats ply its waters, returning with catches of lobster, hottentot and snoek. Artists and photographers find this part of the coastline particularly appealing, with its seclud-

ed bays, rocky coves and kelp-strewn beaches. A weekend at Paternoster's charming hotel is highly recommended. Just south of Paternoster is Tietiesbaai, a rocky cove in the Cape Columbine Nature Reserve, where there are numerous drives and walks (a map will be given to you at the entrance). The Columbine lighthouse was built here in 1936 after two ships, the *St Lawrence* and the *Lisboa,* ran aground there.

Just north of Paternoster, stretching 21 km from Stompneus Point to the Berg River mouth, is St Helena Bay, another of the west coast's great fishing centres. Here beautiful beaches line the bay beneath a ridge of low-lying hills.

Velddrif-Laaiplek

A graceful bridge across the Berg River at Velddrif is the finish point for the rugged, annual 280-km Berg River Canoe Marathon. Waterskiing, boating, fishing and canoeing are popular here. Special attractions are the marina at Port Owen, named after the developer, Owen Wiggins, where you can hire a fully equipped cabana; bokkem (dried fish) factories at Laaiplek harbour; a restaurant specialising in west coast seafood, and a yacht club.

A variety of birds, including flamingoes, spoonbills and avocets, feed off the nutrient-rich waters of the estuary. Rocher Pan, further north near Dwarskersbos, also offers a varied bird life.

Elands Bay

Take a tent along with you, or, if you're going in the flower season, book well in advance at the Verlorenvlei Country Inn, tel. (0265) 724, to savour the stillness of this lovely surfer's paradise off the beaten track. Long, sweeping beaches, a prolific birdlife, and the opportunity to dive for large crayfish bring visitors back time and again. Verlorenvlei, near Elands Bay, is a birdwatcher's wonderland, with more than 230 species, including migrants that come here to escape the harsh European winter. The Eland Hotel has 16 rooms, and there are cottages for hire. At Baboon Point, a cave in the hills is adorned with old San (Bushman) paintings.

Piketberg

This small town lies at the foot of the Piketberg range and is surrounded by golden fields of wheat in summer. The mountains around the town were once the stronghold of the San and Khoikhoi people who have left a legacy of paintings on the walls of the caves. The Piketberg Museum in Hoog Street, furnished in Edwardian style, is worth a visit. It is open weekdays between 14h30 and 16h30.

Citrusdal

Heart of the southwestern Cape's citrus-growing region, this town in the fertile valley of the Olifants River is known by locals as the Golden Valley, because of its enormous wealth of oranges. Stop at any roadside stall near Citrusdal in winter and you can sample some of the country's finest oranges – valencias and navels – and naartjies. The original orchards of Citrusdal were grown from seeds planted in the garden of the 17th century Dutch commander at the Cape, Jan van Riebeeck, and the fruit is of world-class standard.

You can visit one of the largest orange packing sheds in the country at De Goede Hoop Citrus Co-operative, which handles 66 000 tons of fruit annually. Book a tour by phoning (022) 9212211 from March to September, or contact the Citrusdal Municipality at (022) 9212181. An orange tree at Groot Hexrivier, which is over 200 years old, has been declared a national monument.

Other attractions are the town's red and white jerepigo (sweet wines) and its muscadel. There is a hotel and caravan park among the trees on the banks of the river.

You can spend a few invigorating days in the country near Citrusdal at the famous Baths, a radioactive spa with a hot spring, jacuzzis and comfortable chalets run by the McGregor family. Just 18 km from Citrusdal, the area abounds in birdlife, with 128 species in all. For accommodation in chalets, rooms, caravan or camping sites contact The Baths Health Resort, PO Box 133, Citrusdal 7340, tel (022) 9213609. Alternatively, try the luxury chalets of the Piekenierskloof Mountain Resort at the top of the Piekenierskloof Pass, tel. (022) 9212570.

Clanwilliam

Travellers converge on this, one of the 10 oldest towns in South Africa, in spring and summer for two main reasons. Firstly, the Clanwilliam Dam is probably one of the best inland watersport spots in the country, and secondly, the flowers around Clanwilliam are superb.

The focal points of the flower displays are the 125-ha Ramskop Nature Reserve, on the eastern banks of Clanwilliam Dam, and the nearby Biedouw Valley, whose extravagant displays of wild flowers have earned it the name of "Little Namaqualand".

Numerous trails take you through Ramskop reserve and bring you back to a rooftop tearoom which offers panoramic views of the Cederberg Mountains, the Pakhuis Pass and the Olifants River Valley. Also on the outskirts of the town are the two picnic spots of Boskloof and Kranskloof, which offer pretty country rambles. The Clanwilliam Flower Garden in Main Road has its own splendid floral displays.

This quaint town, with its thatched houses and concrete streets, is the growing centre of an aromatic herbal brew known as Rooibos tea, grown from the indigenous rooibos or red bush (*Aspalathus linearis*). Caffeine-free and low in tannin,

The Cederberg Wilderness Area

Among all the wilderness areas of South Africa, the Cederberg has a special magic of its own: ancient, gnarled cedar trees rise up like phantoms in the rocky hills and valleys, where wind and water have sculpted extraordinary formations out of the sandstone bed. The Cederberg Mountains, running north-south for some 100 km, and rising to their peak at Sneeuberg (2 028 m), dominate the area. The Clanwilliam cedars (*Widdringtonia cedarbergensis*), after which the area is named, cling to heights up to 1 500 m, and some are nearly 1 000 years old.

This is a region of streams winding through secret valleys, waterfalls cascading over fern-clad rocks, and crystalline pools basking between corridors of flowers. Above the snowline, the pure-white snow protea (*Protea cryophila*) flourishes in the only habitat it has on earth.

For nature lovers, the Cederberg is a paradise. More than 254 km of remote footpaths and animal tracks take hikers, backpackers, photographers and bird-watchers through deep, silent valleys where they can marvel at the strangely eroded rock formations, listen to the birdsong or revel in the cool waters.

Among the classic rock formations are a 20-m-high pillar called the Maltese Cross, the Wolfberg Arch, and a 30-m cleft called the Wolfberg Cracks.

About 30 mammal species roam the area, including steenbok, grysbok, grey rhebok, klipspringer, caracal, baboon and wild cat.

The centre of the Cederberg, and chief departure point for hikers, is the Algeria Forest Station, which lies in the valley of the Rondegat River. This is reached by a good gravel road. There is a lovely camping ground and picnic site here, and you can swim in the river.

Travel in the Cederberg Wilderness Area is on foot only, but guides or donkeys may be hired to help you get around. It is essential to take a forestry map (available at Algeria) with you, and a compass is recommended.

Spring, summer and autumn are the preferred times to go. More than 1 000 mm of rain falls here in winter and it can get extremely cold. The summers are hot and dry, with temperatures of up to 35 °C.

A word of warning: the 15 species of snake found here include the potentially lethal berg adder and the puff adder, so wear strong hiking boots for protection.

Entry is by permit only. To book a campsite at Algeria or in the Pakhuis Pass (you must book three months in advance) contact the Nature Conservator, Private Bag X1, Citrusdal 7340, tel. (022) 4822812. For other accommodation write to Cederberg Tourist Park, PO Box 284, Clanwilliam 8135, tel (027) 4822807. For other details contact tel. (02623) 2900.

Take along cooking utensils, food, sleeping bags, tents and water (in the summer months).

A popular alternative to the Cederberg is the Groot Winterhoek Wilderness Area to the south, where you may camp under the stars in rare and beautiful surroundings.

Rooibos is experiencing a growing worldwide demand. You can tour Clanwilliam's tea-packing sheds, tel. (027) 4822155 or (027) 4821109

Clanwilliam Dam, on the fringes of the town, is 18 km long and has become a favourite venue for picnickers, waterskiers and powerboat enthusiasts, and more recently, a venue for triathlons.

If you'd like to stop over in Clanwilliam for a day or two, try the Olifants Dam Motel or the Clanwilliam Hotel.

Lambert's Bay

This large fishing village, which was named after the British naval commander at the Cape in 1820, Rear-Admiral Sir Robert Lambert, is best known as the centre of the west coast's crayfishing industry, and a paradise for birdwatchers. The bay's Bird Island, home to more than 150 species of seabird, is possibly the world's noisiest natural airport. Here thousands of Cape gannets, penguins, cormorants, seagulls and other, smaller birds find a perfect refuge and breeding place. Together they produce about 300 tons of phosphorus-rich guano, which is harvested for commercial use. A series of pans at Steenbokfontein and Wagendrift, about 8 km south of Lambert's Bay, are a favourite haunt for aquatic birds and birdwatchers, so take your binoculars along.

The breakwater joining Bird Island to the mainland shelters a large fleet of colourful fishing boats.

Lambert's Bay has a museum, a caravan and camping area with 250 sites, and a comfortable hotel, the Marine Protea Hotel. Although the water is very cold, you can swim in the large tidal pool south of the town, or collect shells along the beach.

For birdwatchers there's a wealth of birds (including flamingoes) at Krompoort, 13 km from Lambert's Bay, on the road to Leipoldtville.

A special attraction at Lambert's Bay is the open-air restaurant called Die Muisbosskerm, which serves delicious seafood in a rough and ready environment.

Springbok

Originally named Springbokfontein, this small town takes its name from the thousands of small fawn-and-white antelope that used to congregate here. Reminders of its early history as a major copper mining town include a prospecting shaft sunk by Dutch Governor Simon van der Stel in 1685, and an old smokestack built by Cornish miners in 1886.

Today it is one of the main stopover points on the highway to Namibia. The main attraction, 15 km east of Springbok, is the Goegab Nature Reserve (incorporating the Hester Malan Nature Reserve) covering 7 000 ha. The reserve features 45 mammal species, including gemsbok, eland and springbok, and 29 reptile species, in a landscape of huge granite domes and broad grassy plains. There is a network of game-viewing roads and three hiking trails of 4,5 km, 5 km and 7 km. The best time to visit is early spring, when the flowers are in bloom.

West coast wine country

The winelands of the west coast region boast the Swartland and Olifants River wine routes, and they extend roughly from Malmesbury (the Swartland) to Vanrhynsdorp (Olifants River) north of Clanwilliam. Comfortable hotel accommodation is available at country towns along both routes, particularly at Malmesbury, Citrusdal and Clanwilliam (see *Accommodation guide,* p. 66).

The Swartland offers deep green valleys and undulating vineyards beneath imposing mountain chains, and is just a 40-minute drive from Cape Town. The low rainfall and warm climate contribute to creating robust wines. Fortified, white as well as red wines can be sampled at three wine cellars and one estate.

The Olifants River Wine Route, sandwiched between the Cederberg Mountains and the west coast, stretches 200 km, from Citrusdal to Lutzville in the north, and includes the towns of Clanwilliam, Klawer, Trawal, Vredendal and Koekenaap. You'll need more than a day to explore this wine route, but it gives you the chance to view the spectacular Cederberg range, and the country's most elevated wine cellar, 900 m above sea level. Two of South Africa's largest co-operatives are situated here. The estates specialise in white wines. The best time to visit is spring and summer.

For full details of various tours available around this part of the west coast, including wine route tours, wild flower tours and crayfish tours, contact the Coast to Coast Tourism Bureau, PO Box 7327, Stellenbosch 7599, tel. (021) 8864669 or the Olifants River and West Coast Tourism Bureau in Kalkrand Street, Klawer, tel. (02724) 61731. Wine cellars to consider are: Cederberg Winery, Citrusdal Co-operative Wine Cellars, Klawer Co-operative Wine Cellars, Lutzville Vineyards Co-operative and Vredendal Co-operative Wine Cellar.

North of Springbok the country opens up into a vast region of scrubveld and scattered grassy plains known as the Richtersveld. Curiosities of the region are the bizarre halfmens (half-human) plant and the quiver trees, used formerly by the Bushmen (San) to make quivers for their arrows.

Richtersveld National Park

This 162 445-ha park is remote, rugged and rough, but it holds one of the most diverse collections of succulents in the world, as well as an interesting community of mammals and birds.

Grey rhebok, steenbok, duiker and Hartmann's mountain zebra are found here, as well as baboons, vervet monkeys, caracals and leopards.

Apart from game-viewing and birdwatching, there's good angling and bathing in the Orange River, but be careful, the river has claimed many lives over the years.

You can get entry, overnight and fishing permits at Sendelingsdrif (open 08h00 to 16h00). There's no formal accommodation in the park, but you can camp at specified spots. If you wish to overnight, take tents, tarpaulins, chairs and bedding; food and drinking water; cooking utensils, toiletries, medicines and refuse bags.

The best way to get there is via the N7 north of Springbok to Steinkopf, and then northwards along the coast to Alexander Bay. From Alexander Bay, it's 93 km to Sendelingsdrif, the park's headquarters. For more information, contact the Warden, Richtersveld National Park, PO Box 406, Alexander Bay 8290, tel. (0256) 506.

THE NORTHERN CAPE

If you're driving from Cape Town to Johannesburg, the national road winds through the massive mountain chains that fringe the northern part of the Cape coastal terrace – the Dutoitsberge, the Hex River Mountains and the Witberge. After Worcester, the road starts ascending a beautiful mountain pass to reach the beginning of a vast, interior plateau, known as the Great Karoo – the largest natural ecosystem in South Africa.

This is a very dry country, and you could be forgiven for thinking there's not much to it, except a flat, endless landscape, punctuated by hillocks (known as koppies) and shallow valleys. But beneath the tussocked grasslands of this plain, and compressed between the layers of shale that form the koppies, rest untold secrets of the country as it was 200 million years ago.

In those days the Karoo was a great swampland inhabited by bizarre fossil-like reptiles that stalked the land. The existence of these amazing creatures, with such names as *Massospondylus, Thrinaxodon,* a mammal-like reptile, and *Rubidgea,* a flesh-eating creature, proved the evolutionary link between reptiles and mammals, and established the Great Karoo as one of the focal points of palaeontologists and geologists worldwide.

About 190 million years ago, huge outpourings of basaltic lava exterminated this world of mammal-like reptiles, but their fossils remain embedded in the Great Karoo, a huge natural museum, whose wares are on display in the serenely beautiful Karoo National Park.

Karoo National Park

Established in 1979, this park is a wonderful place to make a detour on the long road from the Cape to the northern parts of South Africa. It lies just south of the Karoo town of Beaufort West on the N1, about four hours' drive from Cape Town.

The park covers more than 46 000 ha of typical Karoo country, and incorporates part of the Nuweveld Mountains. Among the 61 species of mammals you can see here are springbok, Cape mountain zebra, kudu, gemsbok, red hartebeest, mountain reedbuck, grey rhebok, eland and bat-eared fox. The park also serves as a sanctuary to 20 breeding pairs of black eagles and 183 other species of bird. The 58 or so species of reptile include five tortoises.

Two rest camps offer superior accommodation in tranquil surroundings. The Karoo Rest Camp has airconditioned Cape Dutch-style chalets that are serviced and equipped with crockery, cutlery, bedding, towels and soap. One of the cottages has been adapted for handicapped people.

The Mountain View Rest Camp offers hutted accommodation, with only beds and mattresses provided. There's a communal ablution block here, and you must bring your own bedding, towels and food.

There's a 4x4 trail (maximum eight people), with one overnight stop in a hut on the plains at Afsaal, or accommodation at the Doornhoek Guesthouse.

Apart from the 4x4 trail, there are four main hiking trails: the three-day Springbok Trail, the Fossil Trail, which has fossil exhibits along the way, the Bossie Trail and the 11-km Fonteintjieskloof Trail.

Other attractions are game-viewing, night drives and a swimming pool.

For reservations and enquiries, you can write to the National Parks Board, PO Box 787, Pretoria 0001, tel. (012) 3431991 or Cape Town, PO Box 7400, Roggebaai 8012, tel. (021) 222810.

Augrabies Falls

The name Augrabies comes from the Khoikhoi word "loukurubes" (the noise-making place), and describes the huge gorge in the Northern Cape into which the Orange River plunges on its way to the Atlantic Ocean.

The river flows across a plateau and then very suddenly plunges 56 m down slippery walls of granite into the gorge. When the river comes down in flood, numerous secondary falls are created, accelerating the roar of the Augrabies that can be heard from kilometres away.

The gorge itself is 18 km long, and the river drops a further 35 m along this course in a series of spectacular rapids.

One of the six great waterfalls of the world, the Augrabies provides a magnificent setting for the Augrabies Falls National Park – once the home of the San and Khoikhoi, who fed on the river's fish, and the roots, berries and beans that grow there.

Today the park is a highly recommended stopover point for travellers on their way to the Kalahari Gemsbok National Park.

In his book *To the river's end*, author Lawrence Green described Augrabies as follows: "It is the rock that remains vivid in the memory, the masses of black and grey granite, the steep rock walls of the canyon. Mile after mile of gigantic rock faces, washed and polished by the floods of centuries, naked, slippery, steep and deadly."

A suspension bridge over the falls gives panoramic views of the river and gorge, and there are protected lookout points alongside the falls. Although some of these are easily scaled, this practice is highly dangerous. Five people have been washed over the falls (one survived).

TIPS FOR TRAVELLERS

The altitude and the atmosphere of these regions tend to dry the nasal passages and the skin, so take along a moisturising cream and a balm for the lips. A sun-protection cream is also needed if you're going there from October to March.

Travel as early as possible in the morning, hopefully avoiding the hot hours between midday and 15h00.

For reservations or further enquiries, write to the National Parks Board, PO Box 787, Pretoria 0001, tel. (012) 3431991; Cape Town, PO Box 7400, Roggebaai 8012, tel. (021) 222810.

A rich variety of plant life survives on the meagre rain that falls here. They include the prehistoric-looking kokerboom, the camel thorn, white karee, wild olive and Karoo boerbean.

Animals include rhino, eland, baboon, monkeys, small antelope, such as klipspringer, and birds.

The rest camp is clean, comfortable and shaded by trees. The four-bed, airconditioned chalets, with bathroom, kitchenette and braai (barbecue) area, are a short stroll from a large, à la carte restaurant. There's a museum next to the restaurant displaying the gemstones, rocks and fauna and flora of the area. There's also a camping site.

The three-day Klipspringer Hiking Trail follows the course of the Orange through the Augrabies Falls Gorge, and offers overnight huts with bunks, toilets and braai facilities. Take your own food and cooking equipment.

Kalahari Gemsbok National Park

This beautiful park in the northwestern corner of South Africa is the largest nature conservation area in southern Africa (nearly a million hectares), and one of the truly wild places on the subcontinent. But be warned – it gets extremely hot here in summer, with temperatures often running into the 40s. Those who can take the midsummer heat – from November to February – qualify for a 25 per cent discount off the fare for staying in the park.

Wedged between Namibia and Botswana, it is an ideal place for complete solitude, excellent game-viewing and comfortable accommodation in three rest camps. The roads to the park are long – and often dusty – so if you're driving from Johannesburg or Cape Town, give yourself plenty of time for the journey.

The countryside in the park is typical Kalahari – sand dunes, tinged red by iron oxide, taper off to broad dry, or fossil riverbeds that serve as semi-desert highways for teeming populations of game.

Huge herds of wildebeest, springbok, eland and smaller groups of gemsbok and red hartebeest trample the dry beds of the Nossob and Auob rivers, while lion, cheetah, leopard, wild dog, jackal, brown hyaena and spotted hyaena roam the grassland and thorny scrub between the dunes. Smaller mammals, such as steenbok, duiker, bat-eared foxes and porcupines can also be seen.

More than 215 species of birds, including kori bustards, marabou storks, yellow-billed hornbills and a variety of raptors are to be found here. The most prominent of the winged inhabitants of the park are the sociable weavers, whose huge "sectional title" apartment-nests you will see scattered throughout the park.

There are three rest camps – Twee Rivieren (the largest), Mata Mata and Nossob, all of which offer comfortable family accommodation, with kitchen and bathroom, huts with showers and toilets, and huts with communal ablution blocks. There are camping sites at each camp with ablution facilities.

Twee Rivieren, attractively laid out near the southwestern Botswana border, offers thatched chalets, an enclosed swimming pool, a restaurant and a lapa (walled enclosure) where brunches and evening braais (barbecues) are served.

There's a petrol pump, a landing strip and a shop where you can buy groceries, curios and wine, beer and spirits. You can also hire a car at Twee Rivieren, but book well in advance.

Petrol is also available at Nossob and Mata Mata, and both camps have a shop. Nossob also has a landing strip, and an information centre that tells you about the plant and animal life in the park.

For reservations or further enquiries, write to the National Parks Board, PO Box 787, Pretoria 0001, tel. (012) 3431991; Cape Town, PO Box 7400, Roggebaai 8012, tel. (021) 222810.

THE WEST COAST, NAMAQUALAND AND NORTHERN CAPE AT A GLANCE

When to go: Late winter and early spring (August, September, October), with its feast of wild flowers in Namaqualand, are best. Dress warmly, as the nights can be bitterly cold at this time. The summers are hot and dry, with temperatures reaching the upper 30s in December, January and February. This is a winter rainfall region which, in places, records only 150 mm a year.

Getting around: *Road:* The N7, a wide, well-tarred highway runs north from Cape Town up the west coast to Vioolsdrift on South Africa's border with Namibia. The road runs parallel to the coast, between 50-75 km inland for most of the way, and feeds numerous secondary roads, many of them gravel, that lead to the coast. Some of these roads, particularly the coastal road between Port Nolloth and Alexander Bay, can be in very poor condition (you need a permit to enter Alexander Bay). To get to Port Nolloth take the R382 left off the N7. For Augrabies Falls turn right at Okiep on the R64.

Coach travel: The Namaqualand Bus Service operates between Cape Town and Springbok, tel. (021) 216630 or (0251) 22061. Hylton Ross Travel runs coach trips to Langebaan and Saldanha (see *Tours and excursions,* on p. 65).

Air: National Airlines operates a scheduled weekly service between Cape Town and Springbok, serving Alexander Bay, Upington and Aggeneys en route. For information and bookings, tel. (021) 9314183/4 or (0251) 22061. Regular flights from Lanseria Airport near Johannesburg also service the Northern and Western Cape, tel. (011) 6592750 for information and bookings.

Sea: For cruises in the Langebaan-Saldanha area, contact the Vredenburg-Saldanha Publicity Association, tel. (02281) 41276 or the Langebaan Publicity Association, tel. (02287) 2115. Schaafsma Charters, tel. (02281) 44235, offer west coast cruises. In Cape Town Intec Marine, tel. (021) 473070 offers sailing courses and cruises up the west coast.

Main attractions: Viewing Namaqualand's spectacular display of wild flowers. Sampling delicious seafood dishes (including west coast rock lobster) at coastal resorts. Hiking and climbing trails in the Cederberg. Birdwatching at Langebaan and in the Cederberg. Camping and caravanning. Boating, waterskiing and canoeing at Velddrif, Langebaan, Saldanha and Clanwilliam Dam. Picnicking among the orchards in citrus country.

Tours and excursions: For detailed information on wild flower, crayfish and wine route tours, contact any one of the following: the Coast to Coast Tourism Bureau, PO Box 7327, Stellenbosch 7599, tel. (021) 8864669; the Olifants River and West Coast Tourism Bureau in Kalkrand Street, Klawer, tel. (02724) 61731; Springbok Tourist Forum, 37 Voortrekker Street, Springbok, tel. (0251) 21321; Kamiesberg and Sandveld Tourism Forum, PO Box 30, Kamieskroon 8241, tel. (0257) 858. Alternatively, contact Captours' Visitors' Information Bureau at 3 Adderley Street, Cape Town (outside the station, next to the Translux Building), tel. (021) 4185214; the South African Tourism Board, 3 Adderley Street, Cape Town 8001, tel. (021) 216274; the Lambert's Bay Tourism Association, PO Box 245, Lambert's Bay 8130, tel (027) 432233. Coach tour operators who run tours up the west coast include: Hylton Ross Tours and Holidays, tel. (021) 4381500; Specialised Tours, tel. (021) 253259 and Sealink Tours, tel. (021) 254480.

Walking tours: There are plenty of attractive walks and trails in the west coast region, ranging from scenic rambles in the Cederberg and an overnight trail in the West Coast National Park, to Namaqualand flower trails and long hikes through the Richtersveld from Springbok (see contact numbers above). There are walks of particular interest at: the West Coast National Park, tel. (02287) 22144; the Ramskop Nature Reserve, Clanwilliam; the Rocher Pan Nature Reserve near Velddrif; Yzerfontein Sandveld Trails (for accommodation on Blombos Farm, contact Mrs Wrightman, 14 Higgo Crescent, Higgovale, Cape Town 8001); and the Columbine Nature Reserve, 3 km south of Paternoster (maps available at the entrance).

Beaches and bathing: In general few bathers venture into the waters of the west coast because they are extremely cold (sometimes as low as 12 °C). For the brave, Langebaan Lagoon is safe, but avoid the deeper channels near the village of Langebaan. Hoedjiespunt Beach at Saldanha, Jacobsbaai, Swartriet and Elandsbaai all have attractive, sandy beaches.

Tourist information: Captour, 3 Adderley Street (outside the station, next to the Translux Building), Cape Town 8001, tel. (021) 4185214. South African Tourism Board, 3 Adderley Street, Cape Town 8001, tel. (021) 216274. National Parks Board, PO Box 7400, Roggebaai 8012, tel. (021) 222810. The Langebaan Publicity Association, Bree Street, Langebaan, tel. (02287) 22115.

Festivals, special events: Darling Wild Flower Show (September); Hopefield Fynbos Show (August); Saldanha Sea Harvest Festival (September); Olifants River Wine Show, Vredendal (October).

ACCOMMODATION GUIDE

The quality of hotel accommodation decreases the further up the west coast you go, with the exception of Lambert's Bay, where there is an excellent holiday hotel, the Marine Protea Hotel*** (PO Box 249, Lambert's Bay 8130, tel (027) 4321126) and Citrusdal, where the Cederberg Hotel** (PO Box 37, Citrusdal 7340, tel. (022) 9212221) offers comfortable accommodation and friendly service. Langebaan Lodge in the West Coast National Park offers clean accommodation: PO Box 25, Langebaan 7357, tel. (02287) 22144. Club Mykonos is highly recommended: Private Bag X2, Langebaan 7357, tel. (02287) 22101; Blouwaterbaai Beach Cottages at Saldanha Bay offers furnished cottages that can accommodate six people each, tel. (02281) 41177. To savour the simple pleasures of a genuine west coast fishing village, try the Paternoster Hotel – it has an excellent seafood menu and comfortable accommodation, tel. (02285) 7521703.

For ungraded holiday accommodation, contact Cape Holiday Homes, tel. (021) 4190430.

For accommodation in the Cederberg write to Cederberg Tourist Park, PO Box 284, Clanwilliam 8135, tel. (027) 4822807.

THE SOUTHERN CAPE

Near Gordon's Bay in the southwestern Cape, the blue ramparts of a rugged range, known as the Hottentots-Holland Mountains, rise precipitously from the floor of False Bay's sandy flats. Towering over a hinterland of tiny Western Cape towns, this range heads eastward, tracking the coastline with stupendous peaks, forested gorges and tumbling valleys. Known collectively as the Cape Fold Mountains, these sandstone giants form the dividing line between the narrow, lush coastal terrace, the rugged interior behind it known as the Little Karoo, and the elevated, dry plateau of the Great Karoo, which lies further north.

Between Gordon's Bay and Hermanus these magnificent mountains, carpeted with flowers in winter and spring, come sweeping down to the coastline, and combine with the sea to form breathtaking scenic vistas and a perfect environment for birdwatching, angling, walking and picnicking.

Along the coastline, sheer cliffs melt into gentle bays of pure white sand and pebble-lined beaches. Here and there headlands protrude to form rocky coves and natural harbours. Offshore, southern right whales cruise the depths in the company of dolphins and a huge variety of fish.

Tiny resorts, with clusters of holiday homes hugging the coast, offer caravan and camping sites, country hotels and a variety of outdoor activities, from bathing, boating and sailing, to angling and shell collecting.

Inland, towards the Little Karoo, there are game parks and nature reserves to visit, mountain passes to explore and historic homes to discover.

This part of South Africa is known to travellers as the southern Cape, an area regarded by many as a place of rugged tranquillity and open spaces.

WHAT TO SEE

Strand

Small, flat waves lapping a long, gently sloping shore make this a very popular holiday resort. Melkbaai, the main bathing beach, is 3 km long and flanked by several tidal pools where you can splash about. At the next beach, Die Poort, you can wade 100 m into the sea at low tide.

The southeast blows very hard here (gale force at times) during summer, but you can seek shelter behind dunes at the north end of Melkbaai.

The beach has a waterslide, a main kiosk and change rooms. Beachside cafés and hotels offer refreshments and accommodation.

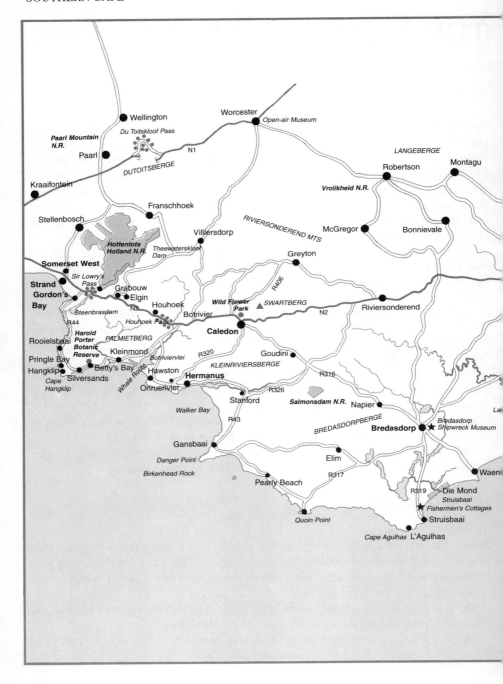

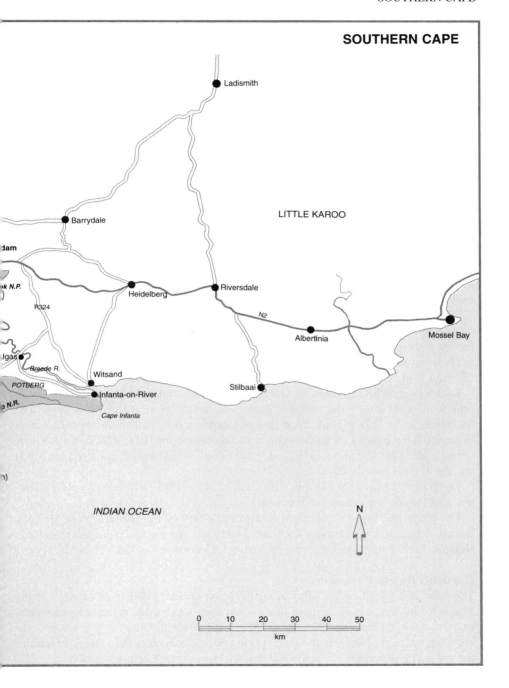

SOUTHERN CAPE

Ladismith

LITTLE KAROO

Barrydale

dam

k N.P.

R324

Riversdale

Heidelberg

N2

Albertinia

Mossel Bay

lgas

Breede R.

Witsand

POTBERG

Infanta-on-River

Stilbaai

N.R.

Cape Infanta

n)

INDIAN OCEAN

N

0   10   20   30   40   50
km

CLIMATE
If you're touring the southern Cape in winter take along a raincoat, umbrella and warm clothing – the winters are cold and wet, with northwest storms moving inland in rapid succession. The summers are hot, with strong southerly to southeasterly winds, reaching gale force at times. The average daily summer maximum temperature at Cape Agulhas, the southernmost tip of Africa, is 23,5 °C, while the daily maximum in winter (July) is 16,4 °C. The daily average minimum temperature in winter is about 10 °C.

Gordon's Bay

Lying in the shadow of the Hottentots-Holland Mountains, Gordon's Bay, originally known as Vischhoekbaai, is a cosy, scenic resort with an old-village atmosphere and two beautiful beaches. Centre of activity is the yachting harbour, where you can stroll about, watch the fishing boats come in and out, or buy fresh fish from the quayside.

Main Beach is a gentle sweep of white sand fringed by a grassy terrace. Bathing is safe here and you can wade a long way into the sea. Nearby, a paved walkway leads to Milkwood Park, where you can have a relaxed picnic under a grove of milkwood trees.

Bikini Beach, a strip of sand adjoining the harbour breakwater, is very popular among sun worshippers, offering shelter from the southeasterly wind, but watch out for the backwash here.

There's a shell shop at the harbour and, above it, an excellent seafood restaurant, Harbour Lights Restaurant, for which you will need to book in advance.

Take a pair of hiking boots to Gordon's Bay, and try the Mayor's Walk, a 7-km mountain jaunt above the sea that gives you beautiful views of False Bay. The Steenbras River Valley Trail, 5 km east of Gordon's Bay, is a short day hike which bypasses three natural rock pools (for a permit, telephone (021) 4003269). Another scenic hike is the Cannon and Wagon Wheel Trail, which starts opposite a lay-by at the top of Sir Lowry's Pass.

The Harbour Master at Gordon's Bay, tel. (024) 561482, will tell you about charters and fishing trips from the harbour.

The place to camp or overnight in Gordon's Bay is the Hendon Park Holiday Resort, which has 93 caravan sites and 54 chalets (for more information, contact Hendon Park, Faure Marine Drive, PO Box 3, Gordon's Bay, tel. (024) 562321).

Gordon's Bay to Hermanus

The drive east from Gordon's Bay along the coast towards Hermanus is known as the Whale Route, because of the pods of southern right whales that come to these waters to calve between June and November. Sheer cliffs that plummet to the sea provide excellent vantage points where you can stop your car to look at the whales, or admire the unfolding panorama of sandy beaches, rocky coves and kelp-covered bays.

Together with Chapman's Peak Drive, this drive ranks among the most scenic in southern Africa and passes snug seaside villages such as Rooi-els, Pringle Bay, Betty's Bay, Kleinmond and Onrusrivier. The last named is a retreat for writers, poets and artists, and has a peaceful, old-world atmosphere to it. There's a small but unsafe beach, a small lagoon, and easy access to mountain and sea.

This coastline is a favourite haunt for fishermen, some of whom have lost their lives – washed off the rocks by what Rudyard Kipling called "the dread Agulhas roll" – the huge, rolling breakers of the Agulhas current. Pringle Bay, about 40 km west of Hermanus, however, has a gentle, curving stretch of white sand that is one of the safest swimming beaches along this stretch of coast, as well as a small lagoon at the river mouth.

Hermanus

Thousands of South Africans converge on this attractive coastal town in summer, for several good reasons. Hermanus has some of the finest bathing beaches in South Africa, dozens of scenic coastal and mountain walks, excellent fishing and boating, and it's only a 90-minute drive from Cape Town. More important perhaps, is the fact that its locality – between mountain and sea – gives it a peaceful, old-world ambience, enhanced by its stately, thatched-roof homes and profusion of indigenous flowers and plants.

Hermanus – known originally as Hermanus Pietersfontein, after the man who founded it in the 1830s – is also the best place for land-locked whale-watchers to be. A 12-km path, the Cliff Walk, which follows the contours of the coast around the town, takes you through secluded glens of milkwood trees, past the fringes of sandy and rocky coves, tidal pools and golden beaches. The walk brings you within 200-300 m of southern right whales as they cruise between the bays. Coves such as Platklip, Bayview Bay and Windsor Point are ideal for this activity. The calves arrive in mid-August, and the cows stay in the bays with their young for about two months.

The most popular bathing beaches are Grotto Beach and Voëlklip, where the water is warm and the slope of the beaches very gentle. Kwaaiwater beach is ideal for shell collecting.

Bathing, canoeing, boardsailing, waterskiing, powerboating and fishing are much in demand at the Klein River Lagoon, east of Hermanus. Two other popular bathing areas are the tidal Fick's Pool and Marine Pool.

During the holiday season (December and January, and at Easter) you can take a launch trip from the New Harbour around Walker Bay. You can also hire a small craft for use on Klein River Lagoon from Lagoon Boat Hire, on Prawn Flats, just beyond De Mond Caravan Park, or join a pleasure cruise on the *Janine*.

Hermanus is a walker's paradise. The 1 500-ha Fernkloof Nature Reserve in the mountains behind Hermanus has 35 km of well-defined footpaths which take you through a floral wonderland of proteas, ericas and other Cape fynbos. Maps, leaflets and free walking sticks are available at the entrance to the reserve.

Set aside a full day for Fernkloof Nature Reserve and a half day for the Cliff Walk, and take a picnic with you.

A particularly scenic drive is along the 4-km Rotary Mountain Way, west of the town, which affords panoramic views of the surrounding mountains and the shimmering expanse of Walker Bay.

The Old Harbour – once the centre of Hermanus' thriving whaling and fishing industry – has been preserved as a museum and national monument. The new harbour area west of the town offers a variety of fresh seafoods for sale – or a deep-sea charter ride to catch tunny. Although Hermanus has traditionally been a rock-angler's paradise, freshwater fishermen can catch trout at De Bos Dam, just a few kilometres inland in the Hemel-en-Aarde Valley.

You can taste the wines of the Hemel-en-Aarde Valley at the Hamilton Russell Winetasting Room on Market Square. There is a bustling craft market on Market Square on Saturday mornings, where local crafters sell their wares.

Accommodation in Hermanus includes two fine hotels, several guesthouses and self-catering farmhouses. For details contact the Hermanus Accommodation Centre, tel. (0283) 700004 or the Hermanus Publicity Association, tel. (0283) 22629.

The Cape Agulhas area

Between Hermanus and Cape Infanta, undulating hills sweep gently towards Cape Agulhas, the southernmost tip of the African continent. This is the Overberg – "the place across the mountain" – a beautifully serene land of blue cranes, milkwood trees and wheatfields dipping down to a wild and rocky coast. Flanking the Overberg in the north are the purple battlements of the Langeberge, bisected by scenic mountain passes and sparkling rivers that tumble through the lowlands to the sea.

Several turn-offs (some tarred) branch southwards off the N2 towards the sea, leading to such coastal resorts as Cape Agulhas and Arniston (Waenhuiskrans). Other gravel roads take you to more isolated attractions, such as the De Hoop Nature Reserve near Bredasdorp, one of the great floral wonderlands of the sub-continent.

Other turn-offs north of the N2 lead you through the Langeberge to the Little Karoo via scenic mountain passes. Two particularly beautiful routes are Garcia's Pass (turn off the N2 at Riversdale to reach it), and the Tradouw Pass, near Barrydale, where the springtime show of indigenous flowers is breathtaking. The Overberg is home to two nature reserves, the Bontebok National Park and the De Hoop Nature Reserve – the latter a refuge for one of South Africa's most diverse bird populations.

Cape Agulhas

South Africa's second-oldest lighthouse, the L'Agulhas Lighthouse (built in 1849), stands resolutely above a tempestuous sea at Cape Agulhas, casting its beam 30 nautical miles out to warn ships off this rocky coast. You can climb up the light-house stairs and peer across the ocean that has claimed so many ships over the centuries. One victim, the *Meisho Maru,* lies on the rocks 2 km west of the lighthouse. It's worth a photograph. Other than that, there's a campsite, two caravan parks and tidal pools at Cape Agulhas.

Bredasdorp Shipwreck Museum
No visit to the southern Cape is complete without visiting this museum. Although it is 24 km from the sea, the flavour is distinctly nautical the minute you walk into the museum's Shipwreck Hall. Tape-recorded sounds of seabirds calling above a crashing sea recreate the mood of dark and stormy nights. There are fascinating showcases of four of this coastline's famous wrecks: HMS *Arniston,* HMS *Birkenhead* (which went down in 1852 with the loss of 445 lives), the *Queen of the Thames,* and the *Oriental Pioneer.*

The museum's Old Rectory and Strandveld Coach House have fascinating displays of 19th century maritime artefacts and furniture.

Arniston
Rustic, whitewashed fishermen's cottages face seaward above the dazzling white sands of Arniston – named after the British transport ship HMS *Arniston,* which ran aground here in the spring of 1815 with the loss of 372 lives. On the western side of the village a huge cavern has been gouged out of the sandstone by the constant sweep of the waves over the millenia. The early settlers who came here thought it resembled one of the giant wagons in which they travelled, so they called the rocky headland that contains the cave "Waenhuiskrans", meaning literally "Wagon House Ridge".

The tiny settlement has grown into a fashionable holiday resort, some of its old fishermen's cottages renovated or newly built into cosy holiday homes. Among these is a small caravan and camping area.

A luxurious hotel overlooks Slipway Beach on the eastern side of the village, where one can bathe in the quite warm turquoise waters (but watch the backwash). The other swimming beach, known as Bikini Beach, has bigger waves and is flanked by rock pools awaiting exploration at low tide. Snorkelling is excellent at Arniston, so take along a mask and snorkel. For superb self-catering accommodation try Arniston Seaside Cottages (pick up the keys from Robert Haarburger behind the hotel).

West of Arniston is Struisbaai, a neat holiday resort with a picturesque fishing harbour and safe bathing beaches. On the way to Struisbaai, stop off at De Mond Nature Reserve.

De Hoop Nature Reserve
This reserve, just 50 km east of Bredasdorp, includes a 5-km marine sanctuary

where you can see southern right whales from one of the most unpopulated coast-lines in southern Africa. On land, the 36 000-ha sanctuary is home to 1 500 species of plants, including a variety of rare lowland fynbos species. De Hoop is a wetland area that has drawn over 250 species of birds to its large vlei and surrounding lime-stone hills.

There are various hiking trails, shorter walks and even a mountain bike trail, introduced in 1994, which takes you right off the beaten track to beautiful spots along the coast.

You're quite likely to see several of the 86 mammal species, which include eland, grey rhebok, baboons, mongooses, caracal and leopard.

For pure tranquillity on the edge of sea and vlei, there's little to match a week-end in one of the reserve's cottages, but bring your own bedding, kitchen utensils and food. The nearest shop is at Ouplaas, 15 km from De Hoop. Contact the man-ager of De Hoop, De Hoop Nature Reserve, Private Bag X16, Bredasdorp 7280, tel. (02922) 782/700.

Swellendam

Stately avenues of oaks line the streets of Swellendam, whose historic, white-washed homes stand proud in the shadows of the Langeberge behind them. Founded in 1746, Swellendam was named after Cape Governor Hendrik Swellengrebel and his wife, Helena ten Damme. This is the third oldest white set-tlement in South Africa and once served as a frontier outpost to the Dutch burghers of the Cape.

The town displays some of the most magnificent architecture in South Africa, notable examples of which are the Drostdy complex in Swellengrebel Street, which was built in 1747, and upgraded to house a cultural history museum in the 1940s, and the Oefeninghuis, a place of worship and a one-time education centre for freed slaves.

Within a few minutes' drive of Swellendam are two beautiful nature reserves, the Bontebok National Park (7 km away to the southeast) and the Marloth Nature Reserve, which sprawls across the Langeberge, and in which flourish spectacular forests of stinkwood and yellowwood, and a large variety of indigenous fynbos, including proteas and pincushions.

The beautiful Swellendam Hiking Trail traverses the Marloth Reserve, and offers picnic sites and overnight huts. Permits to enter the reserve are obtainable from the Swellendam State Forest Station. For further details and booking, telephone (021) 4023043.

Bontebok National Park

This park was established as a protected area for bontebok in 1960, when the ani-mals were threatened with extinction. Today there are about 200 in the park, as well as red hartebeest, Cape mountain zebra, grey rhebok, Cape grysbok, steenbok, duiker, bushbuck, 184 bird species and 470 plant species. You can hire fully equipped caravans, and there's a beautiful camping site next to the Breede River. If you're just passing through, stop here for a picnic and a swim before you move on. There's an information centre and kiosk near the entrance gate where you can get a map of the park. For more information, contact the Park Warden, Bontebok National Park, PO Box 149, Swellendam 6740, or the National Parks Board (see *Tourist information*, p. 76).

Breede River, Cape Infanta, Witsand
If you're travelling eastwards towards Mossel Bay, bear in mind that there are two important turn-offs to the sea, both running parallel to the Breede River. Take the one signposted Cape Infanta, just before Swellendam, or the R324 to Witsand, just past Swellendam. Infanta and Witsand, on opposite sides of the great Breede River, are idyllic seaside hamlets that offer excellent river and sea fishing and the full spectrum of water sports on the river. You can snorkel in San Sebastian Bay, catch kabeljou and grunter at the river mouth or take a boat several kilometres upstream to the famed Malgas Pont, where the waterskiing, canoeing and powerboating are excellent, and, they say, the water is so deep no line will reach the bottom.

At Witsand, you can stay at the Breede River Lodge, tel. (02935) 631, where you can hire a boat (the hotel has its own private harbour, with a slipway and berthing facilities), or you can stay in one of the several guesthouses and cottages for hire. Across the river, at Infanta, there's a tidy caravan and camping site next to the river.

THE SOUTHERN CAPE AT A GLANCE
When to go: November through to April is the best time to go, although south-easterly winds can blow strongly along this stretch of coast from November to February.
Getting around: The N2 is the main highway which links Gordon's Bay with Mossel Bay, but for an excellent alternative route, take the R44 coastal drive, which links up with the N2 near Botrivier. Several secondary roads, some of them gravel, branch off the N2 to the north and south, leading through scenic mountain passes to the Little Karoo, or down to the coast respectively. Most of these roads are in good condition.
Main attractions: Scenic drives. Angling. Swimming, boating, canoeing, sail-ing at coastal resorts such as Gordon's Bay, Kleinmond, Hermanus, Arniston and Cape Infanta. Wild flowers of the Cape Fold Mountains. Historical home-steads in Swellendam. Beautiful mountain passes.
Tours and excursions: *Coach:* The Translux Express runs regular scheduled trips from Cape Town to Mossel Bay, stopping off at several points along the way. For details contact Translux, tel. (021) 4053333 (Cape Town). Intercape Tours offers airconditioned coach tours of the southern Cape regularly, tel. (021) 3862338. For details of other southern Cape tours contact your nearest

travel agency or the South African Tourism Board (see *Tourist information* below).

Rail: An Interpax passenger service connects Cape Town and Port Elizabeth, stopping off at several points along the way, tel. Cape Town (021) 4053018 or Port Elizabeth (041) 5202975. Major international car-hire operators offer cars for hire in Cape Town.

Walking tours: There are hundreds of attractive walks and trails in the southern Cape, including the Swellendam Hiking Trail and walks through the Fernkloof Nature Reserve at Hermanus. For guided walking tours and more information contact the SA Tourism Board (see below).

Launch trips: At Hermanus there are excursions into Walker Bay from the New Harbour; at Witsand powerboats can be hired for fishing trips up the Breede River from the Breede River Lodge (see *Tourist information* below).

Beaches and bathing: Bathing along this coast is generally safe, and the water is warm throughout the year. Strand, Gordon's Bay, Pringle Bay, Hermanus and Arniston are highly recommended for their gently sloping beaches and good swimming conditions.

Tourist information: *Tours:* The South African Tourism Board (Satour), 3 Adderley Street (outside the station, next to the Translux Building), Cape Town 8001, tel. (021) 216274; Captour Visitors' Information Bureau, 3 Adderley Street, Cape Town, tel. (021) 4185214. *Walks, drives and cruises in Hermanus:* The Hermanus Publicity Association, Main Road, Hermanus, tel. (0283) 22629. *Boats at Witsand:* Breede River Lodge, tel. (02935) 631. *Game Parks and Nature Reserves:* National Parks Board, PO Box 787, Pretoria 0001; or PO Box 7400, Roggebaai 8012, tel. (021) 222810.

Festivals and annual events: Hermanus – Festival of the Sea (March); Bredasdorp – Foot of Africa Marathon (October); Caledon – Wild Flower Show, Beer and Bread Festival (September).

ACCOMMODATION GUIDE

There are some cosy, comfortable hotels in the southern Cape. Book well in advance for the peak holiday season in December and January.

SOMERSET WEST

Lord Charles Hotel***** Sumptuous accommodation in beautiful surroundings. 188 rooms; 8 suites. Conference facilities. PO Box 5151, Helderberg 7135, tel. (024) 551040.

GORDON'S BAY

Van Riebeeck*** Highly rated, Gordon's Bay. 78 rooms. Conference facilities. PO Box 10, Gordon's Bay 7150, tel. (024) 561441.

Houw-Hoek Inn** Beautiful mountain setting. Oldest inn licence in South Africa. Table d'hôte. Ladies bar. 33 rooms. PO Box 95, Grabouw 7160, tel. (02824) 49646.

KLEINMOND

*Beach House Hotel*** Beachfront. Highly rated. 23 rooms. Conference facilities for 30. À la carte restaurant specialising in seafood. PO Box 199, Kleinmond 7195, tel. (02823) 3130.

HERMANUS

*The Marine Hotel*** Views of bay and sea. 43 rooms, 10 suites. Conference facilities for 80. Table d'hôte; outdoor and indoor pools. PO Box 9, Hermanus 7200, tel. (0283) 21112.

*The Windsor Hotel*** Close to sea and town. 26 rooms, 4 suites, tel. (0283) 23727.

CALEDON

*De Overberger Country Hotel and Spa*** Luxury hotel in country setting. Mineral springs, 3 pools. Walks in mountain. Gym. 95 rooms. PO Box 480, Caledon 7230, tel. (0281) 41271.

*Alexandra*** Attractive, comfortable. 9 en-suite rooms. Conference facilities for 120; à la carte restaurant; 2 cocktail bars; pool. PO Box 3, Caledon 7230, tel. (0281) 23052.

BREDASDORP

*Arniston*** Neat, luxury, overlooking sea. 23 en-suite rooms; 1 suite. Conference facilities for 20; à la carte (lunch only) and table d'hôte; pool. PO Box 126, Bredasdorp 7280, tel. (02847) 59000.

*Victoria Hotel*** 29 rooms (most en suite). PO Box 11, Bredasdorp 7280, tel. (02841) 41159.

GREYTON

Post House 132 years old; traditional English pub; yellowwood furniture and ceilings. 13 en-suite Beatrix Potter bedrooms. Main Road, Greyton 7233, tel. (028254) 9995.

WITSAND

*Breede River Lodge*** Hotel, time-share at eastern mouth of Breede River. 14 rooms. Fishing expeditions. Table d'hôte; à la carte (lunches); seafood specialities. PO Witsand 6761, tel. (02935) 631.

SWELLENDAM

*Swellengrebel Hotel*** Comfortable hotel close to amenities. 51 en-suite rooms, 1 suite. Conference facilities for 50. À la carte restaurant. PO Box 9, Swellendam, tel. (0291) 42453.

RIVERSDALE

*Royal*** 12 en-suite rooms; à la carte and table d'hôte; pool and sauna. PO Box 5, Riversdale 6770, tel. (02933) 32470.

*Hotel President*** 22 en-suite rooms, 1 suite. Conference facilities for 50; PO Box 1, Riversdale 6770, tel. (02933) 32473.

ALBERTINIA

*Albertinia Hotel*** 16 en-suite rooms. Conference facilities for 30; table d'hôte. Main Street, Albertinia 6795, tel. (02934) 51030.

THE GARDEN ROUTE AND LITTLE KAROO

Emerald valleys, towering rainforests, tranquil lakes and lagoons, a serpentine coastline with secluded coves and wide, sweeping stretches of sand – this is the Garden Route, a region of spectacular scenic beauty.

Nestling between the peaks of the Outeniqua and Langkloof mountains in the north, and the translucent waters of the Indian Ocean in the south, the Garden Route reveals a succession of secluded resorts, linked to the interior by breathtaking mountain passes.

The abundance of rivers, lakes, lagoons and estuaries along this coastal terrace offers unlimited opportunities for bathing, boating, waterskiing, surfing and angling.

For nature lovers there are natural sanctuaries for animals and birds, walking trails through fern-clad forests of yellowwood, blackwood and ironwood, and the chance to revel in the peace and solitude of country hotels, guesthouses and seaside villas. The golden beaches, strung out like pearls along the coast, are warm and inviting, offering safe bathing in warm, temperate waters.

WHAT TO SEE

THE GARDEN ROUTE

Mossel Bay

For travellers heading eastward, the Garden Route begins at Mossel Bay, a bustling seaside town that attracts thousands of holiday-makers to its safe, tranquil beaches every year. Here the rocky promontory of Cape St Blaise shelters the placid waters of Munro's Bay – site of the first landing place of Portuguese explorer Bartholomeu Dias, who became the first European to sail into the bay in 1488. The beaches of Munro's Bay provide year-round safe and sheltered swimming.

One of the more popular beach areas is the "Poort" – a channel between two rocky ridges at Cape St Blaise. Other popular bathing areas which line the curve of Mossel Bay's coastline are the "Bakke", Pansy Beach, Dias Beach and Santos Beach. You can have a meal or a snack at the Santos Pavilion, a beautifully restored Victorian building on the beachfront.

Picturesque camping grounds and grassy caravan sites near the beachfront bustle with activity in summer, and the air is thick with the scent of braaiing (grilling) meat and freshly caught fish.

78

CLIMATE

The Garden Route lies in a temperate transition zone between the southwestern Cape's Mediterranean climate and KwaZulu/Natal's subtropical climate. The summers are warm to hot, the winters cool to cold, but the extremes are far less severe than in the south. The region has summer and winter rain, with more rain falling in summer. Strong winds occasionally buffet the coast in summer, so take a jersey along on long walks. The dry Little Karoo gets much hotter in summer, with maximum temperatures approaching the 40s, and much colder in winter, when sub-zero temperatures are common, with little rain in both seasons.

During the holiday season you can board a motor launch at Mossel Bay Harbour for a sightseeing trip of the bay and a visit to Seal Island, a few hundred metres off Dias Beach, home of about 20 000 seals.

The Bartholomeu Dias Museum complex preserves the history of the town with maritime memorabilia, including a life-size replica of the first caravels to land on these shores. There is also an arts-and-crafts centre housed in Munro's cottages, the old Post Office Tree, where Pedro d'Ataide posted South Africa's first "letter" in 1500, and an international shell collection.

You can walk to Cape St Blaise, bypassing on the way about 200 stone cottages built by Cornish masons during the 19th century. You'll need a day for the more ambitious Cape St Blaise Hiking Trail, along the coast from Bat's Cave to Dana Bay.

At the Point, a lighthouse towers above a cave inhabited by Khoikhoi "Strandlopers" before Europeans first set foot ashore. Nearby, in the old aquarium building, there's an oyster hatchery, where you can sample this delicacy.

East of Mossel Bay is the resort of Hartenbos, which offers a heated swimming pool, a skating rink, bowling green, tennis courts and plenty of holiday accommodation, including caravan and camping sites. There is also a 10 000-seat stadium and the Voortrekker Museum nearby, which houses a unique collection of Voortrekker exhibits, including wagons used in a 1938 trek to Voortrekkerhoogte.

Further east, towards George, are two "brackish" rivers – the Little Brak and the Great Brak, both of which have a lagoon at their mouth. Around them have sprung up two popular villages and holiday resorts.

George

The "prettiest village on the face of the earth", is how English novelist Anthony Trollope described George. French traveller Francois le Vaillant, who visited it in the 1780s, called it "the most beautiful land in the universe". And well it might be, for this principal town of the Garden Route was built in an exquisite setting. Named after England's King George III, it lies on a coastal terrace at the foot of the Outeniqua Mountains, and its gardens are overlooked by the towering heights of George Peak (1 370 m) and Cradock Peak (1 583 m).

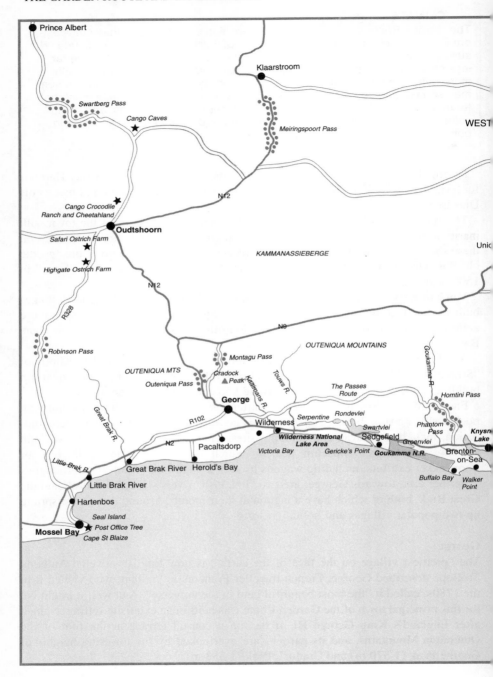

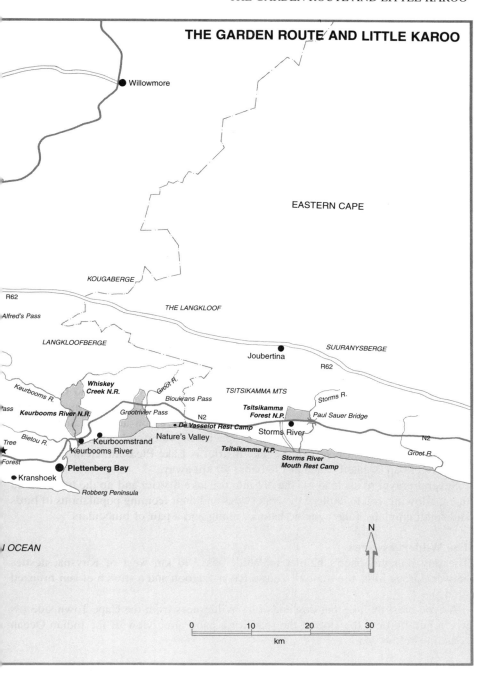

THE GARDEN ROUTE AND LITTLE KAROO

Willowmore

EASTERN CAPE

KOUGABERGE

R62

Alfred's Pass

THE LANGKLOOF

LANGKLOOFBERGE

SUURANYSBERGE

Joubertina

R62

Keurbooms R.

Whiskey
Creek N.R.

Groot R.

TSITSIKAMMA MTS

Storms R.

Bloukrans Pass

ass

Keurbooms River N.R.

Grootrivier Pass

Tsitsikamma
Forest N.P.

Paul Sauer Bridge

N2

De Vasselot Rest Camp

Tree

Bietou R.

Keurboomstrand

Nature's Valley

Storms River

N2

Forest

Keurbooms River

Tsitsikamma N.P.

Storms River
Mouth Rest Camp

Groot R.

Plettenberg Bay

Kranshoek

Robberg Peninsula

J OCEAN

N

0   10   20   30
km

George's fame is due in no small measure to its old, narrow-gauge steam train, the Outeniqua Choo Choo, which huffs and puffs its way through the tall forests and lake district to Knysna. On the way it makes a spectacular crossing of the Kaaimans River bridge. No trip through the Garden Route would be complete without a trip on this remarkable train. It leaves George daily (except Saturdays and Sundays) at 08h00, arriving in Knysna at 11h30 – just in time for a quick pub lunch, before returning at 12h55. You can buy a ticket at the station or book ahead.

The George Museum, in the old Drostdy building, exhibits two horse-drawn hearses from George's early days, the country's largest collection of old gramophones, and the tusks of an old elephant called "Aftand", one of the herd of Knysna elephants, that was shot in the 1970s. In the museum you can buy handmade crafts such as candles and soap.

In front of the Library, which was built in 1850, is a landmark known as the "slave oak', where slaves were bought and sold in the early days.

Other attractions include the crocodile park, 2 km from the town centre, and a 18-hole championship golf course.

The nearest coastal resort to George is Herold's Bay, where there is a tidal pool, good fishing and safe bathing.

The lakes

The battlements of the distant Outeniqua Mountains form a stunning backdrop to the Garden Route's lake district, which stretches for over 40 km, from Wilderness in the west to the Goukamma River valley in the east.

The six lakes in the region are Touws River Lagoon at Wilderness, Island Lake (also known as Lower Langvlei), Langvlei, Rondevlei, Swartvlei and Groenvlei. Jewel of the region is Swartvlei, the largest and deepest of the lakes, which are only 2 000 years old. Birdlife is prolific throughout the region and, at Langvlei and Rondevlei alone, 75 of South Africa's 95 species of waterfowl can be seen.

A popular hotel and resort in the lake district is Lake Pleasant, from where you can drive to an isolated beach at Platbank, 40 km away.

Several gravel roads lead off the N2 into the lake district and up the hills behind them, allowing you to explore the waterways and their teeming populations of birds and small animals. Take a picnic hamper along and a pair of binoculars.

The Wilderness area

The tiny honeymooner's hamlet of Wilderness, 40 km west of Knysna, nestles between green hills, the tranquil Touws River Lagoon and a stretch of sun-bronzed sand.

As you crest the hill that descends into Wilderness from the Cape Town side it's worth pulling onto the side of the road for a panoramic view of the Indian Ocean coastline below you.

▲ 46   ▼ 47

46. The imposing formation of the Wolfberg Arch in the Cederberg mountain range.
47. Sunset over Langebaan Lagoon, Langebaan.

48. A quiver tree near the Augrabies Falls in the Northern Cape.
49. A typical Karoo scene with a windmill in the foreground.
50. The rare and beautiful black eagle is found in the Karoo National Park.

▲ 48   ▼ 49   ▲ 50

51. Wildebeest around a dead tree topped by a sociable weaver nest in the Kalahari Gemsbok National Park.
52. A typical scene in the arid Kalahari Gemsbok National Park.
53. The Augrabies Falls on the Orange River plunge 56 m into the gorge below.

▲ 51   ▼ 52   ▲ 53

▲ 54

▼ 55   ▲ 56

▲ 57

54. The Old Harbour in Hermanus was once the heart of the local whaling industry.
55. A country farm scene near Elim in the southern Cape.
56. The beacon at Cape Agulhas, the southernmost tip of Africa.

▲ 58   ▼ 59

57. One of the quaint whitewashed fishermen's cottages in Arniston.
58. The N2 between Swellendam and Riviersonderend is a scenic drive.
59. Locals await the day's catch on the beach at Arniston, also known as Waenhuiskrans.

60. Farm scene in the Little Karoo with the Swartberge in the background.

61. The Outeniqua Choo-Choo crosses the Kaaimans River on its way from Knysna to George.

62. Sunset over the Swartvlei estuary, at Sedgefield near Wilderness.

▲ 60   ▼ 61   ▲ 62

▲ 63

▼ 64

63. Knysna Lagoon viewed from The Heads.
64. The Heads – where the Knysna Lagoon flows into the sea.

▲ 65

▼ 66 ▲ 67

65. A beach on the Robberg Peninsula at Plettenberg Bay.
66. A huge old yellowwood tree in the Knysna Forest.
67. The long stretch of unspoilt beach at Nature's Valley.
68. Forest blooms in the Tsitsikamma Forest.
69. Storms River Gorge in the Tsitsikamma National Park.
70. A campsite along the Tsitsikamma coastline on the scenic Otter Trail.

▲ 68 ▼ 69 ▲ 70

▲ 71   ▼ 72

71. Ostrich farming near Oudtshoorn in the Little Karoo is a lucrative business.
72. The cavernous main hall in the Cango Caves near Oudtshoorn.

▲ 73

▼ 74

▲ 75

▼ 76

73. Dolphins performing at the Port Elizabeth Oceanarium.
74. A gracious building in High Street, Grahamstown.
75. Market Square in the city centre of Port Elizabeth, with the public library in the foreground.
76. The luxury Fish River Sun on the banks of the Great Fish River.

▲ 77 ▼ 78

▼ 79

77. The Hole-in-the-Wall, an impressive rock formation along the Wild Coast.
78. Elephants enjoying a mudbath in the Addo Elephant National Park.
79. Catch the Apple Express, one of the few remaining narrow-gauge railways left in the world.
80. Traditional Xhosa homes in the hills of the former Transkei.
81. The suspension bridge linking the island to the mainland at Mazeppa Bay.
82. Fishing is a big attraction on the Wild Coast.
83. The Wild Coast Sun lures holiday-makers from all over South Africa.

▲ 80

▼ 81

▼ 82

▼ 83

▲ 84   ▼ 85   ▼ 86

▼ 87

84. Swimming pools entice holiday-makers along the Durban beachfront.
85. Hobies setting out from Addington Beach, Durban.
86. Indian spices for sale in the Victoria Street Market in Durban.
87. Tourists can enjoy a ride around the city of Durban in a ricksha.

▼ 90

▲ 88

▼ 89

▼ 91

88. The rolling green hills and valleys of the Valley of a Thousand Hills.
89. The Durban City Hall, a familiar landmark.
90. A sangoma and her student at Shakaland.
91. A white rhino in the Mkuzi Game Reserve.

▲ 92   ▼ 93   ▼ 94

92. The St Lucia Estuary at sunset.
93. The popular Hilltop Camp in the Hluhluwe
Game Reserve.
94. A hippopotamus giving a threat display,
Zululand.

Wilderness National Park

Lying just off the N2 highway, 4 km from Wilderness, this 10 000-ha national park incorporates 28 km of southern Cape coastline, as well as four lakes, five rivers and two estuaries. It includes the beach at Wilderness, the Touws River Lagoon and the lakes, which provide unlimited opportunities for water sports such as swimming, sailing, canoeing and waterskiing.

You can take a ride through the Serpentine into Island Lake, or up the Touws River.

Highlight of a visit to the national park is the circular Kingfisher Hiking Trail, where you can see five of South Africa's ten kingfisher species. The trail takes you across the Touws River floodplain and onto the beach. Take along your own refreshments and set aside a full day to complete the circuit.

The centre of the park is the Ebb and Flow Rest Camp, which offers two-bed huts with bathroom or shower, two-bed huts with communal ablution facilities and caravan and campsites set under trees. The camp also hires out canoes, rowing boats and paddleboats.

The camp's shop sells curios, essential groceries, soft drinks, bread, meat, eggs and firewood. The nearest restaurants are at Wilderness and George.

The rest camp will supply information about trails and the birdwatching hides at Bo-Langvlei and Rondevlei. For more details contact the Rest Camp Manager, PO Box 35, Wilderness, tel. (0441) 8771197.

Sedgefield

Sedgefield, a bustling holiday town that has grown up on the eastern banks of Swartvlei Lagoon, offers safe swimming, fishing and canoeing. Birdwatching is excellent here, particularly at Kingfisher Creek – a reed-lined channel connecting the sea with the lagoon. You can take a pleasant walk along the beach westwards to Gericke's Point. There are several caravan parks and campsites in and around Sedgefield, but if you intend visiting in December or January, book early (contact the Knysna Publicity Association, see *Tourist information,* p. 94).

East of Sedgefield is the 2 230-ha Goukamma Nature Reserve, which shelters the tranquil waters of the Garden Route's only freshwater lake – Groenvlei (a popular angling and boating area), and the lower reaches of the Goukamma River. More than 150 bird species live here, including the African fish eagle and the marsh harrier.

Several trails crisscross the reserve, including the 14-km Goukamma-Groenvlei Trail, the 8-km Goukamma Nature Reserve Circuit and the 4-km Lake Trail. The 13-km stretch of sandy beach here is most attractive, but bathing can be treacherous due to strong currents and an unpredictable backwash.

Beyond the reserve is Buffalo Bay, a small cluster of holiday homes set on the narrow peninsula of Walker Point. A magnificent beach – popular with swimmers and surfers – stretches eastwards from Walker Point to Brenton-on-Sea. There's a large restaurant on the beach here, where you can get a meal or a snack.

The Passes Route

One of the most scenic country drives in southern Africa, the Passes Route – linking George and Knysna inland – is a panoramic, 82-km ramble through fields and forests, quiet country lanes and hedgerows. Set aside a full day for this drive through one-time gold-mining country, take along a picnic and stop along the way to marvel at the countryside.

The passes that gave the route its name are the Swart River, the Kaaimans River, the Touws River, the Diep River, the Homtini and the Phantom.

Knysna

A picturesque, winding road on the western fringes of the Knysna Lagoon takes you to one of the historic treats of the Garden Route – Belvedere's Gothic-style church, modelled on the architecture of the 12th century Normans. Built in the early 19th century by Thomas Duthie, the son-in-law of one of Knysna's early pioneers, George Rex, the church's beautiful stained glass windows and neat graveyard reflect the peace and tranquillity of Belvedere Estate, one of the elite country suburbs of Knysna. Bishop Robert Gray, who consecrated the church in 1855, described it as "the gem of church architecture in the Colony".

The winding road that takes you to Belvedere continues to the coast, where the golden, bush-fringed beaches of Brenton-on-Sea invite exploration. The preferred swimming beach is about a kilometre to the east. There is a hotel at Brenton-on-Sea, and, at nearby Brenton-on-Lake, chalets and rondavels for hire (for details contact the Knysna Publicity Association, see *Tourist information,* p. 94).

Surrounded by rolling, forested hills, the little town of Knysna faces two towering promontories of rock, known as the Heads, which surge up from the sea to flank a restless channel between them. This treacherous channel serves as a conduit between the rolling breakers of the Indian Ocean and the vast, inland expanse of shimmering water known as the Knysna Lagoon. Knysna is a Khoikhoi word believed to mean "straight down" – a reference to the perpendicular cliffs that guard the ocean portals of the town.

Here, between mountain and lagoon, forest and sea, you will find the very heart of the Garden Route, a place described by the locals as "the gift of God".

The channel between the Heads is deep enough to allow the passage of ski-boats, trawlers and medium-sized vessels, although many ships have come to grief here, among them the naval brig, *Emu,* which foundered in 1817.

The eastern head, accessible by road via George Rex Drive, has a parking area, with beautiful viewsites overlooking the Indian Ocean nearby. A lower road takes you to another parking area alongside a restaurant where there is a small aquarium, known for its Knysna seahorses (*Hippocampus capensis*), and run by the National Sea Rescue Institute. From here you can walk to the base of the eastern head which has some deep caves.

Trails in the Wilderness-Knysna area

The abundance of mountains (the Outeniquas), forest, rivers, lakes and lagoons make the Wilderness-Knysna area probably one of the finest in South Africa for exploring the outdoors. Enchanting forest walks, week-long hikes, mountain bike trails, horse and canoe trails are all available for exploring the coast and hinterland between Wilderness and Knysna. These trails include:

Outeniqua Trail: A 90-km, 5-day hike from Beervlei in the Bergplaas State Forest, to Diepwalle in the east. The starting point is about 20 km east of Wilderness on the N2. Hiking tips: the forest can be very wet and damp, so take along warm clothing. Keep an eye out for elephant, grey rhebok, klipspringer, grysbok and the variety of forest birds, which includes Knysna loeries and black eagles. For permits, contact the Department of Water Affairs and Forestry, Demar Centre, Main Road, Knysna, tel. (0445) 825466.

Millwood Circuit: About 20 km north of Knysna, this trail is a 5,6-km, three-hour circuit that starts and ends at the ruins of the gold-mining village of Millwood and its cemetery in the Goudveld State Forest. You don't need a permit, but you should register at the forest station.

Jubilee Creek Walk: If you're walking the Millwood Circuit, you could do this walk in the same day. It's an easy two-hour walk through natural forest, and shares part of the Outeniqua Trail. No permit required.

Bushbuck Trail: This trail in the Featherbed Nature Reserve in Knysna offers superior views of cliff and sea, a ramble past beachcomber caves, and the chance to swim off the reserve's beaches. For permits and bookings, telephone (0445) 810590.

Terblans Nature Walk: This 6,5-km jaunt will take you right into the depths of the Gouna Forest where the birdwatching opportunities are excellent, and many of the trees are labelled for identification. There's a lovely picnic site and a place to swim. For details telephone (0445) 825466.

Elephant Walk: Bushbuck, vervet monkeys, elephant, baboons and other small mammals populate the forest through which this walk wanders. If you're lucky you may also see narina trogons, gymnogenes and possibly crowned eagles. The full walk takes about eight hours, but there are shorter options. Along the walk you will see King Edward's Tree – a giant yellowwood with a circumference of 7 m. No permits are required. The walk is just off the R339 northeast of Knysna.

If you want a guided tour, Knysna Forest Trails offers a two-and-a-half hour walk through the Knysna Forest every Wednesday and Thursday morning at 10h00 (meet Judith Hopley outside the Rheenendal Post Office). Take a picnic along, which you can have at Jubilee Creek, before heading for Millwood.

For further information, contact the Knysna Publicity Association, Main Road, Knysna 6570, tel. (0445) 825510.

The western head lies in the Featherbed Nature Reserve, which is accessible only by boat from the lagoon.

One of Knysna's legendary sons is the flamboyant George Rex, reputed son of George III, who bought the farm Melkhoutkraal on the eastern banks of the lagoon in 1804, and lived extravagantly with two common-law wives, lavishly entertaining the wealthy of the area. Today, Rex's property forms part of the National Lake Area that encompasses the lagoon.

Since George Rex's days, woodcutting, furniture making and other crafts have been the main industries in Knysna. Today the town centre offers a large variety of craftwork by local artists, including paintings, pottery and furniture. Some of the finest Outeniqua yellowwood and stinkwood chairs and tables in the country are available here at reasonable prices.

An integral part of Knysna's history is Millwood House, erected in Millwood during the gold rush of the 1880s. The house was dismantled, brought to Knysna and now serves as a museum with an interesting collection of period furniture and photographs of shipwrecks and gold diggings.

Don't pass through Knysna without visiting the Oyster Tasting Tavern on the Long Street jetty. The oyster bar is open for tasting, and you can buy oysters to take away.

Knysna Lagoon

The 17-km-long expanse of Knysna Lagoon has some special treats in store for travellers, offering sailing, canoeing and boating with a difference. You can hire a live-in cabin cruiser (which sleeps between two and eight people), and cruise the length and breadth of the lagoon, tying up at secluded spots for a champagne picnic or braai (barbecue).

A recommended cruise is to the Heads, then on to the Featherbed Nature Reserve. Contact the Southern Seas Charter Company and Lightley's Holiday Cruisers for more information on available cruises. You can wine and dine on the *John Benn,* an attractive, 20-ton boat that serves as a floating entertainment centre, and departs from the jetty each morning (see *Tours and excursions,* p. 93).

For an afternoon at a tranquil beach near Knysna, turn off to Noetzie, just east of the town, and take the panoramic 8-km drive to the sea, where five holiday homes, designed like odd-shaped castles, overlook the beach in a fairytale setting.

The Knysna Forest

Giant yellowwood, ironwood and stinkwood trees dwarf just about anything that moves in the dim, green world of the Knysna Forest – except the elephants, of course. A few elephants were translocated to the forest in July 1994 to supplement the last surviving members of a once great population of elephants that lived here. And today, together with vervet monkeys, bushbuck, bushpig, spotted genet and a

---- **TIP FOR TRAVELLERS** ----------------------------------

Busrides offers personalised bus tours from Plettenberg Bay to interesting places on the Garden Route, including Oudtshoorn and the Tsitsikamma area, tel. (04457) 33272.

variety of small forest animals, they form one of the enduring attractions in South Africa for backpackers seeking a refuge in the woods.

Together with the Tsitsikamma Forest, the Knysna Forest, which begins east of Knysna, forms the longest continuous stretch of indigenous forest in South Africa. No trip to the Garden Route would be complete without sampling some of its trails. For walking trails in the Knysna Forest, see the box on page 85.

Plettenberg Bay area

Drive through the forested region east of Knysna known as the Garden of Eden, and you come to the extraordinarily beautiful upmarket resort of Plettenberg Bay (the locals call it "Plet"). Portuguese explorers first named it Bahai Formosa (bay beautiful), but it received its present name from Dutch Governor Joachim van Plettenberg, who proclaimed the land for the Dutch East India Company in 1778.

Huge holiday homes, luxury hotels and various time-share blocks are sprawled across the low-lying hills and valleys between the Robberg Peninsula in the west, and Lookout Beach in the east. From Robberg, a stretch of sand known as Millionaire's Row sweeps towards Beacon Island Hotel, which is linked to the shore by a causeway, and continues as Central Beach, and later as Lookout Beach. Both these beaches are safe for bathing.

There's plenty to do in Plet – boating, swimming, surfing, fishing, skindiving, golf, tennis, bowls and squash, and some lovely coastal strolls along 20 km of excellent beaches.

For launch trips to the Robberg Peninsula and around the bay inquire at the reception desk of the Beacon Island Hotel. Alternatively, hire a motorboat at the Plettenberg Bay Angling Club on the western bank of the Keurbooms River.

Shell collecting – at Shelley Beach, Robberg Beach or Lookout Beach – may reward you with a sought after pansy shell.

If you want to fish, contact the local club, tel. (04457) 31325 or 32941; or to scuba dive, tel. (04457) 31120 or 30303.

The town's culture is preserved in the Gallery of the Plettenberg Bay Arts Association, which displays graphic arts, ceramic work, weaving, jewellery making, beadwork and woodwork – all produced by local artists and craftsmen.

Several camping grounds and caravan parks provide sites close to the sea at Plettenberg Bay and Robberg (contact the Plettenberg Bay Tourist and Publicity Bureau, see *Tourist information*, p. 94).

The Robberg Nature Reserve extends over the 4-km headland of Robberg. A walk

Hikes and rambles

The Garden of Eden, 14 km west of Plettenberg Bay, and the Kranshoek area near Harkerville, both have beautiful forested walks. On the eastern side, the Keurbooms-Bitou Lagoon and the marshy lower reaches of the Bitou River are good for birdwatching and short walks. Within Plettenberg Bay, the Signal Hill Nature Trail, starting at Signal Hill, takes you through the Piesang Valley and onto the beach past the old timber store.

along its back to Cape Seal provides perfect opportunities for viewing local birdlife (whitebreasted cormorants, kelp gulls and oystercatchers). The walk also affords superb views of the precipitous cliffs, secluded coves and the sparkling bay that stretches towards Plettenberg Bay. The peninsula was home to prehistoric man, who left ancient tools in the kitchen middens of the sandstone caves.

Keurboomstrand

The Matjies River Cave at Keurboomstrand is the site of a major archaeological find – 200 skeletons and 3 000 archaeological objects dating back 11 000 years were discovered here.

The Keurbooms River Nature Reserve, home of the purple-flowered keurboom, occupies 760 ha of the riverbank and forest, and lies adjacent to the 3 500 ha Whiskey Creek Reserve at Keurboomstrand. For details of walks, contact the Plettenberg Bay Tourist and Publicity Bureau (see *Tourist information*, p. 94).

The Bitou and Keurboom rivers combine to form a lagoon and estuary here. You can swim in the lagoon but beware of strong currents at the mouth.

On the western side of the river, the Plettenberg Bay Angling Club hires out canoes and motorboats for fishing, waterskiing and sightseeing.

■■■ THE TSITSIKAMMA AREA

"Tsitsikamma" is a Khoikhoi word, meaning clear or sparkling waters, and it refers to the tranquil, shimmering waters of the Indian Ocean that wash the shores of the rugged coastline.

Cool mountain streams slash through the Tsitsikamma Mountains behind the coastal terrace, then plunge through an enchanting world of high forest and tangled bush, where orchids, creepers, indigenous ferns and flowers offer cover for a variety of small animals and birds.

Many visitors to South Africa feel that the Tsitsikamma area is one of the most serene of the country's holiday hideaways – and with good reason. Panoramic mountains provide sweeping views of whales and dolphins cavorting in the sea; numerous trails traverse the Tsitsikamma Forest –the longest stretch of indigenous high forest in southern Africa – and there are innumerable picnic spots along the rivers or under the canopies of giant yellowwood trees, where you can marvel at the quiet splendour of the forest.

Nature's Valley
This sleepy coastal village, bordered on three sides by the Tsitsikamma National Park, lies in a sylvan setting of lagoon, mountain and sea. Fronted by a sweeping expanse of copper sands, it is the beginning and end point of two of South Africa's major hiking trails (see p. 90). Its surrounding forests and coast support a large and diverse population of birds, including kingfishers, oystercatchers, fish eagles and Cape gannets.

The Tsitsikamma National Park
This park, the first marine national park in southern Africa, is one of the very special places you'll find in Africa. An easy 200-km drive from Port Elizabeth, Tsitsikamma National Park is a natural forest- and fynbos-covered playground that stretches 80 km along the coast, from Nature's Valley in the west, to the mouth of the Groot River in the east, and embracing the sea for a distance of 5 km. It also includes the 700 sq km Tsitsikamma State Forest Reserve – on the slopes of the Tsitsikamma Mountains – a hiker's paradise. The forests, mountains and coastal fringe teem with an abundant birdlife and a variety of animals: leopards, chacma baboons, bushpigs, blue duikers, vervet monkeys, caracals, honey badgers and otters.

Storms River Mouth Rest Camp: This is the headquarters of the Tsitsikamma National Park, and it hugs a rocky shore at the base of rolling mountains and gorges. Neatly terraced lawns run down from the fringes of the surrounding high forest, and provide a luxuriant, Garden of Eden-like setting for campers, caravanners and those who prefer more secure lodgings. Comfortable log cabins, chalets and "oceanettes" face the sea, and provide easy access to the tidal swimming pool, snorkelling trail, barbecueing facilities, beaches, angling spots and hiking trails.

All the accommodation units are fully equipped with cooking utensils, crockery, cutlery, bedding, soap and towels.

The spacious camping and caravan sites, surrounded by milkwood trees, offer washing and ironing facilities.

The major attractions at Tsitsikamma park are its beautiful nature trails, the snorkelling and scuba trails, the small wind-protected beach, and some magnificent tidal pools. Angling is permitted within a restricted area, but spearfishing is prohibited. Take along a pair of binoculars, a mask, snorkel and flippers, a fishing rod and some firm hiking boots.

Although it rains throughout the year here, midsummer, between November and February, is the best time to go. The park's gate is open daily from 05h30 to 21h30.

The turn off to the park is clearly signposted on the national road, about 10 km west of the Paul Sauer Bridge, which spans the spectacular Storms River Gorge.

De Vasselot Rest Camp: This part of the Tsitsikamma Park lies in a shady forest

Tsitsikamma's nature trails

The Tsitsikamma park has more trails than any other park in South Africa – they total more than 100 km. The most renowned is the Otter Trail, for some, one of the finest nature trails in the world. The 48-km Otter Trail leads west along the coast, from Storms River Mouth to Nature's Valley, weaving through great coastal forests, fording tidal rivers and mounting gorges of matchless beauty that plummet to the sea. There are four overnight camps in scenic settings: Ngubu Camp, Scott Camp at Geelhoutbos River, Oakhurst Hut and André's Camp. The walk is an unforgettable experience, but don't attempt it unless you are reasonably fit, and make sure you book up to a year in advance.

Other hiking trails in the area are the 64-km, five-day Tsitsikamma Hiking Trail, from Kalander at Nature's Valley to Storms River Mouth, and the shorter trails at Storms River – the Mouth (which takes you to the suspension bridge at Storms River Mouth), the Loerie and the Blue Duiker trails. To book a trail or accommodation, contact the National Parks Board (see *Tourist information,* p. 94), or write to the Warden, Tsitsikamma National Park, PO Storms River 6308, tel. (042) 5411607.

on the edge of the Groot River, 40 km west of Storms River, at Nature's Valley. It's an ideal spot if you want access to beautiful forest walks and the sea.

There are 45 sites for caravans and tents here, and no shortage of space. Ablution and barbecue facilities are available, and there is a scullery and laundry. There is no electricity however, and the nearest shop is 3 km away at Nature's Valley.

■■■■ THE LITTLE KAROO

If you travel northwards from Mossel Bay or George over the Outeniqua Mountains towards Oudtshoorn, the countryside opens out into a vast plain, bordered in the north by the towering peaks of the Klein and Groot Swartberge. The San name for the Swartberge was Kango, which means "place rich in water"; and indeed, although the area only gets 150 mm of rain a year, it is amply watered by perennial streams flowing onto the plains from the mountain fringes.

About 250 km long and 70 km wide, this rugged region of breathtaking mountain peaks and grassy shrubland is known as the Little Karoo. This is ostrich country – a place of leopards, wild flowers and beautifully coloured rock formations.

The passes

The mountain passes that link the Little Karoo to the coastal fringe are quite spectacular, and you should set aside at least a day for venturing through them into the Little Karoo. The direct route between Mossel Bay and Oudtshoorn takes you on to Robinson's Pass (860 m), which bisects the Outeniqua Mountains and offers panoramic views of the fynbos-covered countryside.

Other scenic drives are the 16-km-long Outeniqua Pass (drive north from George to Oudtshoorn), built by Italian prisoners of war, and Montagu Pass (accessible by driving northwest from George to Blanco), which is an historical monument and has a toll house at the start of the pass.

But perhaps the most scenic of the passes is the Swartberg Pass (1 585 m) which links Oudtshoorn with the village of Prince Albert on the southern fringes of the Great Karoo. The pass was designed by roadbuilder Thomas Bain, built with con-vict labour, and opened in 1886. The pass offers stunning views of the surrounding countryside. Drive carefully on this 24-km pass – the gradients are steep, and the curves sharp. At the top of the pass you can turn off to The Hell, an isolated spot in the Gamkaskloof 60 km away which is devoid of human habitation. You will need a permit (available from the Department of Nature and Environmental Affairs in Oudtshoorn), and take along some food and water.

Oudtshoorn

Founded in 1847, and named after Baron Pieter van Rheede van Oudtshoorn, gover-nor designate of the Cape, Oudtshoorn is known as the ostrich feather capital of the world – a reference to the industry which made it famous early this century. Ostrich farms still provide an important industry for the area, and you can see huge popula-tions of these birds around Oudtshoorn (there are about 90 000 birds in the area).

There are three ostrich show farms: Hooper's Highgate, tel. (0443) 227115; Safari Ostrich Farm, tel. (0443) 227311; the new Cango Ostrich Farm, tel. (0443) 224623. Each one offers multilingual guided tours of eggs hatching and ostriches being plucked. A highlight of a visit is an ostrich race in which you can participate, if you have the nerve.

The farms offer refreshments after a tour and you can buy souvenirs in an ostrich showroom.

In Oudtshoorn the large mansions or "ostrich palaces", built by the feather barons of the late Victorian and Edwardian era, still exist today. One, an annexe of the CP Nel Museum in High Street, features the bird and all aspects of the industry, feath-er fashions and period furniture. Other feather palaces are the Dorphuis, Pinehurst, Greystones and Welgeluk.

Apart from the world-renowned Cango Caves, the district of Oudtshoorn has var-ious other attractions, including Rus-en-Vrede, a spectacular waterfall 25 km from the caves, and the Cango Mountain Resort at the foothills of the Swartberge, just 7 km from the caves. The resort offers chalets and a pool in lovely surroundings.

Cango Crocodile Ranch and Cheetahland

Just outside Oudtshoorn is the Cango Crocodile Ranch – home to 400 crocodiles – and Cheetahland, where you can take an elevated catwalk that gives you safe views of cheetahs, leopards and lions. Other attractions are a snake park, a train ride through a deer park and a children's farmyard, where you can see Claude the

---

TIP FOR TRAVELLERS

All the restaurants in Oudtshoorn serve ostrich dishes, and the town is one of the few places where you can get an ostrich steak. Other items available are ostrich egg omelettes and ostrich biltong (strips of dried meat).

Camel, Winston the Warthog, and Twinkle the Otter. You'll also find an excellent curio shop and restaurant here, tel. (0443) 225593.

About 15 km from Oudtshoorn on the Cango Caves road is a unique Angora rabbit show farm where you can hug a bunny, take a donkey cart ride and browse through a showroom with delightful handcrafts. Afterwards you can relax in the restaurant or tea garden. Tours are held regularly between 09h00 and 17h00.

The Cango Caves

Just 26 km north of Oudtshoorn, beneath the slopes of the Swartberg range, is one of the longest underground cave sequences in the world – the Cango Caves. Kango is a Khoikhoi word meaning "a watered place between hills".

This haunting fairyland of weird dripstone formations, enchanted lakes, deep pits and interconnecting tunnels is nearly 3 km long, and attracts about 200 000 visitors every year.

These caverns of glittering stalagmites and stalagtites were discovered in 1780 when a cattle herdsman stumbled into the entrance of the caves. He told his employer, a farmer named Van Zyl, who, accompanied by eight slaves, entered the caves with torches to discover a chamber 98 m long, 49 m wide and 15 m high.

Through the years, a vast sequence of chambers has been uncovered. Today they are known as Cango 1 (which is open to the public), Cango 2 and Cango 3 (which are closed to the public) and Cango 4 (which still has to be charted).

You will be introduced to the caves with a sound-and-light presentation in Van Zyl's Hall. The hall is a popular venue for local concerts and performances, and has a seating capacity of 2 000. Cango's strange dripstone formations (called speleothems) were created over more than 150 000 years by the dripping of water through cracks filled with calcite, a crystallised form of chalk.

Conducted tours of the caves are held every hour on the hour from 08h00 to 17h00 in January, February, April and December. During the rest of the year, tours take place every second hour – at 09h00, 11h00, 13h00 and 15h00.

After visiting the caves, you can browse at a curio shop and have a bite to eat at the restaurant. Enquiries and bookings, tel. (0443) 227410.

THE GARDEN ROUTE AND LITTLE KAROO AT A GLANCE

When to go: *Coast:* Summer, with its average daily maximum temperature of 23,5 °C, is best, but take a jersey along, as strong winds can buffet the Garden Route at this time. *Karoo:* The summers are hot and dry, and the Little Karoo swelters in daytime temperatures of up to 40 °C, so autumn and winter would be a cooler time to visit the interior. The Garden Route is a summer rainfall region.

Getting around: *Road:* The N2 highway which links Cape Town and Port Elizabeth, runs through, or provides a link with, the major attractions of the Garden Route and the Little Karoo. From Mossel Bay the road hugs the coast to Plettenberg Bay, then swings slightly inland past Storms River Mouth.

Coach: A regular coach service, the Translux Express, operates between Cape Town and Port Elizabeth. For details contact Translux tel. (021) 4053333 (Cape Town) or (041) 5072276 (Port Elizabeth). *Rail:* An Interpax passenger service connects Cape Town and Port Elizabeth, tel. Cape Town (021) 4053018 or Port Elizabeth (041) 5202975. A steam passenger train, the Outeniqua Choo Choo, runs between George and Knysna (tickets are available at the George and Knysna railway stations, see p. 82).

Air: National and regional airlines serve George Airport, 10 km from town; regional airlines serve Plettenberg Bay and Oudtshoorn.

Main attractions: *Coast:* Scenic drives. Lakes of the Wilderness. Boating on Knysna Lagoon. Swimming, surfing, skindiving and angling at coastal resorts such as Storms River Mouth, Plettenberg Bay, Great Brak River, Vleesbaai and Mossel Bay. Walks through the Knysna Forest. *Karoo:* The Cango Caves. Wild flowers of the Swartberg and Outeniqua mountain ranges. Scenic drives through the passes. Ostrich farms near Oudtshoorn.

Tours and excursions: *Coach tours:* Garden Route Tours offers a variety of excellent tours of this region, ranging from a three-day George to Port Elizabeth tour, to a seven-day Cape Town to Port Elizabeth tour (contact Central Reservations, PO Box 7169, Blanco 6531, tel. (0441) 707993/4). Swann Travel Promotions offers a comprehensive 10-day New Garden Route Tour (Private Bag 1044, Germiston 1400, tel. (011) 8734033). For further details of Garden Route or Karoo tours contact your nearest travel agency or the local tourism office (see *Tourist information,* p. 94). Major international car-hire operators offer cars in Knysna, George and Oudtshoorn, as well as in Johannesburg and Cape Town.

Walking tours: For guided walking tours and more information contact the local tourism office (see p. 94).

Launch trips: Boat trips are available at many resorts along the Garden Route. At Mossel Bay a motor launch takes visitors on a trip to Seal Island during the holiday season (tickets available at the harbour); at Knysna, scenic cruises on the Knysna Lagoon are available on the *John Benn* pleasure cruiser, tel. (0445)

21693. Lightley's Holiday Cruisers can offer you a cruiser that will accommodate from 2 to 8 people, tel. (0445) 871026.

Beaches and bathing: Bathing along this coast is generally safe, and the water is warm throughout the year. Sheltered swimming is available at the mouths of the Hartenbos, Little Brak and Great Brak rivers, while the waters along the Mossel Bay coast are particularly calm. Herold's Bay, Victoria Bay and Plettenberg Bay are highly recommended for their gently sloping beaches and good swimming conditions, while the Tsitsikamma Coastal National Park has excellent swimming and snorkelling facilities in a very sheltered environment.

Tourist information: *Coast:* For information on tours of the Garden Route contact: The Regional Tourist Information Centre, 124 York Street, George 6530, tel. (0441) 736314 or 744000; the Knysna Publicity Association, Main Road, Knysna 6570, tel. (0445) 825510; or the Plettenberg Bay Tourist and Publicity Bureau, Victoria Cottage, Kloof Street, Plettenberg Bay 6600, tel. (04457) 34066. *Karoo:* For tours in the Karoo contact the Klein Karoo Marketing Association, PO Box 1234, Oudtshoorn 6620, tel. (0443) 226643. For information on game reserves and national parks, contact the National Parks Board, PO Box 787, Pretoria 0001, tel. (012) 3431991 or National Parks Board, PO Box 7400, Roggebaai 8012, tel. (021) 222810.

Shopping: George, Knysna and Plettenberg Bay have numerous small shops selling furniture, arts, crafts and curios. The Tsitsikamma National Park also sells handmade crafts and souvenirs.

Festivals and annual events: Mossel Bay – Fish Festival (September); Knysna – Knysna Festival (June); Wilderness – Wilderness New Year Regatta (December). Little Karoo – Cango Caves Marathon (March).

ACCOMMODATION GUIDE

Visitors have a wide choice of excellent hotels, ranging from Fancourt Country Estate in George to the Karos Wilderness Hotel at Wilderness. Book well in advance for the peak holiday season in December and January.

MOSSEL BAY

Eight Bells Mountain Inn*** Below Robinson Pass, 35 km from Mossel Bay. Highly recommended. Five Swiss-style chalets, 10 rooms, 8 family suites. Pool, bowling greens, tennis and squash. PO Box 436, Mossel Bay 6500, tel. (0444) 951544/5.

Rose and Crown Hotel*** Comfortable family hotel. 10 rooms. Conference facilities. PO Box 302, Mossel Bay 6500, tel. (0444) 911069

Santos Protea*** Well-appointed on the beachfront. 58 rooms; pool. PO Box 203, Mossel Bay 6500, tel. (0444) 7103.

GEORGE

Fancourt Country Estate Elegant luxury. National monument built in 1860. 30 rooms, 5 executive suites. 2 presidential suites. PO Box 2266, George 6530, tel. (0441) 708282.

WILDERNESS

Karos Wilderness Hotel**** Reputation for excellent accommodation and food. Near lakes and sea. 148 rooms; 1 suite. Conference facilities for 400; 2 cocktail bars, swimming pools, bowls, tennis, squash. PO Box 6, Wilderness 6560, tel. (0441) 91110.

Holiday Inn Garden Court – Wilderness*** Elevated position overlooking sea. 149 rooms. Conference facilities for 100; à la carte restaurant; bar, pool and tennis courts. PO Box 26, Wilderness 6560, tel. (0441) 91104.

Fairy Knowe Hotel** On the Touws River. 42 en-suite rooms. Conference facilities for 60; pool. PO Box 28, Wilderness 6560, tel. (0441) 91100.

SEDGEFIELD

Lake Pleasant Hotel*** Cosy, old world near lakeside. English pub, great cuisine. 17 en-suite rooms; pool and tennis courts. PO Box 2, Sedgefield 6573, tel. (04455) 31313.

KNYSNA

Knysna Protea*** Near lagoon; 52 rooms. Conference facilities for 200; à la carte restaurant, pool. PO Box 33, Knysna 6570, tel. (0445) 22127.

PLETTENBERG BAY

Hunter's Country House**** Beautiful surroundings. 15 rooms; 15 suites. Conference facilities; pool. PO Box 454, Plettenberg Bay 6600, tel. (04457) 7818.

The Plettenberg Hotel**** Luxury hotel with magnificent view; 20 en-suite rooms; 6 suites; swimming pool. PO Box 719, Plettenberg Bay 6600, tel. (04457) 32030.

Beacon Island*** Exceptional setting on the sea; 189 rooms, 8 suites. Conference facilities for 250. À la carte and table d'hôte; cocktail bars, pool, sauna and quick access to beach. Private Bag 1001, Plettenberg Bay 6600, tel. (04457) 31120.

TSITSIKAMMA AREA

Tsitsikamma Forest Inn** Tranquil forest surroundings. 41 en-suite rooms. Conference facilities for 60; table d'hôte. PO Storms River 6308, tel. (042) 5411711.

Tsitsikamma National Park Storms River Mouth. Well-appointed, serviced one-bedroom and two-bedroom beach cottages and apartments. Excellent views of sea in wild, forested setting. Restaurant, tidal pools and beaches. National Parks Board, PO Box 7400, Roggebaai 8012, tel. (021) 222810.

OUDTSHOORN

Holiday Inn Garden Court – Oudtshoorn*** 30 km from Cango Caves. 120 rooms. Conference facilities for 85; 2 cocktail bars, à la carte restaurant, pool, tennis court. PO Box 52, Oudtshoorn 6620, tel. (0443) 2201.

Kango Protea Hotel*** In town. 40 rooms in thatched chalets. Conference facilities for 120; à la carte restaurant and carvery, pool. PO Box 370, Oudtshoorn 6620, tel. (0443) 2261.

THE EASTERN CAPE

Rocky promontories, interspersed with great seas of sand, announce the shores of the Eastern Cape, which start some 50 km east of Plettenberg Bay, and sweep right up the coast as far as the former Transkei's border with KwaZulu/Natal.

This Sunshine Coast, so named for its long, sun-soaked days and temperate seasons, is favoured by many South Africans above other coastal holiday spots, because of its rural, mellow atmosphere, its superior bathing, surfing and angling opportunities, and its wealth of other outdoor-related activities inland and at the sea.

Another attraction of the Eastern Cape is its enormous historical value. Before the 15th century it was inhabited mainly by dark-skinned pastoralists and Nguni-speaking tribes. Europeans, led by Portuguese explorer Bartholomeu Dias, made their mark on these shores in 1490, and were followed, in 1820, by 4 000 British immigrants, sent by their government to serve as a "buffer" community between the black Xhosa tribes north of the Fish River and the inhabitants of the Cape Colony in the south. Today, well-preserved garrisons, forts and stockades throughout the Eastern Cape testify to the bloody conflicts which took place between the British settlers and the Xhosas over 150 years ago.

The area further north (known under the old apartheid government as the Ciskei), once the scene of nine frontier wars between the Xhosa and the British, today is a tranquil holiday playground, known for its superb scenic vistas, modern coastal resorts and nature reserves nestling at the feet of towering mountain ranges, such as the Katberge, the Amatola, the Winterberge and Hogsback.

Still further along the coast, beyond the Kei River Mouth, is Transkei, as this former homeland was called, which was reincorporated into South Africa under the new government of national unity in 1994. Here, humpbacked hills of green tumble down to the bronze beaches of the Wild Coast – a palm-fringed paradise where vervet monkeys play on the terraces of casino resorts and hidden hotels.

CLIMATE

This is a winter and summer rainfall region, so take an umbrella along for both seasons. The winters are warmer and drier than the more southerly parts of the South African coast, but it can still be very chilly here in midwinter. The summers are warm to hot. Port Elizabeth has a daily maximum average temperature of 25,2 °C in January (midsummer), and 19,5 °C in July (midwinter). The further inland you move from the coast, the colder it gets.

WHAT TO SEE

Jeffrey's Bay

This surfer's paradise, fishing village and holiday resort, with its magnificent beaches, is one of South Africa's fastest growing resorts.

For water-lovers there's almost every conceivable form of recreational activity: a pleasure cruise in a luxury 10-m yacht, gamefishing, or a ride in a Mississippi type paddlesteamer, the *Belafonte,* (see *Tours and excursions,* p. 111). Near the beach, craft shops offer beautiful shells, pottery, leatherwork and bric-a-brac. Don't miss the Kritzinger Sea Shell Collection in the library on the seafront road.

◼◼ PORT ELIZABETH

South Africa's fifth largest city is a leading South African port and a vibrant, easy-going metropolis, known to locals as "The Friendly City" – a reference to its pledge to "put people first".

The city was named in 1820 by the acting British Governor of the Cape Colony, Sir Rufane Donkin, after his wife Elizabeth, who died in India two years earlier. At the time the settlement was a small, nameless cluster of houses on the coast, protected by Fort Frederick on top of a hill. Since then the city has grown to become the second-largest municipal area in South Africa, with a population of some 700 000 people.

The good-natured ambience, the mellow atmosphere of its lazy beaches and its warm, temperate climate combine to make Port Elizabeth an engaging tourist retreat.

Tucked into the southwestern corner of Algoa Bay, it is ideally placed as a base for coastal day drives to spots such as Bluewater Bay, Skoenmakerskop, Seaview or Van Staden's River Mouth, or inland, to the Groendal Wilderness Area, Addo Elephant National Park or Uitenhage Nature Reserve.

There's no shortage of things to do in Port Elizabeth. You can visit the abundance of historical sites, museums, memorials and monuments dating back to the 15th century; you can take a steam train trip on a narrow-gauge railway; watch performing dolphins and seals at the Oceanarium; climb the Campanile; or snorkel and scuba in excellent diving spots.

If you enjoy other sea-related sports, there's boating, yachting, windsurfing and angling. For strollers, there are plenty of walks through historic parks and nature reserves.

Most of the historical buildings, the docks and several fine restaurants are no more than 10 minutes' walk from the centre of town. To plan your route get a copy of The Donkin Heritage Trail from the Tourist Information Bureau.

Buses to all parts of the city depart regularly from the underground concourse below the Norwich Union Centre in Market Square.

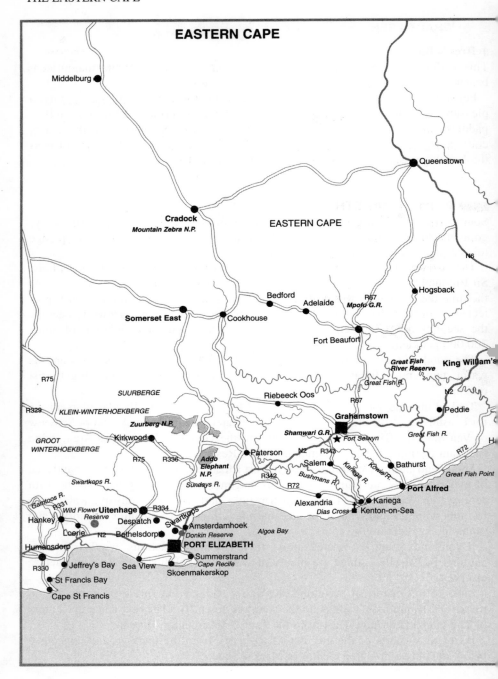

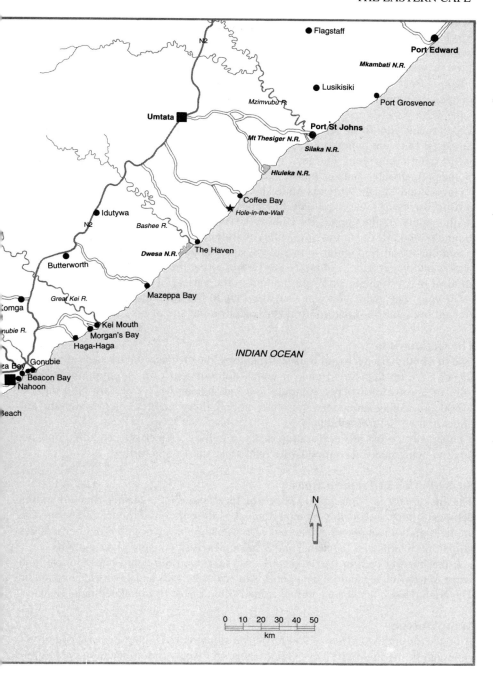

Flagstaff

N2

Port Edward

Mkambati N.R.

Lusikisiki

Port Grosvenor

Mzimvubu R.

Umtata

Port St Johns

Mt Thesiger N.R.

Silaka N.R.

Hluleka N.R.

Coffee Bay
Hole-in-the-Wall

Idutywa

N2

Bashee R.

Dwesa N.R.   The Haven

Butterworth

Great Kei R.

Komga

Mazeppa Bay

nubie R.

Kei Mouth
Morgan's Bay
Haga-Haga

za Bay   Gonubie
Beacon Bay
Nahoon

Beach

INDIAN OCEAN

N

0   10   20   30   40   50
km

Beaches

Port Elizabeth has a good selection of wide, gently sloping beaches that are safe for swimming. The seawater temperatures range from 20-24 °C in summer (November through March), and seldom less that 15 °C in winter.

King's Beach, extending 1,6 km from the harbour breakwater to Humewood, has an open-air amphitheatre, a putt-putt golf course, a supertube and a miniature train – the Seabreeze Express. For a longer train journey, hop onto the Dias Express, which takes you from King's Beach to the Campanile. The train stops at the Humerail Museum, where you can browse among the relics of a bygone steam era, before continuing your journey. The McArthur Bath Complex at King's Beach includes freshwater and sea pools, and change rooms.

Humewood Beach, which is quite sheltered and safe for bathing (the best body-surfing waves in town), leads on to Happy Valley, a quiet garden valley of lawns (with nursery rhyme themes for children), riverside walks, ponds, palm trees and a giant chessboard. In summer the valley is illuminated with coloured lights.

Summerstrand is popular with sailors, and Pollack beach is the haunt of body-surfers and waterskiers. About 24 km further along the coast, Schoenmakerskop is an ideal place to picnic and splash about in the variety of rock pools.

On your way there you can visit the Piet Retief Monument in Summerstrand, erected in memory of the Voortrekker leader on the site of his farm, Strandfontein.

The Oceanarium

One of South Africa's major tourist attractions, the Oceanarium houses a 60-m-long (nearly five million litres) tank in which dolphins perform an entertaining repertoire of acrobatic displays, jumping and ball balancing. Shows are held daily at 11h00 and 15h00. An underwater observation gallery enables you to watch the dolphins in their natural habitat.

Other attractions are performing seals, a colony of jackass penguins, and two large viewing tanks accommodating fish, rays, sharks and turtles.

Snake Park and Tropical House

The snake park is home to 80 species of local and exotic snakes. Snake handling demonstrations with such venomous snakes as the cobra, puff adder and boomslang are held daily in an open pit. There is also a cosmopolitan population of crocodiles, alligators, lizards and leguaans, and a special facility housing giant pythons.

A meandering path in the Tropical House takes you through a dense jungle landscape of tropical vegetation, with pools, streams, waterfalls and an artificial mountain. The Night House features nocturnal animals illuminated by simulated moonlight.

Main Museum

An outstanding exhibition of South African shipwrecks (including salvaged bronze cannons) is the highlight here. Other items on display are archaeological exhibits (early humanoid fossils and artefacts), an historical costume gallery, and a bird hall. 50 000 people annually visit the children's museum with its open wildlife displays, and children are encouraged to touch the displays.

For information and bookings at the Museum, Snake Park, Tropical House or Aquarium, tel. (041) 561051.

Historical buildings

Fort Frederick was built above the Baakens River by the British in 1799 to protect the tiny settlement at Algoa Bay. Although it was designed for a garrison of 350 men and eight 12-pounder guns, no shot was ever fired in anger. The fort is open on weekdays.

A mighty climb awaits you at the Campanile, which was opened in 1923 to commemorate the landing of the 1820 settlers. For a spectacular view of the city and Algoa Bay, climb the 204 steps (51,8 m) to the top. This stately tower has a carillon of 23 bells that peal three times a day.

Another historical monument is the Donkin Pyramid in the reserve of the same name, erected by Sir Rufane Donkin in memory of his wife Elizabeth, who died in India in 1818. A lighthouse, erected in 1861, and a military museum, housing a superb collection of badges, medals, uniforms and other war memorabilia, are situated nearby. A tough climb gets you to the lighthouse's platform, from which you can view the city.

Across the park are the Donkin Street houses, a much-photographed terrace of Victorian houses, each stepped lower than its neighbour. For further information on any of the above places, contact the Port Elizabeth Publicity Association, Donkin Reserve, Belmont Terrace, Port Elizabeth 6001, tel. (041) 521315.

The city hall and surrounds

A replica of the cross planted at the headland Kwaaihoek by Portuguese explorer Bartholomeu Dias in 1488 stands in front of the City Hall, which was rebuilt after it burned down in 1977. The hall overlooks Market Square, where visitors used to outspan their ox-wagons.

The oldest house in the city, Parsonage House, built by the Rev Francis McCleland in 1830, has an attractive display of Victorian furniture. An outside room houses a fine collection of Edwardian and Victorian toys.

Across the road are the Sterley Cottages, one of which was occupied by the city's first policeman, Thomas Sterley.

St George's Park

This 73-ha park, the oldest park in the country, was the venue for the first South African cricket test in 1889, and the first rugby test played two years later. The park also houses the oldest cricket club and bowling green in South Africa. Another feature is the 100-year-old Pearson Conservatory, housing an excellent collection of orchids and water lilies. There's also a large swimming pool with steam baths, a tearoom and recreation areas. Art in the Park, an open-air exhibition of homecrafts for sale, is held here on the first Sunday of every month. At the park's entrance are the Cenotaph and Memorial which commemorate the fallen soldiers of Prince Alfred's Guard, a local regiment dating back to 1877.

Settler's Park Nature Reserve

Indigenous plants, shrubs and trees abound in this 54-ha park – just five minutes from the City Hall. Footpaths and stepping stones take you across the Baakens River, past attractive water features and colourful cultivated displays (the best time to visit is November). Spacious lawns, landscaped terraces and exotic woodland make this a birdlover's paradise, and the ideal place for a picnic.

The Apple Express

One of the few remaining narrow-gauge railways in the world (it was established in 1906), the apple-green Apple Express chugs westwards from Port Elizabeth station through beautiful mountain scenery to Loerie in the Langkloof apple country, crossing Van Staden's River gorge bridge – the highest narrow-gauge bridge in the world. At Loerie you can braai (barbecue) and stroll through the village before returning on the same day.

Two other options are open: you can hop off at Van Staden's bridge, and spend a few hours hiking (or visiting the Van Staden's Wild Flower Reserve nearby), before getting back on the train on its return trip. The other option is to take a bicycle with you (at a nominal fee), and explore Loerie and its surrounds in the saddle. Tourist excursions are run on scheduled dates throughout the year, but you must book ahead. (For details see *Tours and excursions,* p. 111.)

Sea cruises

The tug *Blue Jay* offers cruises around the bay, including a sunset cruise, and a cruise which takes you to Thunderbolt reef to see the wreck of the *Kapodistrias.* The *Nauticat,* a pink pleasure cruiser offers weekend daytime cruises or nightly braai (barbecue) cruises on request (for both cruises see *Tours and excursions,* p. 111).

■■■ AROUND PORT ELIZABETH

The Swartkops River

This wide, slow-moving river east of the city offers some beautiful picnic spots and excellent fishing. The tiny hamlet of Amsterdamhoek, with its wooden jetties leaning into the river near the bridge, provides a tranquil setting for a riverside picnic and a chance to watch a variety of seabirds feeding on the mudflats.

Attractions here include the aloes reserve on the Tippers Creek Road. From Amsterdamhoek onwards, chalets, campgrounds and resort facilities are available at St George's Strand, Joorst Park and the Pearson Park resort on the Sundays River.

The Swartkops River winds its way northwards up to the village of Redhouse, another idyllic picnic spot in a rural setting.

Seaview Game Park

You can watch lions and cheetahs being fed at the Seaview Game Park and Animal Shelter west of Port Elizabeth. Animals in the wild include giraffe, wildebeest, kudu, zebra, nyala, impala, and blesbok. A walking tour of the animal shelter will take you into the company of baboons, caracal, duiker and owls. Light refreshments are available, and there are braai (barbecue) facilities at the campsite. For more information telephone (041) 741702.

Addo Elephant National Park

More than 185 elephants are the major attraction of this 8 595-ha park, proclaimed in 1931 to protect the last of the Eastern Cape's elephants. The elephants were nearly wiped out 10 years earlier, when a hunter hired by local farmers shot 100 of them. The surviving 16 sought sanctuary in the nearly impenetrable tangle of trees and creepers of the Addo bush.

Other animals include black rhino, buffalo, eland, kudu, hartebeest, bushbuck, grysbok and duiker. The 185 species of bird include ostriches, hawks, finches and francolins.

You can hire self-contained rondavels, chalets and six-bed family cottages at reasonable rates. There is also a camping and caravan park, a licenced restaurant, shop and petrol pump. For details contact the Port Elizabeth Publicity Association (see *Tourist information*, p. 112).

Shamwari Game Reserve

This beautiful sanctuary for animals, opened to the public in 1993, is just 72 km from Port Elizabeth on the N2 heading for Grahamstown. It offers four superb lodges for guests who want to get close to nature in the company of the Big Five. Major attractions are the animals and a variety of birds, day and night game drives, tennis courts, a swimming pool, gymnasium and steam baths. To get to Shamwari from Johannesburg, you may book a seat on the Elephant Carriage of the Algoa Express. The coach will stop virtually at Shamwari's doorstep. For bookings and details telephone (042) 8511196.

Grahamstown and settler country

A classic three-day country tour takes in the historic settler towns of Grahamstown, Bathurst, Port Alfred and Salem (for details contact the Port Elizabeth Publicity Association, see *Tourist information*, p. 112). Alternatively, take a day to tour Grahamstown by car (it's one-and-a-half hours from Port Elizabeth).

Established in 1812 as a military outpost, and later as a village and trading centre for the 1820 settlers, Grahamstown's most prominent landmark is the Cathedral of St Michael and St George (1824), which took 128 years to build. Here you can visit the 1820 Settler Monument, the Methodist Commemoration Church (1850), with its Gothic Revival facade, and the City Hall, built in 1870 as a memorial to the 1820 settlers.

Other places of interest are the Albany Museum, the Settlers Wild Flower Reserve and Fort Selwyn.

Port Alfred

This beautiful coastal hamlet just over an hour's drive from Port Elizabeth is known as "the family holiday resort", because it offers just about everything you could want: a temperate climate, clean, white beaches, a long, wide river (the Kowie) with powerboating, canoeing and sailing and a tranquil lagoon. The angling is excellent here and all the other outdoor recreational facilities are available – a fine, 18-hole links, bowls, tennis and squash and many excellent restaurants.

A major attraction at Port Alfred is the two-day Kowie Canoe Trail, during which you sleep under a thatched shelter upriver (see *Tours and excursions,* p. 111).

Zuurberg National Park

Spectacular mountain scenery and rich forested valleys are the highlights in this 20 777-ha park northwest of the Addo Elephant National Park. Unique plants, such as the Zuurberg cushion bush (*Oldenburgia arbuscula*) and the Zuurberg cycad (*Encephalartos longifolius*) flourish here, together with forests of yellowwood, white assegaai and white stinkwood trees.

The valleys and ravines are home to baboons, caracal, bushbuck, mountain reedbuck and grey duiker. There is no overnight accommodation, but you can stay at the nearby Zuurberg Inn, a lovely country hotel nearby that offers a swimming pool, country walking trails, tennis, bowls and horseriding.

Mountain Zebra National Park

This picturesque park southwest of Cradock is home to about 200 of one of the world's rarest large mammals, the Cape mountain zebra. There are 37 km of good gravel roads providing rewarding viewing of 57 species of mammal including eland, springbok, black wildebeest, red hartebeest, blesbok, mountain reedbuck and klipspringer. Black-backed jackal, aardwolf, caracal and Cape fox share this grassland area with about 200 bird species, among which are the rare booted eagle, the black eagle and the martial eagle. For accommodation you can choose between 18 two-bed chalets and the Doornhoek guest cottage – a restored Victorian farmhouse with kitchen and cooking facilities.

Apart from a camping and caravan site, there is a shop, swimming pool, à la carte restaurant and riding stables.

The three-day Mountain Zebra Hiking Trail is very popular. For details contact the Warden, Mountain Zebra National Park, PO Box X66, Cradock 5880, tel. (0481) 2427.

The Fish River Sun
A few decades ago, a cluster of ramshackle fishing shacks lined the banks of the Great Fish River in a sylvan setting of sandy beach and rocky coastline. Today the Polynesian-styled, 300-bed Fish River Sun offers a more luxurious taste of this peaceful part of the Eastern Cape coastline. You can try your luck in the modern casino, dine in a delectable à la carte restaurant or socialise in one of the cocktail bars.

Outdoors, there's a swimming pool, tennis and squash courts and an 18-hole golf course designed by golfing maestro Gary Player.

A major attraction at Fish River is the 64-km Shipwreck Trail, which takes you northwards along the coast to the Ncera River mouth. The walk will take about three or four days, provided you are reasonably fit. Attractions along the way are birdwatching, vast expanses of golden sand, overnight camping on the beach and the wrecks themselves. Take a fishing rod along with you – fine catches are made at the river mouth.

Mpekweni Marine Resort
Another 100-room Sun hotel complex graces the green terraces of Mpekweni as they roll down to the lagoon and sea. On offer are safe swimming in the lagoon, a spectacular swimming pool from which you can order drinks at the bar, river cruises and various outdoor sports, including bowls, tennis and squash. An à la carte restaurant specialises in seafoods.

Amatola Sun
Luxury accommodation in 59 rooms, a casino, several restaurants, cocktail bars and live entertainment are offered in Bisho near King William's Town.

Other reserves
North of the Fish River are three lovely reserves worth visiting: The Tsolwana Game Reserve, a magnificent 1 700-ha park in the foothills of the Winterberg Mountains, offers three fully furnished and serviced lodges, a rustic bush camp, and 48 species of game, including wildebeest, rhino, giraffe and antelope. There are guided walks and pony trails, trout fishing dams and hunting safaris – with a luxury hunting lodge. The Tsolwana Trail offers magnificent scenery and excellent chances to view some of the 117 species of bird in the area. You can walk for three hours or three days along this trail. For details, contact the reserve at PO Box 1424, Queenstown 5320, tel. (0408) 22026.

Mpofu Game Reserve is a 12 000-ha wilderness, 45 km south of Seymour, with a recently completed luxury lodge. It is home to shy forest-dwelling creatures such as the rare blue duiker, bushbuck and bushpig. For details contact Contour, tel. (0401) 952115 or the reserve direct at (040452) ask for 11.

The new Great Fish River Reserve, incorporating the former Double Drift Game Reserve, the Andries Vosloo Kudu Reserve and the Sam Knott Nature Reserve, covers 45 000 ha of the Fish River Valley. Luxury lodges, self-catering cabins and camping sites are available here. Game includes black rhino, red hartebeest, hippo, eland and leopard. For more information tel. (0461) 27909.

Hogsback

Exceptional mountain scenery, fern-fringed forests, tumbling rivers and streams and fine hotel accommodation combine to make a visit to this remote Eastern Cape wilderness quite unforgettable. Waterfalls such as the Madonna and Child, the Bridal Veil, the Swallowtail and the Kettle and Spout are major attractions here. All the hotels and lodges have maps of the area. Holiday bungalows and a camping site nestling in an exquisite forest setting offer true tranquillity in this quiet place.

An attraction is the beautiful clay animals – hogs, horses and kudu – that local craftsmen sell from the side of the road. Keep an eye out for them – vendors tend to jump into the road to peddle their wares. Hogsback is also the site of one of South Africa's smallest churches, St Patrick's-on-the-Hill.

■■■ EAST LONDON

This city – the fourth biggest port in the country – and its magnificent, uncluttered beaches are known as the Romantic Coast. The equitable climate, warm ocean and beautiful hinterland make it the perfect place for a holiday.

Beaches

A 2-km esplanade borders one of the safest beaches in the country – Orient Beach, named after a Russian ship that ran aground here in 1907. The beach, which has its own theatre complex (Orient Theatre) and restaurant, offers umbrellas, beach chairs and beach tents for hire. There's also a nice walk down the esplanade, past the site where the *SA Oranjeland* ran aground a few years ago.

Nahoon Beach is the most popular East London beach, and its reef is internationally renowned among surfers. The beach bus from the city will take you there. There have been isolated attacks on surfers at the reef by Great White sharks over the years. A young surfer died after being bitten by a Great White off Nahoon Reef in 1994. Eastern Beach, opposite Marina Glen, has a sheltered children's playground, as well as a miniature train, the Charity Mail.

There's a lovely tidal pool at Fuller's Bay. Alternatively, cool down in the Joan Harrison or Ruth Belonsky freshwater swimming pools.

Aquarium

Twice daily seal shows are a major attraction of the esplanade's aquarium, which houses 400 species of marine animals. You can also see jackass penguins, and a number of injured or pollution-affected creatures that are being nursed back to health.

Museums

The East London Museum has two unique displays unrivalled elsewhere on earth – the first coelacanth (*Latimeria chalumnae*), a prehistoric fossil-fish, thought to have become extinct 60 million years ago, and the world's only dodo egg (the dodo became extinct in the 18th century). There's also an outstanding collection of Karoo fossils, an exhibition depicting traditional Xhosa and Fingo dress, crafts and customs, and maritime exhibits.

Gately House is named after the town's first mayor, John Gately, and houses Victorian period furniture.

Ann Bryant Art Gallery

This large house in town exhibits works by such well-known South African artists as Battis and Pierneef.

The harbour

Presently handling about three million tons of cargo each year, the harbour has a tanker berth, a huge grain elevator and a container-handling facility. The John Baillie Memorial, erected in honour of Lieutenant John Baillie, who surveyed the harbour area in 1835, is situated in the grounds of the Port Captain's office on Signal Hill. Harbour tours are available (contact the East London Publicity Association, see *Tourist information*, p. 112). For pleasure trips around the bay, see *Tours and excursions*, p. 111.

Queen's Park Botanical Gardens and Zoo

Covering 35 ha between the city centre and the river, these gardens, opened in 1880, are the only natural habitat in the world of the Buffalo River thorn (*Umtiza listeriana*). Indigenous trees and shrubs, interspersed with flowering plants such as strelitzia and flame lily, flourish here. The zoo within the park is home to a variety of antelope, snakes, monkeys, miniature goats and birds.

■■■ AROUND EAST LONDON

Resorts

Attractive coastal resorts between East London and the former Transkei include Beacon Bay, a coastal hamlet on the Quinera estuary that incorporates Bonza Bay. There are a hotel, two nature reserves, with a variety of birdlife, and an attractive coastal forest off the beach. Gonubie Mouth, further north, has a waterfowl sanctuary, with 130 species of birds, and a scenic 4-km coastal drive that takes you to

Gonubie Beach and German Bay (both safe for bathing), and a paddling pool for children.

At Morgan's Bay, just south of the former Transkei border, huge waves crash against humpbacked hills west of the village. To the east, a tranquil lagoon provides excellent swimming, canoeing and waterskiing. Morgan's Bay's twin village, Kei Mouth, is a fishing village noted for its fine catches.

Mpongo Park

This 1 600-ha game reserve, which nestles among rolling hills and valleys just half-an-hour's drive from East London, is home to more than 40 species of mammal, including rhino, giraffe, zebra and various antelope, as well as ostriches. There's a curio shop and a museum, dedicated to the great explorer, Dr WJ Burchell, at the park's entrance. An animal orphanage here houses predators, antelope and reptiles that have been injured or abandoned.

The Huberta Restaurant – named after a famous wandering hippo – offers take-away snacks, or sit-down meals. There are braai (barbecue) facilities on the banks of the Umpongo River (for details contact the East London Metropolitan Tourism Association, tel. (0431) 26015).

■■■■ WILD COAST AREA

Hole-in-the-Wall

A huge dolerite island, with a natural tunnel carved through its centre, provides a remarkable vista on this enchanting part of the Eastern Cape's Wild Coast. A short drive from Coffee Bay, Hole-in-the-Wall was named by the crew of the British survey ship *Barracuda* in 1823. The local Xhosa people call it esiKhaleni (the place of sound) for the amplified sound the tunnel gives to waves crashing through it. The hole has been eroded over millions of years by the Mpako River and the sea.

Take care if you plan to walk to the rock shelf in front of the Hole-in-the-Wall. People have been washed off this shelf by the incoming tide; one swimmer died trying to swim through the tunnel, and people attempting to scale the cliffs have had to be rescued.

You can swim at the beautiful, sheltered beach east of Hole-in-the-Wall, or have a picnic under the milkwood trees, alongside the stream that runs onto the beach. There's a new bungalow-style hotel opposite this beach, with all amenities.

Alternatively, you can stay at one of Coffee Bay's two hotels. Coffee Bay, nestling between mountain and sea, has a kilometre-long beach that provides good swimming, fine shells and a scenic walk, and a nine-hole golf course. The Nenga River nearby is popular among powerboat enthusiasts.

Mazeppa Bay

This pleasant hide-away resort, fringed by wild date palms, offers rare seclusion in

The magic world of the Xhosa

A drive through any of the country roads will inevitably take you past communities of Xhosa people, living in thatch-roofed huts or rondavels, some of which are colourfully painted in various hues.

Although history books speak of the Xhosas "clashing" with northward-migrating Europeans in the 19th century, they were in Transkei – the land beyond the Kei – long before Europeans came to the subcontinent in 1652.

The Xhosa nation is divided up into a number of different tribes, each with its own particular culture, customs and traditions.

Even today witchcraft, divining, exorcism and superstition play an important part in the traditional way of life of the Xhosa. Many rural communities believe in the existence of a hairy, cunning, dwarf-like creature known as *uThikoloshe,* who is said to cause disease in humans and animals. He is only accessible to children and is believed to be a popular playmate of them. *uThikoloshe* is said, among other things, to suck the milk from cows and make some women frigid.

Also much feared by the Xhosa is *impundulu* – the lightning bird, which has a large, hooked beak, long legs and a red beak. This fearsome bird stands taller than a man and is capable of causing death and disease. When it flaps its wings thunder is heard, when it spits, forked lightning flashes.

In the southern Transkei area, there is widespread belief in aquatic semi-deities called *aBantu bamlambo* (the people of the river). Near the Hole-in-the-Wall there is still the belief that *aBantu bamlambo* were responsible for creating the hole in the dolerite island there.

These creatures, about the size of humans, are naked, with flipper-like feet and hair hanging below their shoulders. When someone drowns in the sea, and the body is not recovered, he is said to have been taken by the river people, and is not mourned, as such a death is an honour.

Occupying pride of place in any Xhosa community is the witchdoctor, who is the mediator between the community and revered ancestral spirits. Many witchdoctors are believed to be the reincarnated forms of victims "taken" by the river people.

The Xhosa witchdoctors wear white. Their bushy headdresses are made of animal fur and they sometimes carry a switch (made from the tail of a wildebeest), and an animal horn. Witchdoctors are intrinsically good people who heal and exorcise victims of sorcerers or evil spirits.

serene, subtropical surroundings. Famed for the huge sharks that are caught here, Mazeppa Bay has three broad beaches, and its own island that is linked to the mainland by a suspension bridge. You can swim, snorkel or scuba dive in safe beach conditions.

Coastal dunes, forests and an inland lagoon offer scenic walks. Take along a fishing rod and a pair of binoculars. The Island, Shark Point and the Boiling Pot are excellent fishing spots. Accommodation includes a hotel, a cottage resort and a campsite.

Port St Johns

Two huge sentinels of rock, Mount Sullivan and Mount Thesinger, tower above thick subtropical forest, and the mighty Mzimvubu River at Port St Johns, in one of the most dramatic settings of any coastal resort in South Africa.

The long, quiet road that leads into this resort is lined with stalls offering hand-carved curios, beadwork, batik, cane crafts and subtropical fruits such as mangoes, pawpaws and bananas. There are three beaches to choose from: First Beach is a good fishing spot, but watch out for sharks; Second Beach, site of a cluster of holiday cottages, offers safe, warm-water bathing; Third Beach further south, which lies in the Silaka Nature Reserve, is a holiday paradise, with four-bed chalets, a pebble-lined beach, some great birdwatching (this is a favourite haunt for giant, pied, malachite and brownhooded kingfishers), and excellent rambles along the coast.

Silaka Nature Reserve is home to zebra, blue wildebeest and blesbok, and a variety of indigenous orchids, lilies, mosses and lichen. If you're staying in Port St Johns, pack a picnic hamper, and take a full day to visit Silaka and Third Beach.

Just west of Port St Johns is the lagoon-side resort of Umngazi River, site of the Wild Coast's largest mangrove forest. Here, hillside resort cottages and a hotel peer over dunes that plummet to lagoon and sea. The nearby forest is home to more than 250 species of birds.

This is not only a fisherman's paradise – you can bathe in the lagoon's warm waters, go on a boat trip up the river or take an organised hike.

The day-long coastal hike to Port St Johns is recommended. On the way you will pass the wreck of the *Horizon,* the spouting Blow Hole and the Crack Rock formations.

Wild Coast Sun

This is the most popular upmarket resort on the Wild Coast, combining the luxury of a top-class hotel and casino complex with the rugged grandeur of curving, palm-fringed beaches and subtropical forests.

The resort – the northernmost on this coastline – is set on the banks of a placid lagoon, and offers the full range of water-related activities: swimming in the surf or a freshwater pool, waterskiing, canoeing and sailing at Waterworld, and surf and deep-sea angling.

Top class entertainment includes a modern casino, marvellous restaurant (the Commodore), cabaret and theatre shows. For the sportsman and woman there is a golf course, bowls, tennis and squash.

At Mzamba River to the south are the Mzamba Cretaceous Deposits, fossils of petrified trees and relics of marine life that thrived here 100 million years ago.

To the north of the Wild Coast Sun is the Umtamvuna River and its waterfall.

THE EASTERN CAPE AT A GLANCE

When to go: Summer is best, with its abundant sunshine, warm to hot days and mild nights. Winter, however, can be just as pleasant, especially along the Wild Coast.

Getting around: Well-surfaced tarred roads connect the major and minor towns of the Eastern Cape, but some secondary gravel roads in the former Transkei are in bad shape, with severe potholes and corrugations. Stray animals crossing the road are a hazard in the northwestern parts of the Eastern Cape. From Port Elizabeth, the N2 leads west to Cape Town and northeast to Durban.

Main attractions: Sun, sea and sand of the Eastern Cape's coastal resorts. Scenic drives. The Apple Express. Addo Elephant National Park. Gamefishing. Riding the paddlesteamer at Jeffrey's Bay. Exploring the mountains and forests of the Hogsback and Zuurberg. Walks along the Wild Coast. Boating and canoeing in the rivers, estuaries, lagoons and lakes. Visiting historic homesteads, garrisons and forts.

Tours and excursions: *Coach tours:* Transnet offers 37 routes in the region linking Port Elizabeth with Grahamstown, East London, Graaff-Reinet, Cape Town and Durban. Sightseeing coach tours of the region are laid on by Plusbus, Springbok Atlas and Garden Route Tours. For more information contact Satour (see p. 112).

Car hire: Many major car-rental companies operate in Port Elizabeth, East London, Bisho, Umtata and other Eastern Cape centres; consult the Yellow Pages or your hotel reception.

Walks and trails: There are hundreds of walks and trails in this region, ranging from the 64-km, three-day Shipwreck Trail (from the Great Fish River to the Chalumna River) to leisurely strolls through nature reserves. Highly recommended is the Bushbuck Walk (16 km or shorter), 25 km from Port Elizabeth. For trails in the Eastern Cape contact the Port Elizabeth Publicity Association, Donkin Reserve, Belmont Terrace, Port Elizabeth 6001, tel. (041) 521315, or Satour, 21-23 Donkin Street, Port Elizabeth 6001, tel. (041) 557761.

Launch trips: Lagoon, river and deep-sea boat trips are available at many resorts along the Eastern Cape coast. The major ones are: Jeffrey's Bay: the *Belafonte,* a Mississippi-type paddlesteamer, offers cruises of the inland lake and marina complex, tel. (0423) 920200. Port Elizabeth: The tug *Blue Jay* offers cruises around the bay, including a sunset cruise, and a shipwreck cruise to Thunderbolt Reef, tel. (041) 521315. The *Nauticat,* a pink pleasure cruiser, offers weekend daytime cruises (on request) all year round at 11h00, 13h00 and 15h00. Nightly braai cruises are offered on request. For bookings telephone (041) 553089. Port Alfred: Kowie Canoe Trail (Port Alfred – 21 km) in double canoes. Contact Satour (see p. 112). East London: For pleasure trips around the bay, contact the East London Metropolitan Tourism Association, PO Box 533, East London 5200, tel. (0431) 26015.

Trains: The Apple Express. Booking: Transnet Main Line Ticket Office, Port Elizabeth Station, tel. (041) 5202313. The Dias Express, a steam train service offered on an extended narrow gauge railway line from the Campanile to King's Beach, tel. (041) 5202313.

Beaches and bathing: The warm Agulhas Current creates ideal bathing conditions throughout the year – from 20-24 °C (October to March), and seldom less that 15 °C in winter (April to September). Bathing is safe along most of this coastline, but most of the northern beaches are unpatrolled, so be careful here. Port Elizabeth's Humewood beach, and East London's Orient and Nahoon beaches are particularly safe.

Tourist information: Port Elizabeth Publicity Association, Donkin Reserve, Belmont Terrace, Port Elizabeth 6001, tel. (041) 521315, or Satour, 21-23 Donkin Street, Port Elizabeth 6001, tel. (041) 557761. East London: Satour, NBS Building, Terminus Street, East London 5201, or the East London Metropolitan Tourism Association, PO Box 533, East London 5200, tel. (0431) 26015. Wild Coast: Wild Coast Hotels and Information, Private Bag X5028, Umtata 5100, tel. (0471) 253444.

For details on National Parks contact the National Parks Board, PO Box 787, Pretoria 0001, tel. (012) 3431991.

Shopping: Port Elizabeth: Main Street offers a wide range of retail shopping centres. There's a large undercover complex in Newton Park with chain stores. East London: The Oriental Plaza, Berea Mall and the Vincent Park Centre are the main shopping areas.

Festivals and annual events: Jeffrey's Bay – Shell Festival (March/April); Port Elizabeth – Shakespearian Festival (February), Port Elizabeth Show (April), The Great Train Race (September), Harbour Festival (December); East London – Expo (September), Oktoberfest (October), Oxford Street Carnival (December); Grahamstown – National Festival of the Arts (June/July).

ACCOMMODATION GUIDE

PORT ELIZABETH

Beach Hotel*** Marine Drive, Humewood. Quick access to beaches and aquarium; 63 rooms. Conference facilities for 100. PO Box 319, Port Elizabeth 6000, tel. (041) 532161.

Holiday Inn Garden Court – Kings Beach*** Luxury hotel overlooking King's Beach; 127 rooms, 7 suites. Conference facilities for 900. PO Box 13100, Humewood 6013, tel. (041) 523720.

Holiday Inn Garden Court – Summerstrand*** Walking distance of beach. Summerstrand; 230 rooms, 6 suites. Conference facilities for 250; excellent cuisine; Marine Drive, Summerstrand 6000, tel. (041) 523131.

Marine Protea Hotel*** Cosy Summerstrand hotel near beach; 73 rooms; à la carte restaurant. PO Box 501, Port Elizabeth 6000, tel. (041) 532101.

Clarendon Hotel City centre. Comfortable, close to amenities. 10 rooms. Conference facilities for 120; fine restaurant. Lutman Street, Port Elizabeth 6001, tel. (041) 551558.

EAST LONDON

Holiday Inn Garden Court*** 171 rooms, 2 suites. Conference facilities for 300; pool, 2 bars. PO Box 1255, East London 5200, tel. (0431) 27260.

Hotel Osner*** On beachfront. 110 rooms. Conference facilities for 300; gymnasium, sauna, spa; à la carte restaurant, 2 cocktail bars. PO Box 334, East London 5200, tel. (0431) 433433.

Kennaway Protea*** On beachfront. 83 rooms, 5 suites. Conference facilities for 140; fine restaurant. PO Box 583, East London 5200, tel. (0431) 25531.

Esplanade** On beachfront. 66 rooms. Conference facilities for 25. Beachfront, East London 5201, tel. (0431) 22518.

Amatola Sun Bisho. Luxury accommodation. 78 rooms; 2 suites; casino, several restaurants, cocktail bars; PO Box 1274, King William's Town 5600, tel. (0401) 91111.

PORT ALFRED AREA

Fish River Sun***** Seaside luxury; 119 rooms. Conference facilities for 200; casino, swimming pool, 18-hole golf course. PO Box 232, Port Alfred 6170, tel. (0405) 661101.

Mpekweni Sun Overlooking lagoon and sea; 100 rooms; 1 suite; bowls, tennis, squash; à la carte restaurant specialises in seafoods. Conference facilities; PO Box 2060, Port Alfred 6170, tel. (045) 661026.

WILD COAST

Kei Mouth Beach Hotel** Stately, comfortable hotel above the waves. Superb cuisine. Conference facilities. PO Box 8, Kei Mouth 5260, tel. (0432) 820818.

Cape Hermes Hotel Port St Johns. Near mouth of Mzimvubu River; 58 rooms. Conference facilities for 100. PO Box 10, Port St Johns, tel. (0475) 441236.

Hole-in-the-Wall Hotel Near Coffee Bay. 22 en-suite rooms; family chalets and thatched cottages. PO Box 54, Umtata, tel. (0471) 25344.

Trennery's Hotel Qolora Mouth. Subtropical surroundings overlooking sea. 65 rooms; 11-hole golf course. Private Bag 3011, Butterworth, tel. (0474) 3293.

Wild Coast Sun Mzamba. Luxury hotel-casino complex. 393 rooms; 6 suites. Conference facilities; swimming pool, restaurants, theatre, shops. PO Box 23, Port Edward 4295, tel. (0471) 59111.

DURBAN, THE KWAZULU/NATAL COAST AND ZULULAND

From the soaring peaks of the Drakensberg in the east, South Africa's garden province unfolds in a panorama of rolling hills and emerald valleys that tumble gently towards a warm, subtropical shore. Stretching 600 km, from Mozambique in the north to the former Transkei in the south, this sunshine coastline was named Natal (Nativity) by Portuguese navigator Vasco da Gama, when he discovered it on Christmas Day 1497. With the establishment of a new government in South Africa in 1994, the official name of this beautiful province was changed to KwaZulu/Natal.

Today the sun-bronzed beaches of KwaZulu/Natal and its hinterland of subtropical forests, quiet country fields, tranquil lake districts and teeming game reserves are one of the country's idyllic holiday places. North and south of Durban, lazy holiday resorts merge with golden sands and the turquoise waters of the Indian Ocean. In the north they give way to roller-coasting fields of sugar cane and the fertile, green valleys of Zululand. In this humid, hot region elephant, lion, rhinoceros, giraffe, wildebeest, hippopotamus and a large variety of other animals flourish in game parks that rank among the best in the world.

Durban is South Africa's second largest city, Africa's busiest port, and one of the world's great tourist destinations. With an urban population of one million, and a further two-and-a-half million people living on its outskirts, Durban has been rated as one of the world's fastest growing cities. This expanding port is an exciting, cosmopolitan blend of eastern and western cultures that attracts more than one million visitors to its shores annually. The reason, of course, is because the city lives up to its motto: "The fun never sets in Durban".

The dazzling beaches, the flower-fringed esplanades, the oriental markets, shopping centres, exhibition centres, flea-markets, parks and gardens generate an air of sultry relaxation of the type you might find in Rio de Janeiro or Acapulco.

Perhaps equally important, Durban has a sophisticated transport system that can put you in touch with the rest of southern Africa's tourist attractions, whether you choose to go by air, sea, rail or car. Its well-tarred open highways transport you quickly to game reserves, country curio shops and African communities that were here long before the Europeans arrived.

The city lies sprawled around one of the southern hemisphere's finest natural har-

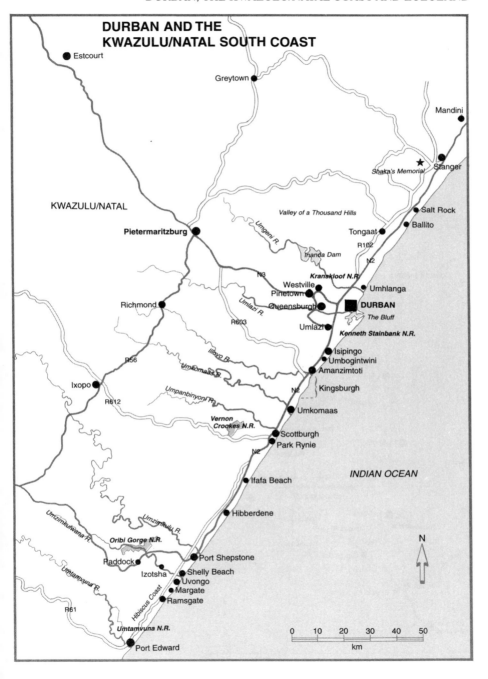

DURBAN AND THE KWAZULU/NATAL SOUTH COAST

Estcourt

Greytown

Mandini

Shaka's Memorial Stanger

KWAZULU/NATAL

Valley of a Thousand Hills

Salt Rock

Pietermaritzburg

Umgeni R.

Tongaat Ballito

R102

Inanda Dam

N2

N3 Kranskloof N.R.

Westville Umhlanga

Pinetown

Richmond

Umlazi R. Queensburgh DURBAN

The Bluff

R603

Umlazi

Kenneth Stainbank N.R.

Illovo R.

Isipingo

R56 Umkomaas R. Umbogintwini

Amanzimtoti

Ixopo Umpanbinyoni R. N2 Kingsburgh

R612

Vernon Umkomaas

Crookes N.R.

Scottburgh

Park Rynie

N2

Ifafa Beach

INDIAN OCEAN

Hibberdene

Umzimkulwana R. Umzimkulu R.

Oribi Gorge N.R.

N

Paddock Port Shepstone

Izotsha Shelly Beach

Umtamvuna R. Uvongo

Margate

Hibiscus Coast Ramsgate

R61

Umtamvuna N.R.

0   10   20   30   40   50

Port Edward km

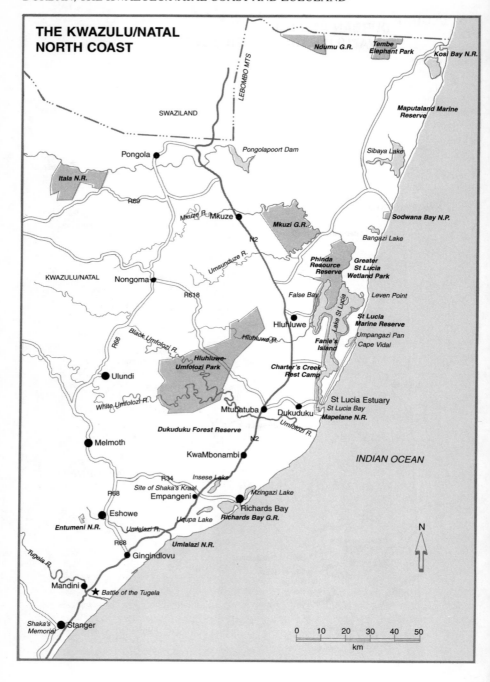

THE KWAZULU/NATAL
NORTH COAST

Ndumu G.R.

Tembe
Elephant Park

Kosi Bay N.R.

LEBOMBO MTS

SWAZILAND

Maputaland Marine
Reserve

Pongolapoort Dam

Sibaya Lake

Pongola

Itala N.R.

R69

Mkuze R. Mkuze

Sodwana Bay N.P.

Mkuzi G.R.

N2

Bangazi Lake

Umsunduze R.

Phinda
Resource
Reserve

Greater
St Lucia
Wetland Park

KWAZULU/NATAL

Nongoma

R618

False Bay

Leven Point

Lake St Lucia

St Lucia
Marine Reserve

Hluhluwe

R66

Black Umfolozi R.

Hluhluwe R.

Umpangazi Pan

Cape Vidal

Fanie's
Island

Hluhluwe-
Umfolozi Park

Charter's Creek
Rest Camp

Ulundi

White Umfolozi R.

Mtubatuba

Dukuduku

St Lucia Estuary

St Lucia Bay

Mapelane N.R.

Umfolozi R.

Dukuduku Forest Reserve

N2

INDIAN OCEAN

Melmoth

KwaMbonambi

R34

Insese Lake

Site of Shaka's Kraal

Empangeni

Mzingazi Lake

R68

Eshowe

Uqupa Lake

Richards Bay

Richards Bay G.R.

Entumeni N.R.

Umlalazi R.

R68

Umlalazi N.R.

N

Tugela R.

Gingindlovu

Mandini

★ Battle of the Tugela

Shaka's
Memorial

Stanger

0   10   20   30   40   50
km

CLIMATE

If you're a sun-seeker, this is the place to be – there are an average of 320 sunny days a year in Durban. The summers can get very hot and sticky (the northern coastal areas are particularly hot). The climate is subtropical, with hot, humid summers, and mild to warm temperate winters. Most rain falls in summer between September and November (the coastline averages 1 300 mm a year), but there is little winter rain. The temperatures range from about 18 °C in winter up to 32 °C in midsummer at the coast – ideal for swimming throughout the year.

---

bours – Port Natal. After the Portuguese explorer Vasco Da Gama had christened the harbour Rio de Natal ("River of the Nativity"), it remained undeveloped for about 300 years – shunned by travellers because of its inhospitable jungle vegetation, mangrove swamps and wild animals.

Then in May 1824, two groups of men led by Lieutenant Francis Farewell and his deputy Henry Fynn sailed into the harbour, hacked their way through the tangled vegetation, and established the first tiny settlement there. The settlers proclaimed a township 11 years later, which they called D'Urban – in honour of Sir Benjamin D'Urban, then Governor of the Cape.

Durban has one of the country's most efficient tourist bureaux – Durban Unlimited, tel. (031) 3044934, which will put you in touch with any number of touring options in KwaZulu/Natal. One of these is "Milescapes", a series of fascinating self-drive round trips of about 100 km that will take you to some delightful destinations in KwaZulu/Natal. You can pick up free Milescapes maps at the Visitors' Information Bureau, top hotels and BP service stations.

Another major attraction is Durban Unlimited's "Walkabouts" – a series of strolling tours organised by the publicity association. They include an "Oriental Walkabout", an introduction to eastern cultures and commercial parts of Durban, the "Durban Experience", a fascinating walk through the ethnic heart of Durban, and the "Feel of Durban Walkabout".

The telephone numbers and addresses of Durban Unlimited are Tourist Junction, 160 Pine Street, Durban 4001, tel. (031) 3044934 and Beach Office, Marine Parade (opposite Seaworld), Durban 4001, tel. (031) 322608.

TIPS FOR TRAVELLERS

If you intend visiting Durban during the summer, book accommodation well in advance. Rates for hotels and other accommodation rise in the peak season.

When driving in the city, be aware that many of the major thoroughfares in town are one-way streets. Parking is at a premium most of the time along the beachfront. Park away from the beachfront, and walk to the beach. If you wish to see central Durban and the oriental quarter, the best option is to find a parking garage and walk.

WHAT TO SEE

▰▰▰ DURBAN

Golden Mile

A carnival atmosphere pervades this 6-km-long strip of amusement parks, playgrounds, pavilions, pools and pleasure emporiums that line the Durban beachfront. Glitzy, five-star hotels peer down on this pavement of pleasure where the squeal of overhead cable cars mixes with the bump and grind of dodgem cars, the drone of surf and the gleeful shouts of sun-seekers enjoying themselves. The air here is thick with the aromas from round-the-clock restaurants and takeaway establishments, and there's plenty for you to do – from riding a ricksha or taking a helicopter flip over the beachfront, to watching sharks at Seaworld aquarium or visiting the snake park.

The nightlife is hectic, and local entertainment ranges from an assortment of beachfront cinemas (there are 12 alone at the Wheel) to cabaret shows and symphony concerts.

The beaches

Addington Beach, at the southern end of Golden Mile, is the first of a series of beautiful bathing beaches along the huge sweep of sand that forms Durban Bay. Like most of KwaZulu/Natal's resort beaches, Addington is patrolled by lifesavers, protected by shark nets, and offers safe bathing in warm water.

Also shark protected and patrolled is South Beach, next to Addington, probably the most popular beach in South Africa. Flanked by lawns, it backs onto an avenue of busy shops and food stalls, with a playpark and paddling pools higher up. Nearby, an aerial cableway north of West Street takes you for a joyride above a sparkling complex of paddling pools, fountains, stepping stones, bridges and the sheltered Rachel Finlayson Seawater Swimming Pool.

Further on are the bronze sands of North Beach and the Bay of Plenty – a surfer's paradise, and the usual venue for the annual surfing spectacular, the Gunston 500. Beware of the strong backwash and current here. Opposite the country club further north is Water Wonderland, an attractive complex of landscaped gardens, pools, waterslides, rapids and ski jumps.

At Funworld in front of the Marine Parade Holiday Inn there's an amusement park, dodgem cars, the aerial cableway and a hair-raising swing boat.

The Fitzsimons Snake Park

This park opposite North Beach houses 80 species of snakes, as well as crocodiles, leguaans and other reptiles. There are four handling demonstrations a day in season, and the snakes are fed on Saturdays and Sundays. The park has a well-stocked curio shop, tel. (031) 376456.

Seaworld

Peer into the gaping jaws of a ragged-tooth shark, or watch dolphins perform amazing acrobatic feats in this spectacular dolphinarium and aquarium complex (linked by an underground tunnel) near West Street. More than 1 000 species of fish, sharks and turtles cruise around the transparent interiors of the huge marine tanks. Bottlenose and dusky dolphins, Cape fur seals and jackass penguins feature prominently in daily shows for the public. At feeding times, 11h00 and 15h00, a diver enters the main fish tank to handfeed sandsharks, rays and turtles. Tickets are available at the aquarium, tel. (031) 373536.

The harbour

Durbanites proclaim their harbour the largest, busiest and safest in Africa. It's also the ninth-biggest in the world, but many areas are out of bounds to the public. The places you can visit are the mole basin, the small-craft harbour, the ocean terminal (which has viewing galleries of the harbour and the city), the floating and graving docks, the fishing jetty and the sugar terminal.

For a real feel of the harbour atmosphere take a round-the-bay trip on the harbour ferry, or for something more luxurious, take a harbour pleasure cruise from the Dick King jetty. Tickets are available at the Pleasure Cruise terminal. The cruise takes just over an hour, and it can get chilly, so take a jersey along.

You can also cruise around the bay or out to sea in the *Sarie Marais* pleasure boat which departs from the Gardiner Street jetty every day, weather permitting. Tickets are available at the main booking office, opposite the aquarium on the corner of West Street and Marine Parade, tel. (031) 3054022.

Worth exploring on foot are Maydon Wharf's grain elevator and sugar terminal (which can store 520 000 tons of sugar), the Prince Edward Graving Dock, one of the largest dry docks in the southern hemisphere, and the yacht basin, with its bustling flotilla of yachts. Between the harbour and the city are the grass-fringed, shaded pavements of Victoria Embankment. Here you can stroll past the statue of Dick King and his horse, Somerset, who together made a courageous 960-km ride from Durban to Grahamstown in 1842, to raise help for British soldiers besieged by the Boers in Durban's Old Fort.

Oriental Durban

The aroma of pungent curries, chilli powders, exotic eastern spices and incense pervade the air at the Victoria Street Market, a bustling oriental bazaar built on the site of Durban's original Indian Market, which burnt down in 1973. Here 80 tightly packed stalls offer a large range of oriental goods: curios, leatherware, basketware, brassware and a variety of luxuriant silks and satins. There's a fish and meat market offering, among other things, crabs from Mozambique and deep-sea prawns. Upstairs, 50 shops invite you to haggle for their wares, and restaurants offer tantalising oriental dishes.

Closer to town, the famed Indian trading area around Grey Street invites exploration. Narrow walkways and avenues bustling with sari-clad shoppers lead past tiny shops jammed with bargain goods of all descriptions, and roadside eateries offer spicy fastfoods such as samoosas, rotis and bunnychows. Towering above it all are the golden domes of the Grey Street Mosque – the southern hemisphere's largest.

Anyone can enter the mosque, but certain formalities must be adhered to: take off your shoes at the entrance, go into the communal ablution block, and wash hands and arms to the elbow, then wash the feet, back of the neck, face, ears and nostrils, and gargle before entering the mosque.

An integral part of oriental Durban is the Hare Krishna Temple of Understanding south of the city, with its magnificent architecture (Austrian Rajaram Das designed it). Within the temple are 557 chandeliers, about 400 sq metres of mirrors and several paintings of Krishna. There are guided tours, an audiovisual presentation, a restaurant and a gift shop. For details contact Satour, 19th Floor, The Marine, 22 Gardiner Street, Durban 4001, tel. (031) 3047144.

The ricksha

No visit to Durban is complete without a ricksha ride, in which a Zulu man, decked out in beaded finery, with large horns above his head, will pull you along in a gaily decorated two-wheeled carriage, leaping into the air with yells as he does so. Originally known as *jinrikishas,* the ricksha was imported from Japan by sugar magnate Sir Marshall Campbell in 1893, and once were Durban's main form of transport. You'll find a ricksha outside the Tropicana Hotel on the Marine Parade. Do remember that if you take a photograph of a ricksha runner, he will expect payment.

African art and curios

Tribal shields, drums, African masks, brightly coloured beadwork, pottery and basketware – an integral part of traditional Zulu culture – are widely available in Durban. The African Art Centre in Gardiner Street is a mecca for collectors of original Zulu craftsmanship. Here you will find wood carvings, screenprinted fabrics and graphics, semiprecious stones, woollen carpets and copperware. Along Golden Mile – particularly in the vicinity of Seaworld – roadside merchants sell the full range of African curios, including impressive displays of wood carvings and beadwork. The Africa Gallery at Umhlanga Rocks sells unique Zimbabwean carvings, contemporary ceramics, hand-blown glass and furniture.

The Wheel

This bustling R90-million entertainment centre, named after a huge, working Ferris wheel mounted on the complex's facade, is one of Durban's busiest shopping and entertainment centres. The Ferris wheel itself is 10 storeys high, 21 m in diameter and carries Indian howdah gondolas, which will give you a wonderful ride for a

Gardens, parks and reserves

Bluff Nature Reserve: A large bird population inhabits this 45-ha reserve of coastal forest and grassland, which has a reed-fringed freshwater pan between two great sand dunes. You can watch the birds from hides or along the reserve's footpaths.

Botanical Gardens: Established in 1849, these 14,5 ha of flowering trees, tropical plants, waterlily pond and tea garden are world-famous for their cycad collection, which includes *Encephalartos woodii,* one of the rarest cycads in the world. The gardens also house a beautiful collection of orchids.

Umgeni River Bird Park: Rated the third best park of its kind in the world, this magical park houses about 2 000 birds, representing some 300 local and exotic species. Ponds, gardens and four waterfalls provide a tranquil setting for the birds, which include flamingoes, cockatoos, Asian hornbills, macaws, lorikeets and other birds from Australia and southeast Asia. The three large walk-through aviaries built into the rockface are an excellent setting for photographing the birds at leisure. You can also sit in a reed-panelled hide overlooking one of the ponds. Light lunches and homemade snacks are served, and there's a playground for children. For more information telephone (031) 5794600.

couple of rand. Several cinemas, restaurants, bars and about 140 shops lure thousands of visitors into the centre's decorative interior. The theme inside is nautical, with lifeboats suspended from davits, and spars, rigging and flags all over the place. Ships' railings separate the shops, the floor is a planked deck and the walls are riveted bulkheads. Each level has a particular theme, with the fashion level on the first, the eastern or Casbah on the second and the Caribbean on the third.

The Durban Exhibition Centre

Established in 1985, this city within a city is set in 30 000 sq metres of plaza and gardens, offering 9 500 sq metres of undercover exhibition space and upmarket facilities to host up to 3 000 delegates.

Museums

The City Hall, one of the finest of its kind in South Africa, was built in 1906, and houses the Natural Science Museum. Lying here in a state of excellent preservation is a 2 000-year-old Egyptian mummy, known as Petea Amen, who somehow ended up in Durban between 1899 and 1910; a life-size reconstruction of the dinosaur *Tyrannosaurus rex* and an egg of the extinct Elephant Bird, *Aepyornis.* Of particular interest is KwaNunu, an authentic insect gallery.

On the second floor is the Durban Art Museum, which features sculptures by Rodin and Dalou, as well as paintings by contemporary artists. Names to look for are Constable, Corot, Lely and Utrillo.

TIP FOR TRAVELLERS ─────────────
There are dozens of small parks and gardens in and around Durban. For details of these and the ones mentioned, contact Durban Unlimited, Tourist Junction, 160 Pine Street, Durban 4001, tel. (031) 3044934.

The Local History Museum has an interesting model of Umgungundlovu, the kraal of the Zulu king Dingane, a replica of the first house in Durban, and reconstructions of a sugar mill, post office and apothecary.

If your interests are nautical, drop in to the Maritime Museum on the Victoria Embankment (opposite the yacht mole), where you can explore two tugs and a minesweeper. There's a delightful pirates' museum here where you can inspect a replica of a pirate's ship.

Minitown

A mini-game park, mini-railway station and harbour, mini-fair and mini-airport – all modelled in excellent detail, and scaled down to four per cent of the real size – are part of this miniature town on Snell Parade. Ships, planes, trains and cars move through the complex, accompanied by sound effects and lights in this ingenious replica of Durban, built in 1960, and based on the Netherlands' Madurodam. Highlights are a mini-drive-in and a funfair.

Nightlife

At night, Durban is Swing City, with an endless variety of cabaret and music shows along the Golden Mile. For details of current shows and venues, consult the local newspapers or call Durban Unlimited, tel. (031) 3044934.

▄▄▄ KWAZULU/NATAL SOUTH COAST

Amanzimtoti

A wide expanse of beach, stretching 7 km northwards from the Manzimtoti Lagoon towards Umbogintwini, is the major attraction of this south coast resort. The main bathing area at Nyoni Rocks is protected by shark nets and offers a mini waterworld with a supertube, a tidal pool and picnic and barbecue facilities. Another excellent bathing beach further north is the Pipeline, which has a freshwater pool. Both beaches offer all the amenities and are patrolled by lifeguards. You can hire a boat at Manzimtoti Lagoon and paddle or row upstream for about 2 km.

Amanzimtoti (the Zulu word for "sweet waters") is a bustling seaside town with upmarket shops, restaurants and cinemas, and an extensive high-rise business district. Funland, an entertainment centre in Beach Road, provides five floors of fun and games for the kids, including dodgem cars, video games, stall games and fast-food outlets.

There are two nature reserves within easy driving distance of the town. The 4-ha Amanzimtoti Bird Sanctuary is home to more than 150 species of birds, including

Egyptian geese, whistling duck, exotic peacock and spurwing geese. You can view these birds around a tranquil lake, fringed with ilala palm trees, and have tea at the kiosk on Saturday and Sunday afternoons. The Ilanda Wilds Nature Reserve is a 18-ha riverine sanctuary with about 160 species of bird, just 2 km from the centre of town. Take a picnic along and walk any one of the three pleasant self-guided trails, the Loerie, Mpiti and Mongoose trails, through the 120 species of indigenous trees and shrubs.

Scottburgh

Built on a headland overlooking the Indian Ocean, Scottburgh is one of the leading south coast resorts. The focal point of summer activity here is Scott Bay, a sheltered bathing beach that offers shark-protected bathing, sand-free sunbathing on terraced lawns adjoining the beaches, a tidal pool and a miniature railway and supertube.

There's a new restaurant and bathing facilities complex on the beach, and a curio shop stocked with African crafts.

Scottburgh lies at the mouth of the Mpambanyoni River, and has several comfortable hotels, holiday flats, attractive camping and caravan facilities and a beautiful golf course.

North of Scottburgh is Crocworld, a spacious and beautiful refuge for crocodiles. Here you can view an aquarium, watch snakes from a glass snake tunnel and visit various crocodile pools and ponds housing Nile crocodiles, alligators, South American caimans and West African dwarf crocodiles. A restaurant offers good food and scenic views. Other attractions are a Zulu kraal, with tribal dancing, and a well-stocked curio shop. For details telephone (0323) 21103.

The Hibiscus Coast

The lower KwaZulu/Natal south coast, from Port Shepstone to Port Edward, is known as the Hibiscus Coast, but these beautiful flowers are not its only tourist attraction.

This subtropical playground of bronze beaches, shimmering surf and lush coastal forests invites visitors to revel in its generous outdoor pleasures. Swimming, deep-sea fishing, scuba diving, nature trails and superior drives are within easy reach. Within one hour's drive of Margate are nine top-class golf courses. For brochures on the "Golf Coast", or other information on the Hibiscus Coast, contact the Natal South Coast Publicity Association in Margate, tel. (03937) 77322. The association will also tell you about the very popular "Wildabout" arts and craft trail that takes you to no less than 14 crafts destinations.

Port Shepstone

Once a busy port serving mainly shallow-draught coasters, Port Shepstone is the commercial, industrial and administrative centre of the south coast. Its main attractions are a bathing beach with tidal pool, the Mzimkulu River (KwaZulu/Natal's largest), which is navigable for 8 km upstream, and is becoming increasingly popular among waterskiers and boardsailors, and an 18-hole golf course. Along the beachfront there's a brand new promenade, change rooms, restaurant and park.

Port Shepstone is the starting point of the Banana Express, a narrow-gauge steam train, powered by a 1939 Garrett engine, that chugs past Shelley Beach inland to Izotsha or Paddock Station. The round trip to Izotsha takes two-and-a-half hours; the round trip to Paddock Station takes six. The train leaves Port Shepstone before 07h15. Dress warmly and take a picnic lunch with you. The trip is an unforgettable experience. For more details telephone Durban Unlimited at (031) 3044934.

Margate

With the safest shark-protected beaches on the KwaZulu/Natal south coast, Margate is a vibrant mecca for swimmers and sun-seekers. Major attractions are a beachfront amusement park, bowling alley, skating rink and an 18-hole golf course. In summer beauty competitions and variety shows are held on the beach. Nightlife here is excellent with good restaurants, discotheques and cabaret shows. For something different, try a microlight flip. Flights depart from Margate Airport, Hanger No. 3, tel. (03937) 77322.

Oribi Gorge Nature Reserve

Orange-red sandstone cliffs soar 370 m above this magnificent 110 837-ha reserve in the Umzimkulwana River Gorge. The valley's dense forests of trees, creepers and flowering plants provide cover for leopards, baboons, bushbuck, vervet and samango monkeys, blue duiker, grey duiker and a variety of birds.

There are nature trails and hutted camps in the reserve, and spectacular viewsites from the top of the gorge such as the Pulpit, Baboon Castle and Overhanging Rock. For details telephone (03930) 91644.

Port Edward

The South African Police holiday resort – on the seafront overlooking Splash Rock – is the best one in town, and is open to all members of the public. Here you can hire rondavels, chalets, huts and campsites. Behind the beach are the forested slopes of Tragedy Hill, where the descendants of Henry Francis Fynn, founder of the Port Natal colony, were massacred by the Zulus in 1881.

South of Port Edward is the Umtamvuna Nature Reserve, a 3 257-ha expanse of riverine forest and steep gorges. The reserve is home to vervet and samango monkeys, caracals, servals, baboons, bushbuck, reedbuck, grey and blue duiker, and more than 700 species of plants, including 35 orchid species. The 250 species of bird include the rare Cape vulture, the crowned eagle, fish eagle and the peregrine falcon.

Self-guided trails enable you to view the scenic delights of this riverside paradise. Maps are available at the reserve. For details telephone (03930) 32383. There

---

TIP FOR TRAVELLERS

There's a daily bus service called Margate Mini Coach that operates between Margate and Durban. For details telephone (03937) 76406.

---

is plenty of accommodation at Port Edward or the nearby Wild Coast Sun Hotel and Casino complex.

▨▨▨ KWAZULU/NATAL NORTH COAST

Umhlanga Rocks

Luxury hotels, high-rise time-share palaces, plush private homes and a plethora of curio shops draw the crowds to this extremely popular beach resort north of Durban. Bathers, surfers and paddleskiers flock to the warm, shark-protected bathing beach north of the candy-striped lighthouse at Umhlanga throughout the year. A paved walkway along the beachfront provides quick access from most points at Umhlanga, and gives fine views of the ocean and the sweep of the coast-line to the south.

At low tide you can see the wreck of the *John Williamson* which went down in 1961 without loss of life. In Lighthouse Road is a small bird sanctuary. It also offers pony rides and refreshments.

On a hill overlooking Umhlanga are the Natal Sharks Board premises. Established in 1964 after a spate of shark attacks, the board services and maintains shark nets that protect about 45 beaches along the KwaZulu/Natal coastline. The board conducts presentations on the life cycle and feeding chain of sharks. Tours are conducted on Tuesdays, Wednesdays and Thursdays, and on the first Sunday of the month, tel. (031) 5611017.

The Umhlanga Lagoon Nature Reserve, with its dune forest and red milkwood trees, and the adjacent, privately owned, Hawaan Bush Reserve, noted for its wild mango trees, attract a variety of birds and small mammals. You can explore the lagoon reserve by trail, or telephone the Wildlife Society, (031) 213126, to organ-ise a visit to Hawaan Reserve.

Valley of a Thousand Hills

A river which the Zulus call Mngeni (the place of the acacia trees) has carved a huge, 64-km-long rift valley between Pietermaritzburg and Durban. Once the scene of savage tribal battles – the Debe tribespeople who live there were decimated in bloody clashes with the Zulus – the valley is highlighted at its western end by a massive sandstone mountain called KwaZulu/Natal Table Mountain or emKhambathini (place of the giraffe acacia trees). You can walk up here from the Pietermaritzburg side for breathtaking views of the KwaZulu/Natal Drakensberg on the one side and the sea on the other.

Densely populated in some places, sparsely inhabited in others, the Valley of a

Thousand Hills is rich in flowering plants such as aloes, fire lilies, snake lilies, arum lilies and Mexican sunflowers.

Recommended stops in the valley are the Rob Roy Hotel, which has an excellent curio shop (Selkirk's Curio Gallery) and carvery, and the Nagle Dam, where you can have a picnic and watch displays of tribal dancing. Other major attractions in the Valley of a Thousand Hills are the two Phezulu kraals, which feature authentic lifestyles of the Zulu people (including tribal dancing), well-stocked curio shops and witchdoctors throwing bones. Alongside the Phezulu kraals is The Pottery Art of Living Studio, which has an excellent range of pottery, crafts and gifts, and an entrancing coffee shop called the Pot and Kettle. For more details telephone (031) 7771405, or contact Satour, 19th Floor, The Marine, 22 Gardiner Street, Durban 4001, tel. (031) 3047144.

Assagay Safari Park also offers a Zulu village with tribal dancing, a crocodile and snake park (one of the residents is Junior, one of the largest crocodiles in captivity), a natural history museum, a botanical garden and a restaurant, as well as a curio shop, tel. (031) 7771208.

■■■ ZULULAND

Between the Tugela River and the borders of Swaziland and Mozambique lies the kingdom of the Zulus. Known as Zululand, this region incorporates much of what is known as KwaZulu – ten different blocks of land formally declared a "national state" in the 1970s. Within this region are the premier game sanctuaries of KwaZulu/Natal.

For sheer variety of big and small game, the six major game reserves of northern KwaZulu/Natal – Hluhluwe, Umfolozi, Mkuzi, Itala, Ndumu and the vast St Lucia complex – must rank among the finest in the world. In a lush subtropical environment of acacia savannah thornveld and thick bush, these parks serve as natural sanctuaries for tens of thousands of animals, ranging from elephant, lion, giraffe, hippopotamus and rhino to buffalo, zebra, leopard, cheetah, crocodile, kudu and impala. The reserves also support several hundred bird species – bateleur eagles, fish eagles, Narina trogons, whitebacked vultures, ground hornbills and a host of others.

All the reserves are easily accessible by road from Durban and provide excellent accommodation.

Take note of the tips for travellers (see p. 127) when planning a visit to KwaZulu/Natal's fabulous game parks. Contact the Natal Parks Board, which will give you comprehensive brochures and friendly advice for your stay at its parks: PO Box 1750, Pietermaritzburg, tel. (0331) 471981.

The Hluhluwe-Umfolozi Park
Two of the world's great game sanctuaries, Hluhluwe and Umfolozi reserves, have

---

TIPS FOR TRAVELLERS

Most of the reserves lie in a malaria belt, and you will need to take a course of pills before you go.

Some reserves have a shop, others don't. Many of the camps do not supply basic provisions (and some don't provide fuel), though they generally provide cooking utensils and the services of a caretaker and cook for your bungalow or hut.

Check what services and facilities are available at your selected park. Also establish what time the park's gates open and close. The usual opening and closing times are sunrise and sunset.

No pets are allowed in Natal Parks Board reserves.

Bathing in rivers and lakes is prohibited in some parks because of crocodiles and hippos, so make enquiries before you leap into the water.

---

recently been formally amalgamated as one reserve, and with a combined area of 96 000 ha, they now form one of the largest game parks in Africa.

About three hours' drive from Durban, the Umfolozi and Hluhluwe sections are joined by a single corridor of land.

The Umfolozi section

Umfolozi, which covers 47 753 ha of rolling hills, is real big game country. Elephants, lions, black and white rhino, giraffe, blue wildebeest, leopard and a variety of antelope roam the dense acacia savannah thornveld, and there are about 400 species of birds.

The summers are hot and humid, the winters cool to warm. Winter, when the vegetation is not too dense, is the best time to spot game.

Umfolozi serves as a sanctuary for about 1 000 white rhinos – a very impressive number, considering that the species faced extinction until the Natal Parks Board launched a campaign to save them in the 1960s.

You can come face to face with these huge creatures – and others – on one-day or three-day wilderness trails in the company of a game ranger. There is an extensive network of game-viewing roads.

Two hutted camps, Masinda and Mpila, offer serviced chalets or rondavels where you can sit on grassy terraces, braai (barbecue) under the stars and listen to the sounds of wild Africa around you. There are two bush camps used as overnight stops on wilderness walking trails: the Sontuli Bush Camp on the banks of the Black Umfolozi River, and the Nselweni Bush Camp, further downstream. Be sure to take your own food to Umfolozi.

The Hluhluwe section

Formerly the hunting grounds of Zulu royalty, this section was named by the Zulus after umHluhluwe, a thorny monkey rope, which grows on the banks of the beautiful Hluhluwe River. Among the 84 species of mammal which live in the tangled bushveld and riverine forest flanking the river are elephant, black and white rhino, lion, leopard, cheetah, buffalo, Burchell's zebra, hippo and crocodile, and 425 species of bird. Guided walks, nearly 90 km of game-viewing drives, hides and a Zulu village museum are the main attractions here. Hluhluwe's Hilltop Camp, upgraded in 1992, offers 20 attractive self-catering thatched chalets, with more luxurious accommodation at Mtwazi Lodge. There's also a rustic bush camp among the trees at Muntulu. There is a shop at Hluhluwe, but take your own groceries. The best times to visit are the winter months from April to September.

Itala Game Reserve

Nestling in the mountains and valleys of northern KwaZulu/Natal, Itala boasts the finest of the Natal Parks Board Camps – Ntshondwe. Here, among rugged rocks and natural bush, a restaurant overlooks a waterhole, and thatched chalets peer over a swimming pool set among the boulders.

Nearby, elephant, leopard, giraffe, cheetah, white and black rhino, nyala, tsessebe, eland, red hartebeest and many other species of mammal roam the magnificent countryside.

Special attractions are the three isolated bush camps – Thalu, Mbizo and Mhlangeni – comprising rustic reed-and-thatch cottages that capture the true spirit of Africa, conducted tours and night drives in open safari vehicles, and escorted walks through the bush with game guards.

Three-day wilderness trails take you into the heart of the bush where you sleep under canvas near the fireside. Fishing is allowed in the river in front of two of the bush camps, and bilharzia-free water enables you to cool down in summer.

Mkuzi Game Reserve

Proclaimed in 1912, this recently enlarged 34 000-ha reserve, lying between the Mkuze and Umsunduze rivers, consists of thick bushveld, interspersed with riverine and sycamore forests and fever trees. At the heart of the reserve is Nsumu Pan, home to crocodile and hippo, where two hides offer superior views of many bird species, including fish eagles, pinkbacked pelicans, hamerkop and various herons and storks.

There are 84 km of road through thick bush inhabited by black and white rhino, giraffe, hippo, blue wildebeest, warthog, kudu, zebra, eland and a variety of other antelope.

Four delightful hides, concealed at the edge of the Kubube, Kumasinga, Kwamalibala and Kumahlala pans, give excellent opportunities to watch and photograph game coming down to drink. Popular visitors to the waterholes are impala (more than 7 000 live in the reserve), warthogs (2 300), nyala (4 000) and kudu.

Special attractions are night drives, the 57-km Mkuzi auto trail, and the Fig Forest Trail. Three-hour foot trails, led by a game ranger, are also available.

Accommodation is provided in rest huts, bungalows and cottages. A particularly attractive camp is the Rustic Camp, which has rondavels surrounded by bush. Two bush camps, Nhlonhlela (hutted) and Umkumbi (tented) offer the services of a personal cook, and a game guard to take you on escorted walks in the bush.

Ndumu Game Reserve

This reserve, on the floodplain of the Pongola River, is a natural haven for waterbirds – if you like birdwatching, you have a choice of more than 400 species, including fish eagle and Pel's fishing owl. Hippo and crocodile share the waterways with tigerfish, tilapia, barbel and bream.

Game-viewing drives, guided tours in open vehicles around the pan and day walks will bring you into close contact with white and black rhino, giraffe, buffalo, zebra, impala, nyala, bushbuck, grey duiker, aardwolf, aardvark, striped polecat and water mongoose.

Two delightful camps offer stunning views in scenic surroundings. The new Ndumo Wilderness Camp on the edge of Banzi Pan offers eight tented rooms; Ndumo Main Camp has seven three-bed bungalows.

The Greater St Lucia Wetland Park

This park, one of the great marine wilderness areas of Africa, is a jigsaw puzzle of many pieces, embracing an estuary, a lake, a pan, a beautiful forest, the highest dunes in the world and the sea.

For the tourist, nature lover and birdwatcher it is a natural paradise, with several large and small mammals, 36 species of amphibians, protected reptiles and more than 420 species of birds, including fish eagles, white pelicans, flamingoes and herons. Seabirds include albatrosses, petrels, skuas and prions. Among the larger mammals are humpback whales, hippo, crocodile, buffalo and rhino.

Phinda Resource Reserve

Officially opened in 1991, Phinda is a 15 000-ha wildlife sanctuary, wedged between Mkuzi Game Reserve and the Greater St Lucia Wetland Park.

The luxury and architecture of its game lodges is unique among the bush camps of the subcontinent, offering tree-level views of birds and the surrounding bush. At Forest Lodge the glass-walled suites are raised on stilts, giving treetop views of elephants, rhinos, giraffes and – if you're lucky – lions. Phinda also offers game and aerial safaris, access to deep-sea fishing trips and cruises on Maputaland's Lake Sibaya.

For more details telephone (011) 8038421 or write to Central Reservations, PO Box 1211, Sunninghill Park 2157.

St Lucia estuary and lake

This 36 826-ha shallow wetland area includes the St Lucia estuary and its lagoons and islands, and is home to 600 hippos and numerous crocodiles. You can see dwarf crocodiles, long-snouted crocodiles and Nile crocodiles being fed at the Crocodile Centre near St Lucia Village on Saturdays at 15h00.

The Natal Parks Board offers two self-guided walks, and boat trips up the estuary to see the hippos and the prolific birdlife, which includes a large breeding population of fish eagles and up to 2 000 pairs of white pelicans. Book early to reserve a seat. A new 80-seater launch, the *Santa Lucia,* with bar and catering facilities, offers three guided tours of the estuary daily.

You can stay in a hotel at St Lucia where there are curio shops selling souvenirs and local crafts. The main Parks Board office at St Lucia provides bait, fishing licences and campsite bookings.

Mapelane

This forested reserve on the southern bank of the Umfolozi River has a sheltered bay for paddling and excellent surf fishing. The reserve is home to over 170 species of bird and small mammals.

Camping and accommodation in fully-equipped log cabins is available, but take your own groceries.

Mfabeni section

A day trip to Mission Rocks from St Lucia will reveal some fascinating rock pools on this lovely stretch of coastline on the eastern shores of Lake St Lucia. A lookout point on the dunes here affords excellent views of the lake, the eastern shores and the sea. Take along a picnic and a camera.

The Mfazana Pans has a short trail from the car park, leading to the two hides. Three one-day trails cover the beach and the shore of the lake.

Cape Vidal

A sheltered bay for swimming, excellent snorkelling on coral reefs, a self-guided trail and excellent fishing lure holiday-makers to the seaside camp here.

The Indian Ocean off Cape Vidal is a playground for humpback whales and their calves. Other gentle giants are whale sharks, 18 m long and weighing up to 40 tons, manta rays and leatherback turtles weighing up to 900 kg. Camping and hutted accommodation are available, but there is no restaurant here.

False Bay Park

You'll probably see hippos and crocodiles in this tranquil reserve, which has access to the lake for boating and fishing. There are two self-guided hikes, one taking you to a beautiful rustic hutted camp, Dugandlovu, overlooking the Hluhluwe floodplain.

There are picnic sites for day visitors, and hutted accommodation and camping sites for those wishing to stay longer. You can get provisions in the town of Hluhluwe.

Fanie's Island

An excellent birdwatching spot, this small camp on the shores of the lake offers a trail that takes you through coastal forest, open parkland and a beautiful swamp forest on the banks of a stream.

There is a swimming pool in the hutted camp and boats for hire. Swimming in the lake is not allowed because of crocodiles. Take your own provisions.

Charter's Creek

On the southern shores of the lake, this attractive camp offers boating, fishing, two self-guided trails and birding. Hutted accommodation is available, but take your own provisions. Swimming in the lake is forbidden, but there is a pool at Charter's Creek.

Sodwana Bay National Park

It's a little-known fact, but Sodwana Bay is the closest beach resort to Johannesburg and, undeniably, one of the loveliest. The huge diversity of fish and invertebrates on the coral reefs attract scuba divers and fishermen to its crystalline waters from all over South Africa. Anglers enjoy some of the world's best marlin fishing, and four-wheel-drive enthusiasts have plenty of bushwhacking trails available.

During summer, loggerhead and leatherback turtles come out of the water to nest, and the Parks Board offers night-time turtle tours in December and January. The best fishing month is November. Camping and hutted accommodation is available in a beautiful campsite beneath a coastal forest. Basic provisions (excluding alcohol) are available.

Kosi Bay Nature Reserve

This reserve covers a surface area of 11 000 ha, and is the northernmost KwaZulu/Natal sanctuary. The bay itself is a series of four lakes around which are mangrove swamps, fig forests and marshes separated from the Indian Ocean by a barrier of forested sand dunes.

Escorted trails (less than a day) enable you to see crocodiles, hippos, samango and vervet monkeys, blue and red duiker, bushpig, and more than 250 species of bird. There are also turtle-viewing tours and a three-day wilderness trail. Kosi Bay Rest Camp offers three thatched lodges and 15 attractive camping sites among the trees.

DURBAN, THE KWAZULU/NATAL COAST AND ZULULAND AT A GLANCE

When to go: The KwaZulu/Natal coast, with its subtropical climate, is a summer and winter playground. Sun-seekers and beachgoers prefer the summer months (October to April) when it is very hot and humid; winter, however, with its temperate, warm days and cool nights is the best time to visit the game reserves of the north coast and Zululand.

Getting around: *Durban:* The Mynah minibus service is probably the best way of getting around Durban quickly, safely and cheaply. The service operates daily from the city centre to the North and South Beach areas, and to Durban's outlying suburbs. Regular bus services operate throughout Durban. You can hail small, three-wheeled scooters called tuk tuks anywhere in central Durban. You'll also find them in the parking area on the beachfront (pay before you ride).

South coast: The N2 links Durban with the south coast as far as Port Shepstone, and after that the R61 continues to Port Edward. *North coast:* The N2 (an excellent road) runs parallel to, but out of sight of the coast, towards Richard's Bay, then sweeps inland to Swaziland. *The game reserves:* There are innumerable self-guided and escorted trails, and fascinating drives throughout the game parks and nature reserves of KwaZulu/Natal. Some roads are tarred, others are gravel, but all are in good condition. For details contact the Natal Parks Board, PO Box 662, Pietermaritzburg 3200, tel. (0331) 471981.

Main attractions: *Durban:* Swimming and sunbathing. Golden Mile's amusement centre, Seaworld and cableway ride. Boating. Fishing. Day drives to game parks, nature reserves and the Valley of a Thousand Hills. Visiting oriental markets. Fine restaurants and hotels. *South coast:* Sun, sea and sand. Boating, paddling, skindiving and surfing. Crocodile farm. Nature reserves. *North coast:* Game-viewing and game trails. Boat trips on St Lucia estuary. Birdwatching. Beachgoing. Zulu art and culture.

Tours and excursions: For organised tours contact Durban Unlimited, Tourist Junction, 160 Pine Street, Durban 4001, tel. (031) 3044934, or Satour (South African Tourism Board), 19th Floor, The Marine, 22 Gardiner Street, Durban 4001, tel. (031) 3047144.

Coach tours: These include a city tour, an oriental drive, a bay cruise, trips southward to Crocworld and the Wild Coast Sun, and north to the Valley of a Thousand Hills. There are also coach tours to the KwaZulu/Natal midlands, the Drakensberg and the game parks and reserves. Coaches leave daily from the Durban Transport Management Board kiosk in Marine Parade. Springbok Atlas Safaris runs a two-and-a-half-hour tour of Durban and one to the Valley of a Thousand Hills. 1001 Hills Tours include the Valley of a Thousand Hills as a specific destination or as part of a broader country tour. Transkei Tours offers a five-day tour of the Wild Coast. For details contact Satour, tel. (031) 3047144.

Adventure trips: Like to try abseiling, paragliding, mountain biking or whitewater rafting? Contact Itchy Feet, tel. (0332) 305613/4

Parasailing: A novel way to see the Golden Mile from the air. Daily on the hour in front of Addington Hospital.

Helicopter flips: Court Helicopters runs night flips over Golden Mile and city from Virginia Airport, tel. (031) 839513.

Boat cruises: Durban harbour: pleasure cruises daily (11h00 and 15h00) from Dick King jetty, tel. (031) 3054022. *Sarie Marais* departs Gardiner Street jetty every day. Tickets from main booking office, opposite aquarium, corner West Street and Marine Parade. St Lucia Estuary: the *Santa Lucia,* a new, 80-seater launch (bar and food) offers guided tours of the estuary three times daily; contact Natal Parks Board at PO Box 662, Pietermaritzburg 3200, tel. (0331) 471981.

Deep-sea fishing: For details of firms offering marlin and tunny fishing contact Durban Unlimited, Tourist Junction, 160 Pine Street, Durban 4001, tel. (031) 3044934.

Beaches and bathing: Safe, gently sloping beaches are a feature of the KwaZulu/Natal south coast. North of Durban the beaches bank more steeply and you must be careful in the water. Along the KwaZulu/Natal coast 45 beaches are shark protected, and most of the popular beaches are patrolled by lifeguards. They include Durban's South and North beaches, Amanzimtoti, Kingsburgh, Scottburgh, Margate, Ramsgate and Umhlanga Rocks.

Tourist information: Durban Unlimited, Tourist Junction, 160 Pine Street, Durban 4001, tel. (031) 3044934. Satour (South African Tourism Board), 19th Floor, The Marine, 22 Gardiner Street, Durban 4001, tel. (031) 3047144.

Shopping: In Durban, the Workshop, in Pine Street, is an enormous shopping complex housing 120 speciality shops; nearby are numerous flea markets. Upmarket speciality shops trade in the Arcade opposite the Pine Parkade. The Wheel is a jazzy beachfront shopping mall.

Festivals and annual events: Dusi Canoe Marathon (January), Durban International Film Festival (April-May), Comrades Marathon (May), Rothmans July Handicap (July), Gunston 500 surfing contest (July), Durban Tattoo (October).

ACCOMMODATION GUIDE

Durban is excellently geared to cater for the huge annual influx of tourists to its shores. Hotel accommodation ranges from five-star luxury to small, one-star establishments in the suburbs.

DURBAN CENTRAL

Royal***** Smith St. Stately hotel, excellent cuisine and good service. One of South Africa's best. 250 rooms, 22 suites. Conference facilities. PO Box 1041, Durban 4000, tel. (031) 3040331.

GOLDEN MILE

Elangeni Sun**** Good service and great views over Indian Ocean. Large and luxurious. 444 en-suite bedrooms, conference facilities. PO Box 4094, Durban 4000, tel. (031) 371321.

Holiday Inn Marine Parade**** 336 rooms; 8 suites. Conference facilities for 300. PO Box 10809, Marine Parade 4056, tel. (031) 373341.

Karos Edward Hotel**** Marine Parade. Colonial atmosphere in elegant surroundings. 88 rooms, 10 suites. Conference facilities. PO Box 105, Durban 4000, tel. (031) 373681.

Beach*** Overlooking sea. Good value. 106 rooms, conference facilities. PO Box 10305, Marine Parade 4056, tel. (031) 375511.

Blue Waters*** Good rates. 300 rooms. Conference facilities. PO Box 10201, Marine Parade 4056, tel. (031) 324272.

City Lodge Durban*** Friendly, economical hotel with quick access to beaches. 161 rooms. Conference facilities. PO Box 10842, Marine Parade, Durban 4056, tel. (031) 321447

Four Seasons*** Just off Golden Mile. 194 rooms. Conference facilities for 140. PO Box 10200, Marine Parade 4056, tel. (031) 373381.

Holiday Inn Garden Court – North Beach*** Good value for money. 245 rooms; 25 suites. Conference facilities for 600. PO Box 10592, Marine Parade 4056, tel. (031) 327361.

Holiday Inn Garden Court – South Beach*** 380 rooms, 8 suites. Conference facilities. PO Box 10199, Marine Parade 4056, tel. (031) 372231.

UMHLANGA ROCKS

Beverly Hills Sun***** International-class, luxury hotel. 81 rooms, 13 suites. Conference facilities. PO Box 71, Umhlanga Rocks 4320, tel. (031) 5612211.

Cabana Beach*** One of KwaZulu/Natal's largest hotels. 1 200 rooms. Conference facilities. PO Box 10, Umhlanga Rocks 4320, tel. (031) 5612371.

Umhlanga Sands*** Luxury accommodation in 237 self-contained suites. Conference facilities for 150; 3 restaurants. PO Box 223, Umhlanga Rocks 4320, tel. (031) 5612323.

SOUTH COAST

Crayfish Inn** Ramsgate. 14 rooms. Conference facilities for 30. PO Box 7, Ramsgate 4285, tel. (03931) 4410/1.

Margate Hotel** 69 rooms. Conference facilities for 600. PO Box 4, Margate 4275, tel. (03931) 21410.

NORTH COAST AND ZULULAND

Karridene Protea Hotel*** lllovo Beach. Complex comprises hotel, flats and caravan park. Hotel: 21 rooms, 2 suites. PO Box 20, lllovo Beach 4155, tel. (031) 963332.

Zululand Safari Lodge*** Luxury accommodation in game ranch; 41 en-suite rooms; à la carte restaurant; breakfasts in the bush. Conference facilities for 40. PO Box 116, Hluhluwe 3960, tel. (03562) and ask for 63/64.

THE KWAZULU/NATAL INTERIOR AND DRAKENSBERG

Between Durban's subtropical coastline in the southeast and the Free State border in the northwest lies a country garden 200 km wide, called the KwaZulu/Natal midlands. Starting at sea level, this region slowly climbs through lake districts and grassy downland, until, at 1 200 m, it rises precipitously for more than a kilometre up the face of South Africa's most spectacular mountain range – the Drakensberg (literally "dragons' mountain").

In this cradle of land between mountain and sea lie tourist opportunities probably unequalled in South Africa. They include historical battle sites, where savage conflicts were played out between Briton, Boer and Zulu in the 18th and 19th centuries; the scenic mountain resorts and game reserves of the Drakensberg; arts and crafts rambles through country villages; waterfalls, lakes and dams and Zulu villages and crafts.

WHAT TO SEE

■■■ PIETERMARITZBURG

Halfway between the sea and the Drakensberg, nestling in a green valley of bougainvilleas and azaleas, is KwaZulu/Natal's capital city, Pietermaritzburg. Colourful parks and gardens, jacaranda-lined streets, gabled red-brick Victorian and Edwardian mansions and old churches and museums combine to give it a peaceful character, reminiscent of the colonial era.

In 1838, the Dutch-speaking Voortrekkers established a village between the Umsindusi River and the Dorp Spruit (stream), which they called Pietermaritzburg.

The British turned the hamlet into a military garrison town five years later, and laid the foundations for its strongly colonial atmosphere.

For visitors what makes Pietermaritzburg so special is its proximity to the golden beaches of the north and south coasts, the game reserves of Zululand, the battle sites of the interior, and the Drakensberg resorts – all of which are within half a day's drive of the city.

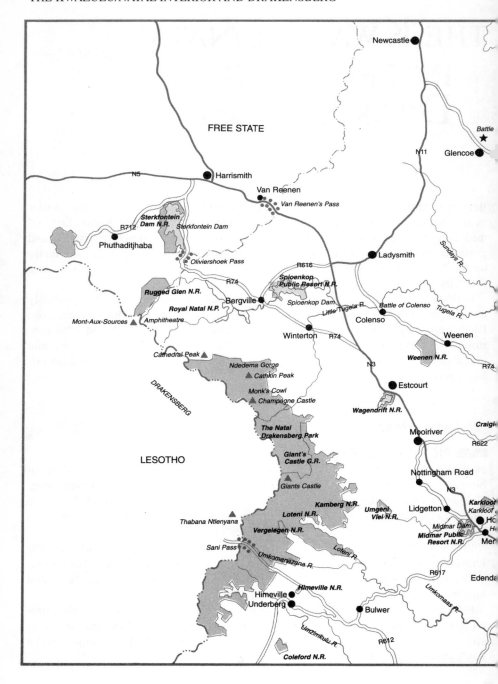

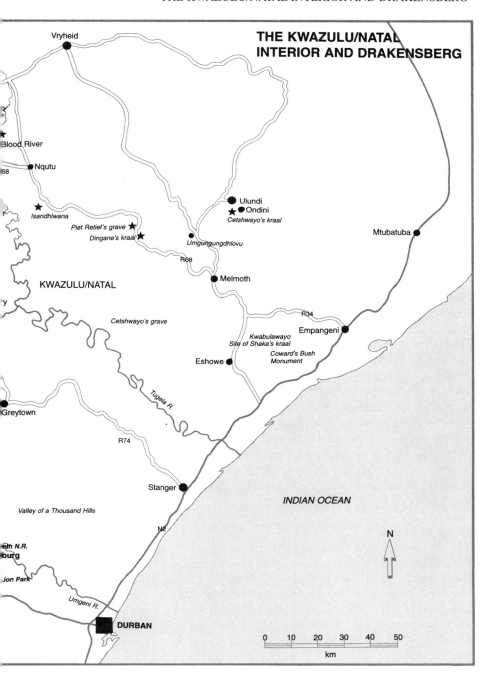

CLIMATE

The KwaZulu/Natal interior has a temperate climate, with warm, wet summers and cool, dry winters. In the Drakensberg the summer days are warm to hot, with crystal-clear air; in winter the days are crisp and sunny, the nights cold and bracing, with snow on the peaks. Summer thunderstorms in the Drakensberg can be violent, with lightning. The wettest months are January, February and March; the driest, June and July.

Within the city, historical streets, monuments, memorials and no less than 13 museums form the basis of several fascinating town trails. You can get a copy of "Pietermaritzburg Town Trails" from the Publicity Association's offices at Publicity House, 177 Commercial Road, tel. (0331) 451348. Enumerated trails start at the City Hall, the largest all-brick building south of the equator, and once the site of the Voortrekkers' Volksraadsaal (people's council hall).

Other attractions in Pietermaritzburg are its art galleries, particularly the Tatham Art Gallery, and its lovely gardens, notably the Botanical Gardens, Alexandra Park and Queen Elizabeth Park.

Natal Museum

This excellent museum in the city centre houses, among other items, one of the most important collections of Zulu crafts in the country, a reconstruction of a Drakensberg cave, with replicas of Bushman (San) paintings on the walls, and a fascinating display of ships wrecked on the southern African coast. For nature lovers, it also houses the finest collection of "Big Game" in Africa, including every species of antelope imaginable. Such rare species as bongo, addax and okapi are displayed. The dinosaur gallery features life-size replicas of such fearsome creatures as *Tyrannosaurus, Stegosaurus* and *Triceratops*. There's also a magnificent section on old Pietermaritzburg, with houses and shops just as they were in the 1850s, as well as authentic Victorian furniture. But perhaps the most acclaimed exhibition is the Marine Gallery, which displays a spectacular variety of marine animals, including sharks, shellfish and a real specimen of the prehistoric coelacanth fish.

Other museums

The following museums should be on your itinerary during a visit to Pietermaritzburg: Macrorie House, 11 Loop Street; Grey's Hospital Museum, Town Bush Road; Natal Steam Railway Museum, Hilton Railway Station; Howick Museum, Fallsview, Howick; Natal Provincial Administration Collections, 330 Longmarket Street; Tatham Art Gallery, Church Street; Comrades Marathon House, 18 Connaught Road, Scottsville; Natal Parliament Building, 239 Longmarket Street; Midmar Historical Village, Midmar Nature Reserve and Project Gateway, Burger Street.

The Church of the Vow

This museum, not far from the City Hall, was built in 1841 to commemorate the Boer victory over the Zulu army at the battle of Blood River on 16 December 1838. It was used as a place of worship until 1861, and opened in 1912 as the Voortrekker Museum. Alongside the museum is the new Church of the Vow, with imposing statues of Pietermaritzburg's founders, Great Trek leaders Piet Retief and Gert Maritz.

Fort Napier

This historic fort, established in 1843 on a hill overlooking the city, is just a few minutes' drive from the city centre. The British Army's 45th regiment camped here, and stayed in KwaZulu/Natal for 15 years. The fort's St George's Church was built in 1897.

Botanical Gardens

Spring displays of azaleas and camellias bring a surge of colour to the beautiful, lakeside Botanical Gardens, which include a 22-ha section of exotic flowers. There's a 24-ha indigenous garden, featuring the rich abundance of subtropical plants that grow in the KwaZulu/Natal interior.

Parks

Alexandra Park, with its tranquil walks beneath the trees, is an ideal spot for a picnic. It was founded in 1863 and named after Princess Alexandra of Denmark. Here you'll find a grand old bandstand, with a roof shaped like a mandarin's hat, which was built just over 100 years ago.

Queen Elizabeth Park (101 ha), on the outskirts of Pietermaritzburg, is the headquarters of the Natal Parks Board, and a most attractive place to take one of several nature walks among the indigenous fauna and flora.

■■■ AROUND PIETERMARITZBURG

Natal Lion and Game Park

Lions roam free in the Natal Lion Park's large enclosures 22 km south of Pietermaritzburg. A 7-km drive takes you right into the midst of these lions, and, elsewhere in the park, past a variety of such wildlife as eland, giraffe, zebra, ostrich, nyala, impala, blesbok, wildebeest, vervet monkeys and birds. Take a camera with you, and don't even think about getting out of the car.

The park's Pet's Corner features lion cubs, dwarf goats from the Cameroons and exotic birds. Facilities include a licenced hotel and a well-stocked curio shop.

Howick

The Umgeni River cascades 102 m into a gorge at Howick to create the beautiful Howick Falls. Proclaimed a national monument as long ago as 1951, these falls offer a safe viewsite, restaurant and caravan park nearby. There's a tragic history to the falls: the son of the first settler at Howick was carried to his death over them, and since then there have been several fatalities.

Attractions at Howick are the Howick Town Trail – a walking tour of the historic village, and the Dargle River Trail, a 6-km walk along the river. Places to stay at Howick are the Old Halliwell Country Inn, tel. (0332) 302602 or the Howick Falls Hotel, tel. (0332) 302809.

Umgeni Valley Nature Reserve

Black and crowned eagles, hornbills, paradise flycatchers and wood owls are just some of the 200 different bird species that live in this tranquil reserve, just below Howick Falls. There's a variety of large and small mammals too, including giraffes, Burchell's zebras, blue wildebeest, impala, nyala, eland, vervet monkeys, clawless otters and spotted genets.

For a true wildlife experience, nature walks, fishing or canoeing in the Umgeni River, book the Mhlangweni Cottage (sleeps five), or the dormitory-style huts catering for adults and children, tel. (0332) 303931.

Karkloof Falls

The spectacular Karkloof Falls, which tumble 115 m into a deep, wooded gorge, is a 15-minute drive away, in the 936-ha Karkloof Nature Reserve. The reserve is a sanctuary for bushpig, duiker, bushbuck and leopard, and a large variety of birds that make their homes in the branches of soaring yellowwood and black stinkwood trees. While you're here visit the Wodehouse Falls, and a few kilometres away, the Cascade and the lovely Shelter Falls. This is an ideal setting for a picnic.

The Midmar Dam Public Resort and Nature Reserve

This 1 618-ha dam and public resort, half an hour's drive north of Pieter-maritzburg, is an outstanding boating, sailing and fishing spot, which also offers tennis and squash courts, boats for hire and safe swimming – either in the dam or swimming pool.

A major attraction at Midmar is a replica of an old Victorian village, and a museum which houses a 1950s ex-SAAF Shackleton aircraft, two old steam locomotives and a tug boat, the *JE Eaglesham*. A Zulu kraal is the scene of informal dancing on Sundays, and there is a narrow-gauge steam train for children. Refreshments are available. A booklet explaining the village, "Step back in time", is available at the entrance.

Adjoining the resort is a game reserve accommodating white rhino, wildebeest, antelope and a large variety of birds. Several game-viewing trails offer excellent opportunities for birdwatching. Chalets are available for hire. For bookings contact the Natal Parks Board at PO Box 662, Pietermaritzburg 3200 or telephone (0331) 471981.

The Midlands Arts and Crafts Routes

Three lovely arts and crafts rambles make their way through the KwaZulu/Natal midlands: the Midlands Meander, the Last Artposts and the KwaZulu/Natal Midlands Experience.

The most popular is the Midlands Meander, which winds through 100 km of rolling farmlands and cosy country villages between Nottingham Road and Lidgetton.

Although you can do the journey in a day, you would be well advised to stay overnight at one or two of the seven country hotels regarded as official stops along the way.

The roughly circular route – the pioneer of craft routes in South Africa – is just one and a half hours' drive from Durban, and 30 minutes from Pietermaritzburg.

Highlights of the meander are visits to Hillford Pottery, the Birdman Gallery, Shuttleworth Weaving and Dargle Pottery.

For a map of the Midlands Meander, and details of the other craft routes, contact the Pietermaritzburg Publicity Association at (0331) 451348.

The northern KwaZulu/Natal Battlefields Route

This popular route takes you right onto the historical battlefields (see box on p. 142), and incorporates the garrison towns of Ladysmith, Dundee, Newcastle and Vryheid, which played pivotal roles in the Anglo Boer War.

There are a number of specialist tour guides – all registered with the South African Tourist Organisation (Satour) – who will escort you along this route, and organise accommodation and catering for the duration of the tour. For details see *Tours and excursions,* p. 151.

If you would rather go it alone, a three- or four-hour drive from Pietermaritzburg or Durban will take you right into these historical battlegrounds, and suggested routes can be provided by the Pietermaritzburg Publicity Association, Durban Unlimited or Satour (see *Tourist information,* p. 151).

Ladysmith

Part of the Battlefields Route, this charming country town, named after the Spanish wife of Cape Governor Sir Harry Smith, made world headlines in 1899 when Boer forces encircled and laid siege to it for 120 days. Many of the historical monuments, cemeteries, cairns and old buildings date back to that period. The town hall, built in 1893, was used as a hospital during the siege. A short drive from Ladysmith is the famous battle site of Spioenkop.

Spioenkop

More than 2 000 Boer and British soldiers died on the slopes of this hill in January

Battlefields of KwaZulu/Natal

The KwaZulu/Natal interior and Zululand have witnessed the full fury of several conflicts and battles, spanning some 200 years, that left the green fields and valleys of the midlands drenched in blood. Among these were the highly successful military manouevres launched by the black Napoleon of Africa, Shaka king of the Zulus, against other chiefdoms during the early part of the 19th century.

This was followed by the Anglo Zulu War and ferocious clashes between Briton and Zulu at Isandlwana, Rorke's Drift and Ulundi. The third conflict – between the Afrikaans Voortrekkers from the Cape Colony and the Zulus – was decided at Blood River.

Another decisive conflict was the South African War between the British Army and the Boer forces, which reached its savage peak at the battles of Colenso, Spioenkop and Majuba. For a first-hand taste of these famous battles, take a week or two to tour the KwaZulu/Natal midlands.

1900, in one of the fiercest engagements of the South African War. There's a resident historian on site to guide you round the area, a self-guided trail to the battle site, and an interesting exhibition of war memorabilia.

Nearby is one of KwaZulu/Natal's best-kept secrets – the Ntenjwa Bush Camp in the Spioenkop Nature Reserve, flanking Spioenkop Dam, just 15 km north of Winterton. Here you can stay in the secluded comfort of a thatched, A-frame hut in a true wildlife setting.

The Spioenkop Reserve offers a wide range of water sports, from swimming and waterskiing to boardsailing and canoeing. The main camp has 30 fully equipped chalets and a campsite catering for 400; Ntenjwa Bush Camp has four A-frame thatched huts.

Other attractions here are the 10-km Discovery Trail and other walks through the 400-ha game park, where you will see a variety of antelope, wildebeest, zebra, rhino and giraffe. For bookings, contact the Natal Parks Board at PO Box 662, Pietermaritzburg 3200 or tel. (0331) 471981.

Colenso

Several battles were fought in this region during the South African War, including the Battle of Colenso, during which Lord Roberts' son, Freddy, was killed. The Boers captured Winston Churchill here when they ambushed his train in 1899.

Dundee

This quaint town, the heart of the KwaZulu/Natal Battlefields Route, serves as an excellent departure point for the battle sites of Talana, Isandlwana, Rorke's Drift and Blood River. In fact, there's a whole lot more to see and do in the Dundee dis-

---

TIPS FOR TRAVELLERS

How to get to the battle sites: *Isandlwana and Rorke's Drift:* Travel west from Dundee on the R68 to Nqutu, and follow the signposts to Isandlwana. To get to Rorke's Drift, double back on the R68. Shortly after crossing the Buffalo River, you'll see a signpost for Rorke's Drift. You can stay over in the attractive Fugitive's Drift Lodge, 9 km from Rorke's Drift, or at the Isibindi Lodge, 12 km from the battle site. The proprietors will tell you everything you want to know about the battle. Alternatively, the Babanango Lodge, closer to Isandlwana, offers superior accommodation and good food.

Blood River: From Dundee go west on the R33. Just before you cross the Buffalo River, a signpost will direct you to the Blood River Monument.

---

trict, once you've established a base there. Two fine hotels, El Mpati Hotel and the Royal Hotel in Victoria Street, and the Kamnandi Guesthouse and Craft Centre, a charming Victorian home, offer comfortable accommodation and reasonable food.

The Talana Museum, on the site of the Talana battlefield just southeast of Dundee, houses military memorabilia from the days of the Voortrekkers, the Anglo-Zulu and Anglo-Boer Wars and other historical artefacts from the early days in Dundee. Take the Talana Trail (two hours) to two British forts built on top of the hill. Just 25 km southwest of Dundee is the Kameelkop Game and Cattle Farm where there are 16 species of game, swimming spots and nature trails, tel. (0341) 23600. For more details of historical sites near Dundee and trails, telephone the Dundee Publicity Association at (0341) 22677.

Isandlwana

Just over an hour's drive from Dundee is a windswept hillside known to the Zulus as Isandlwana, where the pride of the British Empire was shaken to its roots when a force of 1 500 British soldiers was annihilated by 14 000 Zulus in 1879.

An observation post overlooking the scene of former devastation has a detailed model portraying the positions of the forces during the battle. There are also memorials to those who died.

Rorke's Drift

The British soldiers who survived Isandlwana fled to Rorke's Drift, where a small British garrison was stationed. There, in another bloody encounter, they repelled 4 000 Zulus, and earned 11 Victoria Crosses between them. There's a beautiful Zulu handcraft centre at Rorke's Drift where you can buy hand-woven rugs and tapestries, pottery and hand-printed fabrics.

Blood River

In December 1838, Andries Pretorius, a pistol-packing farmer from Graaff-Reinet, led 464 Voortrekkers into the KwaZulu/Natal midlands on a mission to avenge the death of fellow trek leader Piet Retief at the hands of Zulu king, Dingane.

On the banks of the Ncome River he formed a 64-wagon circle – or laager – and faced an advance by 10 000 Zulus. The attacking waves of warriors were repulsed again and again, and when they took to flight, Pretorius and his men chased and routed them. When it was all over, 3 000 Zulus were dead, their blood staining the river red. From then on the Ncome became known as Blood River. The Voortrekkers didn't suffer one casualty. Today a bronze replica of the original laager stands on the site at Blood River.

The Zululand Route (Shaka's Way)

Before the election of the Government of National Unity in 1994, there were isolated outbreaks of violence near parts of the Zululand Route, but peace has been effectively restored, and the route now is quite safe.

This scenic circular drive takes you from Durban eastwards on the N2 to the colourful trading centre of Mtubatuba, and then inland to the very heart of Shaka's kingdom, before coming down to Eshowe and linking up with the N2 again.

On the way you will drive past Ulundi, the Zulu capital of KwaZulu, where a British force led by Lord Chelmsford defeated a Zulu army of 20 000 in 1879 and burnt down the kraal of the Zulu king, Cetshwayo. Archaeologists have restored the royal kraal at nearby Ondini, and you can visit it and the Ulundi Cultural Museum for a first-hand view of the Zulu nation's proud culture and heritage. Just down from the museum, you can spend the night in one of the traditional huts. For details contact the KwaZulu Monuments Council, PO Box 523, Ulundi 3838, tel. (0358) 791223.

A short drive from Ulundi is Umgungundlovu, where Voortrekker leader Piet Retief and 100 of his followers were killed by the Zulu king Dingane on 6 February 1838. Retief's grave is nearby. Further south, two interesting stops are the hilltop and monument which mark the site of Shaka's great capital, Kwabulawayo, and Coward's Bush, where Zulu warriors who had returned from war without their weapons had their hands speared to a tree. If they flinched during the process, they were killed.

For accommodation along the Zululand Route, telephone the Hluhluwe Publicity Association at (035) 5620353.

Zulu kraals

Not far from Eshowe are three Zulu kraals where you can sample traditional life as it was in Shaka's days.

The largest of these kraals is Shakaland, which was built for the film sets of *Shaka Zulu* and *John Ross*, and which was intended to be an authentic reconstruction of a typical 19th century Zulu community. Set on a hill overlooking the Goedertrouw Dam, the kraal offers beautiful views and Western comforts in tribal surroundings. You can stay in luxurious, traditional beehive huts, with bathroom and toilet. The dining area and bar are under thatch.

Attractions at Shakaland include Ngoma dancing, Zulu stick fighting, spear-making and Zulu women making handcrafts. Highlight of the stay is a fireside Zulu tribal dance to the accompaniment of drums, and a typical traditional meal.

You can either visit Shakaland for lunch and watch the Ngoma dancing, which together take about two hours, or stay overnight. Be sure to book in advance. Write to PO Box 103, Eshowe 3815, tel. (03546) 655.

The most authentic kraal is at Stewart's Farm, and was built to preserve the traditional culture of the Zulu people for posterity. Here too you can overnight in Zulu beehive huts (they are quite comfortable and are equipped with shower and toilet), eat traditional Zulu food and watch an outstanding display of ceremonial dancing. The owner, Graham Stewart, will guide you through the kraal with an informative commentary on Zulu life styles.

There is a dining area and lounge under thatch and a well-stocked curio shop, which serves snacks. You must book in advance for overnight accommodation but you can stop off for the morning without advance booking. Write to Stewart's Farm, PO Box 4, Nkwalini 3816, tel. (03546) 748.

The third kraal is that of KwaBhekithunga (advance booking is essential), where lunchtime visitors are met at the gate by dancing Zulu maidens, who lead them down a path to the hut of the headman. Other attractions are Zulu dancing and singing, traditional meals, and visits to a spirit medium and the beer-making hut.

A large curio shop offers a wide range of locally crafted goods, from wooden carvings to beadwork. For bookings write to PO Box 364, Eshowe 3815 or telephone (03546) 867.

■■■ THE DRAKENSBERG

The Drakensberg is a majestic mountain holiday paradise, described by Reg Pearce, author of *Barrier of Spears,* as "a world of basalt giants that stand as sentinels on the roof of Africa". Upon this roof in the clouds is an unspoilt wilderness of cliffs, emerald valleys and rivers that plummet to the sprawling plains below.

Easily accessible by road, the mountain resorts are two-and-a-quarter hour's drive from Durban, and three-and-a-quarter hours from Johannesburg. Most hotels offer to pick up guests at suitable points along the main bus route between Johannesburg and Durban. For details contact the Pietermaritzburg Publicity Association at (0331) 451348.

Where to go

There are three major tourist areas in the Drakensberg: the Amphitheatre and Mont-aux-Sources section in the north; the Cathedral Peak, Champagne Castle, Giant's Castle section in the centre and the southern Drakensberg below Sani Pass, which includes the villages of Himeville, Underberg and Ixopo. If you're visiting the area for the first time, the Amphitheatre, site of the Royal Natal National Park and the most breathtaking scenery in the Drakensberg, is the place to go.

Rules of the Berg

Don't walk alone in the Berg. If a sudden mist sets in and disorients you, stay where you are until it lifts.

The making of fires is prohibited.

The walks and trails suggested in the Natal Parks Board's brochures do not include actual climbs. If you intend climbing, discuss the routes carefully with the proprietor of your hotel or resort, and do not attempt any strenuous walks and climbs if you are unfit.

Thunderstorms – with lightning – can move in very quickly in summer, especially in the Amphitheatre region. To avoid storms, set out early in the morning and return to your base by lunchtime.

Where to stay

There are no less than 18 mountain resorts in the northern and central Drakensberg, complemented by the numerous country cottages, mountain inns and guest farms of the southern Drakensberg.

One of the favourite places to stay is the Tendele Rest Camp in the Royal Natal National Park, but advance booking is essential. The Royal Natal National Park Hotel and the Mont-aux-Sources hotels in the park are also recommended.

Other quality resort hotels in the Drakensberg are the Drakensberg Sun (near Cathkin Peak), Champagne Castle, Cathedral Peak Hotel and Little Switzerland.

In the south, the luxury Sani Pass Hotel is popular, as are the Drakensberg Garden and Bushman's Nek hotels, both attractive for their lovely mountain environment.

At Sani Top Chalet you can have a drink in the highest pub in southern Africa, and ski on the snow-covered slopes in winter.

There's bungalow, chalet and cottage accommodation in Tendele camp, and large en-suite bedrooms. There are also beautiful campsites with ablution blocks at Mahai and Rugged Glen, but you must supply your own equipment. Access to Tendele is between sunrise and sunset, so plan your trip to arrive there before the gates close. For reservations, contact the Natal Parks Board at PO Box 662, Pietermaritzburg 3200 or telephone (0331) 471981.

What to do

The natural setting of all the Drakensberg resorts puts visitors in touch with the full spectrum of outdoor pursuits – from mountain climbing to pony trails to trout fishing. Hiking trails abound in this mountain wonderland, and range from short, easy strolls to strenuous climbs up sheer rock faces.

The rewards for such walks are tantalising: the caves and sheltered rock faces of the Drakensberg – particularly those of the Giant's Castle and Ndedema areas – carry about 40 per cent of all the Bushman rock art in southern Africa.

There is an abundance of wildlife in such beautiful reserves as the Royal Natal

▲ 95   ▼ 96   ▼ 97

95. The loggerhead turtle which nests on the shores of the Sodwana Bay National Park.
96. The reefs of Sodwana Bay National Park are a paradise for divers.
97. A beautiful fig-tree forest, Mkuzi, Zululand.

▲ 98   ▼ 99   ▲ 100   ▼ 101

98. The brick façade of the elegant Pietermaritzburg Town Hall.
99. Four-wheel drive vehicles on the beach near Sodwana Bay.
100. The beautiful Howick Falls plunge 102 m into the gorge below.
101. The British monument and graves at Spioenkop, in the Spioenkop Nature Reserve.

▲ 102   ▼ 103

102. The Policeman's Helmet – an interesting rock formation in the Royal Natal National Park.
103. The Drakensberg Amphitheatre, with the Tugela River in the foreground.

▲ 104

▲ 105

104. A splendid view of the towering formations of the Drakensberg.
105. San (Bushman) paintings in Ladybrand.
106. The Tugela River as it falls over the edge of the Drakensberg Amphitheatre.

◄ 106

▲ 107   ▼ 108   ▼ 109

107. The Johannesburg city skyline at twilight.
108. A scene in Rockey Street, Johannesburg's
arty neighbourhood near the city centre.
109. An old shaft on a gold mine on the Reef,
just outside Johannesburg.

▲ 110

▲ 111

▼ 112

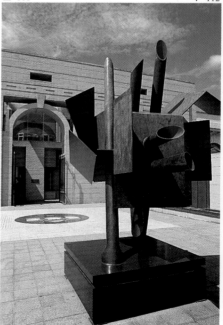

110. The Market Theatre Complex, a vibrant hub of theatre and art in South Africa.
111. A street musician in Johannesburg, part of the city's colourful cultural life.
112. The entrance to the Johannesburg Art Gallery in Joubert Park.

▲ 113   ▼ 114   ▼ 115

113. Christmas lights bring a festive air to the Johannesburg city centre.
114. Selling curios on the streets of Hillbrow.
115. A makeshift shop typical of South Africa's informal settlements.

116. October is jacaranda time in Pretoria.
117. The Paul Kruger Monument in Church Square, the centre of Pretoria.
118. The Voortrekker Monument in Pretoria commemorates the Great Trek of the 1830s.
119. The Union Buildings in Pretoria, where President Nelson Mandela was inaugurated on 10 May 1994.

▲ 116

▼ 117

▲ 118

▼ 119

120. A mountain stream in the Magaliesberg.
121. Ballooning is a popular sport in the Magaliesberg, and provides panoramic views of the Highveld.
122. Yachts on Hartbeespoort Dam, a popular weekend destination for the residents of Gauteng.
123. Tourists on a game drive in the huge Pilanesberg National Park.

▲ 120   ▼ 121   ▲ 122   ▼ 123

▲ 125 ▼ 126

▼ 124

124. The extravagant Palace of the Lost City, the luxury hotel at the epicentre of the multi-million-rand Lost City complex.

125. Gambling at the Sun City Casino.

126. An astonishing variety of water sports is available to visitors to Sun City.

127. Sun City's golf course, the venue for the Million-Dollar Challenge, which attracts world-class golfers.

▼ 127

▲ 128

▼ 129

128. The magnificent Blyde River Canyon where the river flows into the Blydepoort Dam.
129. A bull elephant browsing in the Kruger National Park.

▲ 130 ▼ 131

▲ 132 ▼ 133

▼ 134

130. Viewing a cheetah with its kill on a game drive in Mala Mala Game Reserve.
131. An early morning game drive at Londolozi Game Reserve.
132. Trailists on the three-day Nyalaland Trail in the Kruger National Park.
133. One of the famous white lions of Timbavati.
134. A colourful whitefronted bee-eater in the Kruger National Park.
135. The Madonna and Child formation in the Sudwala Caves.
136. These cycads in the Modjadji Nature Reserve are one of the world's oldest plant species.
137. The Long Tom cannon at the top of the Long Tom Pass.

▲ 135   ▼ 136   ▼ 137

▲ 138

▼ 139

138. The beautiful rock
formations at Bourke's Luck
are the result of the abrasive
action of sand and pebbles.
139. The spectacular Mac-Mac
Falls on the road between
Sabie and Graskop.

▲ 140

▼ 141

▼ 142

▼ 143

140. The quaint town of Pilgrim's Rest marks the place were alluvial gold deposits were discovered in the Eastern Transvaal.
141. The Royal Hotel in Pilgrim's Rest is still as it was in the old mining days.
142. Ndebele women of the Eastern Transvaal in their brightly-coloured traditional dress.
143. Shangaan dancers in the Eastern Transvaal.

144. The Blouberg (Blue Mountain) in the Northern Transvaal.
145. A magical baobab tree, typical of the far northern parts of the country.
146. A venomous puff adder – these snakes are abundant in the dry Northern Transvaal.
147. The beautiful purplecrested lourie of the Northern Transvaal.

▲ 144   ▼ 145   ▲ 146   ▼ 147

National Park, the Giant's Castle Game Reserve and the Kamberg, Loteni and Vergelegen nature reserves.

Scenic drives, such as that up the Sentinel (2 622 m), which takes you to the highest driveable point in South Africa, afford magnificent views of the KwaZulu/Natal Drakensberg and the midlands.

In the foothills, the large number of dams offer excellent fishing and a variety of water sports such as boating, canoeing, boardsailing and swimming.

If your tastes are more domestic, most berg hotels offer tennis, bowls, squash, croquet and volleyball, as well as snooker, bridge and family games. Some have golf courses, and most have swimming pools.

The Amphitheatre and Mont-aux-Sources

A huge island of rock, known as the Amphitheatre, surges skywards from the green valleys of northern KwaZulu/Natal to form one of the natural wonders of southern Africa. The Amphitheatre is 4 km long, and flanked at one end by a stately pedestal of rock known as the Eastern Buttress. On its northeastern end is a fang-shaped peak known as the Sentinel (3 165 m), which leads to a summit called Mont-aux-Sources (the mountain of springs).

Two French missionaries, Rev T Arbousset and Rev F Dumas, were the first Europeans to see Mont-aux-Sources in 1836, and since then it has been regarded as one of the most spectacular sights of the KwaZulu/Natal Drakensberg. Its heights (snow-covered in winter) provide an extraordinary vantage point of the other great peaks of the Drakensberg to the south: Cathedral Peak, Cathkin Peak and Giant's Castle.

The Amphitheatre is the source of the Tugela River, which plummets 2 000 m over its plateau – its second drop of 213 m making it one of the highest vertical falls in the world.

At the base of the Amphitheatre are the green valleys and plains of the Royal Natal National Park.

The Royal Natal National Park

Many regard this natural fairyland of flower-covered mountains, tranquil glens, ice-blue streams and waterfalls as the finest place in the Drakensberg.

Covering 8 094 ha, this mountain paradise is inhabited by an abundance of game, ranging from eland, mountain reedbuck, klipspringer and bushbuck, to baboon, black-backed jackal and porcupine. The 180 bird species include black eagle, bearded vulture and Cape vulture.

There are 31 walks and climbs and 96 km of bridle trails, if you like riding. Most of the walks start from the Royal Natal National Park Hotel and include:

The Gorge: This is the most popular and scenically spectacular walk in the park. Time: 1 day.

Castle Rocks: A very rocky area containing several caves, including the area known as King Solomon's Mines. Time: 3-4 hours.

Mont-aux-Sources: If you're fit and energetic, you can hike up to the Amphi-theatre's plateau, but take provisions and a tent along. Time: 2 days.

Fairy Glen: This short walk is at its best in summer when the rocks in the Glen are covered with begonias and streptocarpa. Time: 1 hour.

Cascades: An attractive route for all ages which passes the trout hatchery. Time: 1 hour.

Gudu Falls: The falls, lying at the head of a large, natural forest, is a lovely picnic spot on hot days. Time: 3 hours.

Sunday Falls: This walk gives a scenic view of the falls from inside the natural for-est below the falls. Time: 2 hours.

The Crack and Mudslide: A fairly strenuous trip will be rewarded with excellent views of the park, and the whole face of the Drakensberg as far down as Cathkin Peak. Take along a camera. Time: 7 hours.

Cathedral Peak

This peak soars skywards in a mountaineer's paradise, boasting some of the most difficult and dangerous climbs of the Drakensberg. They include the Bell (2 918 m), the Pyramid (2 914 m), the Column (2 926 m), the Outer Horn (3 006 m) and the Inner Horn (3 017 m). A series of peaks known as the Organ Pipes, or as Qolo la maSoja (ridge of soldiers) to the Zulus, are particularly spectacular.

Formidable as these peaks are, the climb up Cathedral Peak itself is well within the ability of most fit people, but requires at least a day. There is accommodation at the nearby Cathedral Peak Hotel, which also offers horseriding trails and hikes. Leisurely strolls take you to the scenic delights of Rainbow Gorge, Doreen Falls and Mushroom Rock. In the nearby Mlambonja River valley, you can picnic along-side the cool waters of the river.

Cathkin Peak

The Cathkin Park area in the foothills of Cathkin Peak offers some beautiful hotels and resorts which provide easy access for exploring the area.

Giant's Castle Reserve

The main attraction of this mountainous 35 000-ha reserve is its wealth of Bushman paintings – a 20-minute walk from the hutted camp will take you to one of the country's most prolific exhibitions of Bushman rock art. In the Main Caves are no less than 500 individual paintings. A fascinating museum here depicts the cave life of these nomadic artists as it used to be for several thousand years, long before Europeans came to this part of the world.

A guide leads you through the caves and museum with a commentary on the life and ways of the Bushmen. Battle Cave in the Injasuti valley has even more rock art – some 750 paintings.

The reserve is home to a dozen species of antelope, including eland, South

┌─── **TIPS FOR TRAVELLERS** ───────────────────────────

There are several very good books on the Drakensberg, which will give you an overview of the scenery, the walks and the accommodation available. They include:
Drakensberg walks by David Bristow (Struik, Cape Town); *Mountains of southern Africa* by David Bristow (Struik, Cape Town), with photographs by Clive Ward; *The Royal Natal National Park* compiled by the Natal Parks Board; *The building of the Berg* by AR Wilcox. TV Bulpin's *Discovering southern Africa* is crammed with informative text on the Drakensberg.

Africa's largest antelope. The mountain peaks are home to 140 species of bird, among which are a variety of raptors – species include the lammergeier (bearded vulture) and the lappetfaced, hooded, whitebacked and Cape vultures. There's a special hide from which you can watch these birds at close quarters.

Scenically, Giant's Castle is quite staggering. To the northwest, the Njesuthi Dome rises 3 410 m above sea level. In the south, the basalt wall of the Giant's Castle buttress looms high above the surrounding countryside. All around, the skyline is pierced by surging peaks: Champagne Castle, Monk's Cowl and Cathkin Peak.

There are three camps at Giant's Castle, the most popular of which is the Natal Parks Board's hutted camp, overlooking the Bushman's River. Here you can hire a self-contained cottage or a bungalow sharing a communal kitchen. Bring your own food – it will be prepared for you.

Major attractions are two- to five-day horseriding trails, but you must be a competent rider, and be prepared to rough it overnight in a cave. The departure point for these trails is Hillside Camp, and you must be there before 09h00 on the departure date. The Natal Parks Board supplies everything, including sleeping bags, but bring your own food.

There are 26 different walks and trails at Giant's Castle, with special expeditions led by game rangers. You don't have to be a climber to join a walk, but you must be reasonably fit. For overnight hikes, accommodation is available in three mountain huts (very basic shelters) and two caves. They are Giant's Hut at the foot of Giant's Castle Peak, Bannerman Hut at the bottom of Bannerman Pass, and Meander Hut overlooking the Meander Valley.

A 9-km hike from the Solitude Mountain Resort will take you to the lower Injasuti Cave, the most spectacular in the entire Drakensberg. Take along a sleeping bag, crockery, cutlery and food. Any overnight stay in these huts or caves requires a permit, available from the Giant's Castle warden.

Loteni Nature Reserve

Less than an hour's drive from Nottingham Road, this reserve offers spectacular scenery, magnificent birdlife and trout fishing in the Loteni River. The Settler's Museum exhibits 19th century furniture and household accessories. There's a swimming pool, the circular Eagle Trail and horseriding. Accommodation is in a hutted camp with 12 bungalows, two cottages and a campsite. A rustic cottage, accommodating 10 people, can also be hired. For bookings contact the Natal Parks Board at PO Box 662, Pietermaritzburg 3200 or telephone (0331) 471981.

Sani Pass

This, the only road link between KwaZulu/Natal and Lesotho through the Drakensberg, is one of the highest passes in the world, and offers staggering views of a primitive and rugged landscape. Bear in mind that the 25-km pass is not for those who suffer from vertigo – the climb is very steep and the road narrow and winding.

The pass follows the Mkomozana River, which tumbles through the gorge in a series of cascades. Accessible from the road are caves and rock shelters adorned with Bushman (San) paintings.

The Sani Pass Hotel, one of the luxury hotels of the Drakensberg, lies at the foot of the pass and offers four-wheel-drive trips to the top. Two walks from the hotel take you to the site of Bushman paintings. The paintings at Good Hope Caves, an hour's walk from the hotel, are not as varied or intact as those on Ikanti Mountain, two hours from the hotel.

At the top of Sani Pass, just inside the Lesotho border, is the recently refurbished Sani Top Chalet, at 2 865 m the highest licenced premises in southern Africa. For booking information, telephone (033) 7021069.

Himeville Nature Reserve

You can hire a boat and cruise across the tranquil lakes, or fish for trout in this peaceful reserve. There are 10 campsites in the reserve, or you can stay in the near-by Himeville Arms Hotel, tel. (033) 7021305.

THE KWAZULU/NATAL INTERIOR AND THE DRAKENSBERG AT A GLANCE

When to go: All year round, but summer is best in the mountains, with its warm days and crystal-clear air.

Getting around: Most people use the N3 highway linking Johannesburg to Pietermaritzburg and Durban as the primary access route to the Drakensberg resorts. For the northern Drakensberg resorts branch off the N3 at Harrismith on to the R74. After 49 km, signposts indicate where the resorts are. The central Drakensberg is accessed via Winterton. From Pietermaritzburg, take the N3 to the Ladysmith junction north of Shell Ultra City, then turn left onto the R74. The southern resorts are reached via Bulwer and Underberg. Take the Merrivale turn-off from the N3 near Howick, and watch the signposts.

Main attractions: Scenic wonders of the Drakensberg. Hiking, horseriding and mountain climbing. Bushman rock art. Historic battle sites. Nature reserves of the midlands. Arts and crafts routes. Zulu kraals and culture. Boating, sailing, swimming, trout fishing in dams and rivers.

Tours and excursions: *Coach:* Translux, Transcity and Greyhound Citiliner run intercity trips (Johannesburg and Durban daily) regularly. City Hopper runs trips between Pietermaritzburg, Durban and Durban International Airport. Contact Pietermaritzburg Publicity Association for details at (0331) 451348. Local minibus tours (on request), local scenic flights (Midlands Aviation) and battlefields coach tours and town trails are available regularly. Contact Pietermaritzburg Publicity Association, tel. (0331) 451348 or the Drakensberg Publicity Association, PO Box 1608, Estcourt 3310, tel. (0363) 24186).

Battlefields: Air: Magnum Airlines runs scheduled flights from Johannesburg and Durban to Newcastle and Vryheid, telephone Magnum at (03431) 22602. Tours: Specialist tour guides for the battlefields are: Ben Henderson, tel. (031) 7642261; Pam McFadden, tel. (0341) 22654; David Rattray, tel. (03425) 843 and Maureen Richards, tel. (0361) 22231. Coach: Greyhound runs a daily bus service between Johannesburg and Durban, with stops along the way. Car: Avis and Imperial offer hire-cars from Johannesburg and Durban airports.

Walking tours: There are hundreds of walks and trails in the Drakensberg and the KwaZulu/Natal midlands, full details of which are available from the Natal Parks Board and the Pietermaritzburg Publicity Association (see below). Mpila Adventures offers hiking and bike trips into Lesotho and the KwaZulu/Natal Drakensberg for two to five days. Camping gear is provided.

Tourist information: Drakensberg Publicity Association, PO Box 1608, Estcourt 3310, tel. (0363) 24186. Pietermaritzburg Publicity Association, Publicity House, 177 Commercial Road, Pietermaritzburg 3201, tel. (0331) 451348. Natal Parks Board, PO Box 662, Pietermaritzburg 3200, tel. (0331) 471981. Durban Unlimited, Tourist Junction, 160 Pine Street, Durban 4001, tel. (031) 3044934.

Festivals and annual events: Pietermaritzburg: Dusi Canoe Marathon (January); Midmar Mile Swimming Race (February); Royal Agricultural Show (May); Comrades Marathon (May); Art in the Park (June); Food and Wine Fair (August); Oktoberfest (October); South African Invitation Stakes, Scottsville (November); Natal Witness National Book Fair (November).

ACCOMMODATION GUIDE

Luxury city hotels, mountain lodges and remote country inns combine to offer a diverse range of comfortable accommodation in the KwaZulu/Natal interior and the Drakensberg.

PIETERMARITZBURG

The Imperial*** 500 m from City Hall. Named after Prince Imperial of France. 55 en-suite rooms; 3 restaurants serving alfresco meals; action bar; live entertainment nightly. Conference facilities for 2 000. PO Box 140, Pietermaritzburg 3200, tel. (0331) 426551 .

Karos Capital Towers*** Luxury hotel in Commercial Street. 101 rooms; à la carte restaurant, carvery, bar. Conference facilities for 250. PO Box 198, Pietermaritzburg 3200, tel. (0331) 942761.

CENTRAL NATAL

Granny Mouse's Country House*** Charming country inn set on 50 acres overlooking Lions River, near Balgowan. Birdwatching, croquet, trout fishing. Thatched riverside cottages. PO Box 22, Balgowan 3275, tel. (03324) 4071/4532.

The Hilton Hotel*** Tudor-style country house near Pietermaritzburg. Tennis, bowls, croquet, pool. Three restaurants. 38 rooms. Conference facilities for 300. PO Box 35, Hilton 3245, tel. (0331) 33311.

NORTHERN DRAKENSBERG

Drakensberg Sun**** Near Cathkin Peak, 29 km from Winterton. Luxury accommodation with superb restaurant and bar. Tennis, bowls, volleyball, water sports, nine-hole golf course, horseriding. 144 rooms; 4 suites. Conference facilities. PO Box 335, Winterton 3340, tel. (036) 4681000.

Cathedral Peak Hotel*** Exclusive family mountain hotel. Beautiful setting; new ladies bar; health centre, putt-putt golf, tennis, bowls, squash, swimming, horseriding. 86 rooms. Conference centre. PO Winterton 3340, tel. (036) 4881888.

Cayley Lodge*** Overlooking Champagne Castle and Cathkin Peak. Surrounded by 236 acres of its own parkland and forest. 18 double, 6 superior rooms. PO Box 241, Winterton 3340, tel. (036) 4681222.

Karos Mont-aux-Sources*** In the lap of the Amphitheatre. Spectacular views. 61 rooms; 29 suites; 3 conference venues; lovely bowling green. Private Bag X1, Mont-aux-Sources 3353, tel. (036) 4386230.

Little Switzerland*** Countryside setting in Mont-aux-Sources area; horseriding, bowls, swimming, tennis, squash and sauna. Furnished, thatched cottages set among gardens and lawns. Private Bag X1661, Bergville 3350, tel. (036) 4386220.

Cathkin Park** Family hotel. Good country cooking; log fires in winter. Tennis, swimming, bowls, horseriding. 45 rooms. Conference facilities for 200. Private Bag X12, Winterton 3340, tel. (036) 4681091/2.

Champagne Castle Hotel** Close to Monk's Cowl. One of the highest Drakensberg resorts. Cottages, rondavels and en-suite family rooms. All-weather tennis courts, bowling greens; excellent walks and horseriding. Private Bag X8, Winterton 3340, tel. (036) 4681063.

The Nest** Spectacular views of Champagne and Cathkin peaks. Mountain walks, swimming, tennis, horseriding, bowls, snooker, trout fishing, golf and snooker. 60 rooms. Private Bag X14, Winterton 3340, tel. (036) 4681068.

Royal Natal National Park Hotel** Spectacular mountain setting near the Amphitheatre. Excellent walks, horseriding, bowls, tennis, swimming and fishing. 65 rooms. Private Bag 4, Mont-aux-Sources 3350, tel. (036) 4386200.

Sandford Park Lodge** Century-old lodge and coachhouse in foothills of Drakensberg. Excellent personal service. PO Box 7, Bergville 3350, tel. (0364) 381001.

Hlalanathi Drakensberg Resort Mont-aux-Sources area. Comfortable thatched chalets, swimming pool, walks and fishing. Private Bag X1621, Bergville 3350, tel. (036) 4386308.

SOUTHERN DRAKENSBERG

Drakensberg Garden Hotel*** Family hotel in beautiful setting. Farmyard and zoo animals. Tennis, squash, swimming and walks. Post office, shop and service station. 80 rooms, PO Box 311, Underberg 4590, tel. (033) 7011355.

Sani Pass Hotel*** Excellent facilities include spa centre with squash court, sauna, jacuzzi and masseur. Also horseriding, tennis, bowls, and golf. 66 rooms, 3 suites. Conference facilities for 150. PO Himeville 4585, tel. (033) 7021305 or 7021320.

GAUTENG AND THE NORTH-WEST PROVINCE

JOHANNESBURG

Prospectors, lured by the promise of great wealth, swarmed into the barren Transvaal highveld in 1886, after an itinerant Australian digger named George Harrison discovered gold. Harrison didn't know it then, but he had touched the tip of an iceberg – a vault of mineral wealth so great that it would catapult the nation into the ranks of the world's richest suppliers of gold.

As luck would have it, Harrison sold his Discoverer's Claim for a mere ten pounds, then moved on. But the thousands of merchants, miners, entrepreneurs and fortune seekers who followed him stayed, and laid the foundations of South Africa's richest, most populated city.

During the past 100 years, Johannesburg has undergone a spectacular transformation. From a shabby assembly of mud and corrugated huts before the turn of the century, the mining town has developed into a sprawling metropolis. Around it, mushrooming satellite towns have crept closer and closer towards its own suburbs, forming the world's fastest-growing conglomerate – the Witwatersrand or "the ridge of white waters".

It is the centre of the country's industrial, mining, financial and commercial operations, contributing about 60 per cent of the entire country's gross product, and also the hub of the country's education and research, art and culture. Its assets include a bustling entrepreneurial spirit; more sunshine than the French Riviera; an efficient communications network that puts you in touch with the game parks, beaches and mountain resorts of southern Africa, and a dazzling nightlife, with a profusion of upmarket restaurants, cinemas, theatres and cabaret shows.

South Africa's largest city and brand new capital of Gauteng wears the glitzy trappings of a mining town that outgrew itself in a hurry. Modern skyscrapers pierce the thin highveld air above narrow city streets and distant hills of yellowish sand – the debris of gold mines that made Johannesburg wealthy and famous.

The 166-shop Carlton Centre, in the middle of town, dominates this concrete city, its observation deck, the Carlton Panorama, on the 50th floor giving giddy 360° views of the Witwatersrand. To the north, Hillbrow's flatland, one of Africa's most densely populated residential areas, creeps skywards, dominated by the JG Strijdom Tower;

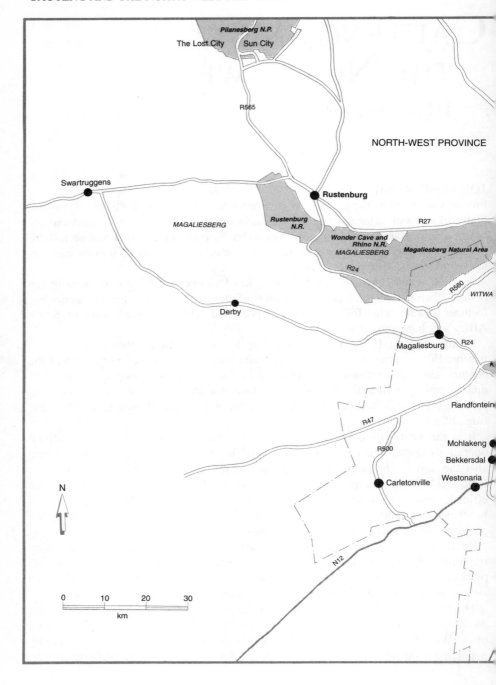

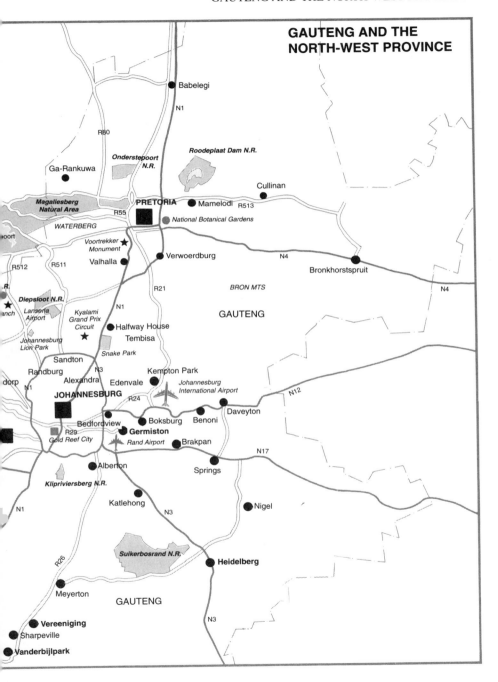

GAUTENG AND THE
NORTH-WEST PROVINCE

155

CLIMATE

Johannesburg has an exhilarating climate, with crisp, dry winters marked by sunny days and cold, frosty nights. Summers are warm to hot with regular, violent, afternoon thundershowers, sometimes accompanied by brief showers of hail. The average rainfall is 850 mm. The daily temperature swings between an average midsummer (January) maximum of 26,3 °C to a winter minimum of 4,1 °C (although sub-zero temperatures are quite common in winter). Pretoria's climate is very similar, but is warmer and more humid in summer and winter. Both cities average about nine hours of sunshine a day.

---

further north, the more affluent, tree-lined suburbs of Johannesburg spread out interminably. To the east are Reef towns such as Edenvale, Benoni, Brakpan, Germiston and Springs; to the west, South Africa's largest black city, Soweto, and the satellite towns of Krugersdorp, Roodepoort and Randfontein merge with the hazy highveld horizon.

Although this vast metropolitan sprawl is not particularly pretty, it conceals a multitude of fascinating things to see and do: in the city centre, historical buildings, art galleries and museums rub shoulders with five-star restaurants, theatres, cinemas, speciality shops and African craft centres. The huge Gold Reef City complex is the place to be for wining and dining, non-stop entertainment and an intimate view of Johannesburg during the gold rush days.

Out of town, you can visit a range of recreational and wildlife retreats, among them the Johannesburg Zoo and Zoo Lake, the Lion Park, the Transvaal Snake Park, and numerous parks and gardens scattered throughout the suburbs.

WHAT TO SEE

■■■■ JOHANNESBURG
Gold Reef City
You can spend a few hours or a few days at Gold Reef City, which is situated at Crown Mines, 6 km south of the city centre. And, depending on your tastes, you could have a roaring good time. Gold Reef City is actually an authentic replica of Johannesburg as it was in the rough and tough pioneer days of the gold-rush era (1888-1890), when fortunes were made in minutes, and men died of greed and cirrhosis of the liver. Here, special recreations of the old gold-rush days include a public house, Chinese laundry, an old-fashioned newspaper and an early example of the stock exchange.

Today there's nothing but celebration at Gold Reef City. About a dozen restaurants, taverns (Barney's Tavern is recommended) and beer-gardens compete with other amenities for your attention. There are gumboot dancers, African choral performers, even a penny-whistler, whom you can hire for entertainment at an hourly rate.

TIPS FOR TRAVELLERS

There's a spirit of "real" Africa in downtown Johannesburg, where street-market stalls spill over onto the pavements, and bargaining and haggling are fierce. But there are problems such as traffic congestion, parking problems and rampant unemployment.

Downtown Johannesburg is not the place to walk about at night. If you're going somewhere in town, drive or take a cab. And, if you are driving, avoid unfamiliar or suspect areas: a spate of several hundred car hijackings was reported in central and suburban Johannesburg during 1994. Keep your car doors locked at all times, and don't talk to strangers at traffic lights.

If you're looking for a good restaurant, telephone Restaurant Line at (011) 7881516 or write to them at PO Box 842, Northlands 2116.

At night, there's non-stop cabaret (including can-can dances) to choose from. For superior nightclub entertainment, try Rosie O'Grady's.

On the upper terrace you can wander through mine houses, listen to a band playing in a gazebo on the village green, or watch children ride the carousel at the Victorian funfair.

Just beyond the village green, you step into "The Crush", change into waterproofs, gumboots and hard hat and descend 210 m down a real gold mine to Kimberley Reef, where you can see how gold is mined.

You can also ride in a steam train or horse-drawn omnibus. Speciality shops feature pottery, laceware, glassware, copperware, leatherware, diamonds, coins, curios and stamps.

At the heliport at Gold Reef City you can charter a helicopter for trips anywhere in South Africa. Regular pleasure flights take place at weekends and on public holidays.

There are daily scheduled tours of Gold Reef City lasting from three to four hours, with transport provided from the following hotels: Protea Gardens, Johannesburg Holiday Inn, Johannesburg Sun and Carlton Hotel. For more details, contact the Johannesburg Publicity Association, telephone (011) 3364961 or (011) 3376650.

Mine dancing

You can arrange a visit to a working mine, or watch traditional tribal dances at various Johannesburg mines on the first, second and fourth Sunday mornings of each month. Dances begin at 09h30 and last about two-and-a-half hours. To book, contact Satour or the Chamber of Mines in Hollard Street (see *Gauteng at a glance*, p. 170).

The Johannesburg Botanic Garden

Californian redwood, English oak, Portuguese and Spanish cork oaks and a huge variety of indigenous plants and trees in beautiful surroundings combine to make a visit to these gardens an essential part of your visit to Johannesburg. Fringing

Emmarentia Dam, half an hour's drive from the city, the Botanic Garden offers a kaleidoscope of springtime colours in its flowering cherries and displays of roses. You can arrange to see the nursery complex, which houses more than 2 500 species of succulents, have refreshments at the Tea Pergola (weekends only) or stroll past cascades and fountains feeding dams and ponds. Birds here include crowned plovers, crested grebes, Egyptian geese and yellowbilled ducks. For more information, telephone (011) 7820517.

George Harrison Park
This, the site of the discovery of gold on the Witwatersrand, features an old Jarrah wood stamp mill, once used to crush ore. A viewing point above the shafts enables you to see the layers of the Main Reef conglomerate that triggered the gold rush of 1886. Admission is free.

African arts and crafts
There are numerous arts and crafts for sale in Johannesburg. Outlets particularly recommended are: Transafrica Art Trading, Shop No. 11, Smal St Mall, Johannesburg, which has a beautiful collection of original African paintings, wood carvings, painted ostrich eggs, beadwork and sculptures; Africa Under One Roof, 43 Juta Street, Braamfontein, the largest warehouse of its kind in Africa, offering the widest range of African curios imaginable; Indaba Curios, Shop U7, Sandton City, Sandton and the Bead Barrel, Shop 7, Willow Centre, 379 Jan Smuts Avenue, Craighall Park.

Market Theatre complex
One Johannesburg journalist said that if you suffer from an overdose of bad news, get down to the amiable bonhomie of the market, and you'll come away well-inoculated. If you're a theatre-goer or bookworm, music lover or artist, insatiable collector of second-hand goods, or if you just want to have a great meal and listen to some good music, the Market Theatre complex is the place to be in Johannesburg. Not far from the new MuseumAfrica, this complex has a colourful, upbeat tempo to it – perhaps radiating from the ever-popular Kippie's Jazz Bar (named after local jazz great, Kippie Moeketsi), or from the excellent local productions staged in one of the three theatres.

Other attractions include several bustling clothes and jewellery boutiques, the Flower Market, the Indian Fruit Market and a shop selling Africana. A lovely second-hand bookshop, "Out of Print Antiquarian Books", has those special type of books you can't get anywhere else.

Other attractions include a photographic gallery, two art galleries and a music-drama venue called "The Warehouse". If you can, visit the complex on Saturday mornings, when it becomes a venue for dozens of stallholders selling just about anything.

Museums

MuseumAfrica: For an overview of the cultural history of South Africa, you shouldn't miss this museum (formerly the Africana Museum), which moved into its new Newtown building in 1994. The early voyages of discovery, Cape homes of the 17th and 18th centuries, the Anglo Boer War, the economic development of Johannesburg, including gold mining, and other South African-related themes are on display. There's also an outstanding collection of South African artefacts, showing the historical growth of African-speaking and Bushman cultures. Artefacts include hunting implements, beadwork, tribal love letters, life-size replicas of huts adorned by tribal artists, and musical instruments.

Other fascinating items are an old doll collection, Cape silver, a Victorian peep show and replicas of a public house and an apothecary. Of special interest is the model of the Battle of Rorke's Drift, fought in 1879 between the British and the Zulus.

Kleinjukskei Motor Museum: Here is the largest private collection of vintage cars, model cars and motorcycles in South Africa. Among the period models on show are a 1900 Daimler, a 1904 De Dion, a 1908 Delage and a 1912 Ford T. There is a pleasant tea garden in the 11-ha picnic-grounds.

Johannesburg Art Gallery: This gallery in Joubert Park has valuable collections of English, Dutch, French and South African art. It features artists such as Picasso, Van Gogh, Rodin, El Greco and Henry Moore. A print cabinet contains more than 2 000 prints, including those of Dürer, Rembrandt and various contemporary artists. Lectures, poetry readings, film shows and concerts are held regularly. The gallery is open from Tuesday to Sunday between 10h00 and 17h00. Groups of six or more visiting the gallery must book two weeks in advance.

Joubert Park itself, established in 1887 on 6,43 ha of vacant land, is the best known and oldest park in Johannesburg, and features a giant chess board, with pieces 1 m high, a greenhouse of tropical plants, a restaurant and fountains.

There's also an open-air art market that sells direct to the public.

The Union Limited

This is the name of a lovely old steam train, with vintage coaches dating back to 1912, that has been brought back into service to run steam safaris from Johannesburg to some of the most beautiful places in South Africa. Regular day tours, such as the Heidelberg Express and the Magalies Valley Steamer, take you out of Johannesburg into the highveld, while a more comprehensive, 15-day tour takes you all the way to the Victoria Falls. On the way, you will be served traditional cuisine in a vintage wooden interior dining car. There are organised photographic stops for you to take pictures.

The Union Limited also offers specialised rail tours for companies wishing to host mobile conferences or functions (for details see *Tours and excursions* under *Gauteng at a glance,* p. 171).

Hillbrow
Rising up above the metropolitan sprawl of Johannesburg is the tallest building in Africa, the 269-m JG Strijdom tower, on Hospital Hill. Known by residents as the Hillbrow Tower, it carries a revolving restaurant and souvenir shop near the top and dominates the densely populated flatland of Hillbrow. The suburb itself is cosmopolitan and crowded and has a large variety of retail outlets, restaurants, cinemas and nightclubs. Unfortunately, the area attracts many vagrants, drug addicts and dropouts.

Oriental Plaza
The aroma of spicy curries and exotic incense will lead you to this colourful world of some 280 Indian-owned shops and stalls, crammed with goods of all descriptions. Oriental fabrics, carpets, hand-carved goods, crockery and clothing are some of the items you can get here, but take time to haggle – you will invariably get a better price than the opening one.

After shopping, you can try a curry in one of the three restaurants, the Golden Peacock Curry Pavilion is particularly good, or get a snack at one of the many kiosks in the plaza.

Santarama Miniland
South Africa is featured in perfect miniature in this scale model of various buildings and landmarks – including Cape Town's Castle and Kimberley's Big Hole. The miniland, which is based on Holland's Madurodam, also features a replica of the *Drommedaris,* the ship that brought the first Dutch governor, Jan van Riebeeck, to the Cape in 1652.

Other attractions include cruises on a paddle-steamer, train rides, a restaurant and souvenir shop.

The Planetarium
See the southern skies in minute detail at this attractive planetarium, which changes its shows every six weeks. You can also buy star charts, telescopes, binoculars, astronomy books and posters.

Johannesburg Lion Park
See lions at close quarters, or hold a lion cub in this small lion reserve north of the city. Other animals in the park include zebra, impala, wildebeest and springbok. You can spend the day here as there are picnic and braai (barbecue) areas, a restaurant and a nice swimming pool. There's a special Pet's Corner for children.

Florence Bloom Bird Sanctuary

There are two hides in this 10-ha sanctuary, from which you can view some of the 200 species of bird which flock to the perimeters of two small dams. The reserve is the headquarters of the Wildlife Society, and features an environment centre with exhibition halls, an aquarium and a meditation room.

Johannesburg Zoological Gardens

More than 3 000 species of animals and birds (30 of which are on the endangered list) live at Johannesburg Zoo – next to Pretoria Zoo one of the most attractive of its kind in Africa. Highlights of a visit to the zoo are its white lions, a fascinating community of primates (chimpanzees, orang-outangs and gorillas), a "walk-in" aviary, a polar bear enclosure, and an animal farm for children.

A new attraction at the zoo is guided night tours, which enable you to meet wild animals face to face in the dark. The tours are held twice a week from 18h30. For more information and details of opening times, contact the zoo director, tel. (011) 6462000.

Also on the well-manicured lawns of the estate is the Museum of South African Rock Art, with its prehistoric rock engravings. A restaurant and kiosks serve meals and snacks. At the east end of the zoo's grounds is the South African National Museum of Military History, which has showcases of military hardware, uniforms, medals and paintings from the Anglo-Boer War and the two world wars. Nearby Zoo Lake is a haven of tranquillity in the midst of suburbia. Here you can hire a boat to row around the lake, relax on the grass and watch the ducks go by, or picnic under the willows that fringe the dam. Above the lake are a public swimming-pool, tennis courts, a tea garden and a restaurant.

To get to the Zoo and Zoo Lake from town, catch bus No. 79 from the corner of Kerk and Loveday streets.

▬ AROUND JOHANNESBURG

African tribal life

An authentic Zulu village called Phumangena Zulu Umuzi is the highlight of a visit to the excellent Aloe Ridge Game Reserve. The village is occupied by a Zulu community living as they have done for centuries. It was built with materials imported from Zululand, and portrays traditional Zulu crafts, customs and clothing as they existed in the days of the great Zulu king, Shaka. You can buy many of these age-old crafts – including pottery, beadwork and baskets – in the handicraft centre.

In Phumangena you can also watch a sangoma (witchdoctor) throw the bones, taste ethnic Zulu food, and sample home-brewed beer. To cap off an exciting cultural experience, you can stay overnight in the specially constructed beehive huts and enjoy a royal Zulu dinner as you watch tribal dancing.

The 1 500-ha Aloe Ridge Game Reserve is home to a variety of large and small mammals, including hippo, buffalo, eland, gemsbok, kudu, black wildebeest, nyala, waterbuck, blesbok and zebra. Birdlife is prolific, with some 230 resident species. Game drives are available in a 14-seater open safari vehicle. The Aloe Ridge Hotel offers luxury accommodation in a rural setting. For details contact PO Box 3040, Honeydew 2040, tel. (011) 9572070.

Not far from Phumangena is the Heia Safari Ranch, where the famed Mzumba African dancers play out ritual tribal legends to the beat of drums and the eerie ululations of handclapping women. These include a rain and python dance, a ritual sacrifice, and a Zulu war dance.

Transvaal Snake Park

Indian and Egyptian cobras, alligators, boa constrictors, rattlesnakes and other exotic species mix with a large variety of local species in this park, which has one of the largest reptile collections in South Africa. You can watch milking demonstrations, when venom is removed from some of the species, twice daily at 11h00 and 15h00. There's also a python-handling display on Sundays and public holidays every hour from 11h00 to 16h00.

Apart from the snakes, the park houses cotton-topped tamarins and Bolivian squirrel monkeys, both of which are endangered species. Other attractions are the Terraquarium (the first in the southern hemisphere), which houses the world's only venomous lizard, the Gila monster; a curio and gift shop selling African art and curios, and a restaurant. For more details tel. (011) 8053116.

Soweto

South Western Townships (Soweto) is the largest residential area in the country, and the fourth largest city on the African continent. Population estimates vary considerably, but there are believed to be at least two million people living in Soweto. In the apartheid years it was regarded as a dormitory town of Johannesburg, serving the labour needs of whites in the city.

Today Soweto exhibits an extraordinarily colourful mix of cultures, languages and religions. But it's not the place to roam the streets alone at night. The crime rate in Soweto is double that of New York City. The South African Police's Flying Squad gets more than 450 crime-related calls a week, and at least four people die violently in the city every day.

Poverty is rife, with 60 per cent of adults unemployed in Soweto. But western-style affluence has made its mark in the "Beverly Hills" section (also known as Millionaire's Row), where BMWs and Mercedes Benz's line the driveways of graceful mansions.

There are several tours available to Soweto, on which you can visit a shebeen (African pub), Nelson Mandela's mansion or the kraal of a local witchdoctor, where you can hear women singing traditional songs. Some tours stop at an institution for the handicapped, a crèche and even private homes. For tours of Soweto, see *Tours and excursions,* p. 171.

Suikerbosrand Nature Reserve

This 13 337-ha sanctuary of open grassland, wooded gorges and acacia woodland south of Johannesburg is a triumph for nature conservation, in that it accommodates a large variety of animals in their natural habitat, right on the doorstep of one of the most densely populated areas in South Africa. You can see cheetah, brown hyaena, black wildebeest, Burchell's zebra, eland, kudu, springbok, red hartebeest and other animals in the wild, as well as about 200 species of bird.

Attractions include a six-day trail (with six trail huts along the way), and shorter hiking trails of 4,5 km, 10 km and 17 km. There are two camping sites, Aventura Heidelbergkloof and Aventura Kareekloof and a 60-km game-viewing drive, picnic sites and braai (barbecue) facilities. For details contact Satour, see *Tourist information,* p. 172.

Vaal Dam

Locals and visitors flock to the tree-lined shores of this huge 300 sq km dam about two hours' drive south of Johannesburg. The dam in general, and Vaal Dam Nature Reserve in particular, are popular for water sports such as boating, fishing, water-skiing and swimming. The Jim Fouche holiday resort on the southern banks of the dam offers camping and caravan sites, picnic and braai spots, a swimming pool, tennis court, riding stables and a restaurant. For more details contact the Johannesburg Publicity Association, tel. (011) 3364961 or (011) 3376650.

Wonder Cave and Rhino Nature Reserve

Eight white rhino and about 20 other species of game roam around this 1 000-ha reserve at the foot of the Swartkop Mountains. Just 30-minutes' drive northwest of Johannesburg, the reserve is a lovely country getaway for beleaguered city slickers, and has some pleasant surprises. One is the secluded rest camp, which has three attractive thatched chalets for guests wanting to spend the night. Another is the restaurant, which offers barbecue packs for picnickers. There are game drives, walking trails (maximum eight people), and conference facilities, but you must book in advance. For information and bookings tel. (011) 9570106/9.

The Wonder Cave at Kromdraai was opened to the public in 1991, and offers some spectacular dripstone formations of stalagtites and stalagmites. The cave is 125 m long and 50 m wide. There's a restaurant near the cave where you can relax and enjoy the views of the Swartkop Mountains. For details of the nature reserve and cave, tel. (011) 9570106/9.

▮▮▮ PRETORIA

In October 70 000 jacaranda trees burst into bloom, lining the streets and covering the gardens of Pretoria in a parasol of rich mauve, which gives the city its alternative name – the "Jacaranda City".

Just a 45-minute drive from Johannesburg, Pretoria was founded in 1855 by

Monuments and museums

Voortrekker Monument This awesome monument was erected to commemorate the Great Trek of the 1830s, when a number of pioneering Afrikaners braved incalculable risks by taking their ox wagons into the wild hinterland.

The monument was built of granite quarried at a site in the Northern Transvaal, and was completed in 1949, although the foundation stone was laid 11 years earlier.

Intended to symbolise the courage, fortitude and indomitable spirit of the Voortrekkers, the monument is 40 m by 40 m at its base and stands 40 m high. The monument is surrounded by a circular laager of 64 ox wagons, and guarding three of its four corners are busts of Great Trek leaders Piet Retief, Andries Pretorius and Hendrik Potgieter.

At the entrance is Anton van Wouw's rivetting sculpture of a Voortrekker mother with her children.

A domed hall within the monument, the Hall of Heroes, is adorned by a 92-m-long frieze of 27 panels depicting various stages of the Great Trek. Another, lower, hall is the site of a granite cenotaph with the inscription "Ons vir jou, Suid Afrika" (we for you South Africa). At exactly noon on 16 December each year, the date commemorating the 1838 Battle of Blood River, when about 500 Afrikaners fought off an army of 10 000 Zulus, a ray of sunshine falls through a hole in the domed roof and illuminates this inscription.

A stairway of 260 steps leads from the lower hall to the roof, where you will get panoramic views of the whole of Pretoria and the Gauteng highveld. Near the monument is a museum, exhibiting models of the Great Trek, antiques, costumes and tapestries, a large amphitheatre and a relief map showing the main routes of the Voortrekkers across southern Africa.

The Police Museum For a spine-chilling encounter with some of the country's most notorious murderers, and graphic displays of their hideous crimes, you can stalk through this original museum in Compol Building at the corner of Volkstem Avenue and Pretorius Street.

Murder exhibits include those of the Boksburg Lake murderer Ronald Burch, poisoner Daisy de Melker and the feared Pangaman of Pretoria, who chopped up his victims. Political crimes such as espionage and general terrorist weapons such as handgrenades, petrol bombs and mines are also featured. Certainly one of Pretoria's most original museums, this one should not be missed, tel. (012) 211678.

National Cultural History and open-air museum You'll be impressed by the historic Cape Dutch furniture, coins, medals, silverware, glassware and the country's largest collection of rock art on display here. And if that's not enough, there's a 2 000-year-old Egyptian mummy lying in state in the archaeology room.

Pretoria Art Museum This museum houses parts of the Michaelis Collection of Flemish and Dutch paintings, and features works by some of South Africa's leading artists – Van Wouw, Pierneef and Frans Oerder. There's also an art library. Guided tours can be arranged. Contact the Pretoria Information Centre, tel. (012) 3137694.

Transvaal Museum of Natural History This museum houses the Austin Roberts Bird Hall, depicting the huge and diverse world of southern African birds. It also has showcases showing the early development of man. Robert Broom, the world- renowned archaeologist, did much of his pioneering work on Australopithecines here. Attractions include audio-visual presentations and a bookshop.

Marthinus Wessel Pretorius, who named it after his father, Andries Pretorius, the Voortrekker leader who played a pivotal role in the battle of Blood River (see p. 143).

With a population of just over half-a-million people, it is a bustling, busy city where modern skyscrapers stand cheek by jowl with mementos of last century's Great Trek, such as the Voortrekker Monument, Burger's Park (where tired trekkers used to rest), and the house of Paul Kruger, President of the South African Republic from 1883 to 1900.

But there's more to Pretoria that its historic buildings. The city is the headquarters of the country's defence force, home for dozens of foreign diplomatic missions, and a centre of culture and learning. The University of South Africa (Unisa) to the west of the city is the largest correspondence university in the world. If you're interested in culture, you will find the State Theatre and a number of museums and art galleries comparable to those of any major European city, and are well worth a visit.

If you enjoy shopping, there are numerous pedestrian malls giving easy access to large retail stores, and scores of smaller shops, where you can buy anything from African crafts to clothing.

Outside Pretoria, the Magaliesberg Mountains and Hartbeespoort Dam are principal attractions, and offer hiking trails, boating, swimming and a host of other outdoor pursuits.

In 1994, the world spotlight fell on Pretoria, when Nelson Mandela, the country's first democratically elected president, was inaugurated at the Union Buildings. The ceremony was attended by representatives from more than 100 countries.

For those who want to sample the wealth of museums, monuments, historical buildings and fine statues that date back to the days of the Great Trek, there's a recently established Culture Route (see p. 172), that takes you from one end of the city to the other. Another fine tour is the Jacaranda Route, which includes visits to the city's major parks. A new set of tours, "Alternative tours", has been organised mainly for foreign tourists who wish to visit homes in the black residential areas of Pretoria. The tourists may stay over with their hosts for a few days (for details of these and other routes, contact the Tourist Rendezvous Travel Centre, tel. (012) 3231222).

But Pretoria is more than an open archive: its restaurants compete with the best in the Western world, its zoo is the biggest of its kind in Africa; there are luxury hotels, cinemas, theatres, swimming pools and plenty of beautiful parks and gardens.

The Pretoria Zoo

This is undoubtedly one of the best zoos in the world, if not for its diversity of animals (there are more than 3 500 creatures living here), then for its beautiful layout. Among the 140 mammal species you'll find four large apes, a Malayan tapir, the rare South American maned wolf and a giant eland – the only one of its kind in captivity.

The park-like surroundings are also home to 320 species of bird. Night tours – with a braai (barbecue) afterwards – can be arranged for Wednesday and Friday nights.

An aquarium houses 300 freshwater and marine fish species and a number of amphibians and invertebrate species. A nearby Reptile Park features reptiles from all over the world.

The aerial cableway will give you a bird's-eye view of the wonderland of animals below as it swings you across the zoo.

There are informative, guided tours of the zoo and lessons in ecology and bird recognition, but be sure to book well in advance (contact Satour, see *Tourist information,* p. 172).

You can also watch the carnivores being fed in the mid-afternoon and the seals being fed mid-morning.

The zoo shop offers souvenirs, and refreshments are available at a restaurant and kiosks throughout the zoo. Handcrafts are on sale outside the zoo's grounds.

Union Buildings

Next to Table Mountain, the Union Buildings, site of President Mandela's inauguration in 1994, are probably South Africa's most famous landmark. Designed by Sir Herbert Baker in 1910 and completed in 1913, the red sandstone buildings peer proudly from their perch on Meintjies Kop above rolling terraces that descend towards the city of Pretoria.

This is a favourite picnic place among the locals, who come to stroll among the trees, watch their children flying kites or to stare at the monuments to South Africa's famous generals – Botha, Smuts and Hertzog. The Union Buildings is also the site of the Garden of Remembrance, the Delville Wood Memorial and the Pretoria War Memorial.

Kruger House

This house of the president of the South African Republic from 1883 to 1900 reveals the simplicity of the man's tastes in furniture, personal belongings and assorted memorabilia. The house was given to him in 1884 by his people, whom he used to greet from its wide verandah. Sometimes he used to lead the service at the Dutch Reformed church across the road.

Parks and nature reserves

Pretoria is a garden city with an abundance of parks, picnic areas, bird sanctuaries and glens where you can have a quiet day under the trees. Among these is the 11-ha Austin Roberts Bird Sanctuary, which protects about 170 species. There's a hide from which you can view the waterbirds attracted to a small dam.

The Fountains Valley Nature Reserve is a popular recreation area offering a camping site, picnic sites with fireplaces and a pool. There's also a 500-ha area inhabited by game species.

The Pretoria National Botanical Garden houses some 5 000 indigenous plant species. There are two-hour tours of these 77-ha gardens, a slide show and a visit to a nursery (for details contact Satour).

Wonderboom Nature Reserve is a superb picnic site with a nature trail, and a giant wild fig tree believed to be more than 1 000 years old. The tree is 23 m high, has a spread of 50 m and has 13 trunks growing from the same roots. Wonderboom is also the site of the ruins of one of four forts built to defend Pretoria after the Jameson Raid in 1896.

Van Riebeeck Nature Reserve supports 1 300 animals, including four rhino, Burchell's zebra, springbok, red hartebeest, steenbok, duiker and oribi. For anglers there's the large Rietvlei Dam, stocked with bass, barbel and yellowfish. For details of bus tours to the reserve, contact the Tourist Rendezvous Travel Centre, tel. (012) 3231222.

■■■ AROUND PRETORIA

The Magaliesberg

A fun-filled mix of outdoor pursuits – from hiking and hang-gliding to birdwatching and ballooning are available in and around this 125 km range of rugged mountains east of Pretoria – named after one Chief Mohale of the Po tribe in the 19th century.

Not to be missed is a trip on the longest cableway in South Africa, which takes you on a six-minute ride to the top of the Magaliesberg for scenic views over Hartbeespoort Dam and the highveld. At the top, you may see the rare Cape vulture, which breeds in these mountains. The cableway is open every day from 08h00 (weather permitting) and children under three ride free (for details, see *Tours and excursions,* p. 171).

To get there you can take the Magaliesberg Steamer, which leaves Johannesburg station regularly (see *Tours and excursions,* p. 171), or drive (it is less than an hour from Johannesburg or Pretoria).

Hartbeespoort Dam

One of the principal attractions in the region, this dam attracts thousands of visitors from all over Gauteng to the holiday resorts and picnic spots that have mushroomed around it.

Holiday homes, permanent homes, camping sites and caravan parks provide quick access to a zoo, snake park and a freshwater aquarium with seal shows daily.

The Magaliespark Holiday Resort is highly recommended for a weekend get-away, and offers 113 fully equipped African-style chalets, three restaurants, pleasure cruises on the dam (try a champagne cruise in the Yellow Ferry) and a variety of water sports, from boating and angling to swimming and waterskiing. There are also squash courts, a golf course, children's play park, a fully equipped sports centre, beauty salons, barbecue areas and nature trails.

The Hartbeespoort Dam Nature Reserve covers the 12 sq km surface of the dam, and a number of small conservation areas protecting a rich birdlife and a small quantity of game (kudu, bushbuck and Burchell's zebra).

Other attractions include horseriding trails run by Glenwood Stables, a 280-ha farm near the Hartbeespoort Dam. The stables provide an ideal refuge from the rat race and an opportunity to explore the Magaliesberg on horseback. For details see *Tours and excursions,* p. 171.

Tant Malie se Winkel, a fascinating country trading post that displays such intriguing items as a century-old cart and brandy still, serves traditional food (home-baked bread, pap and sauces), and sells curios and home crafts, including pottery, preserves and farm food. There are thatched braai (barbecue) spots at Tant Malie's if you want to linger for lunch.

Sterkfontein Caves

These caves south of Hartbeespoort Dam are the site of one of the great palaeontological finds of the 20th century – a skull one million years old, which its discoverer, palaeontologist Dr Robert Broom, named *Plesianthropus transvaalensis,* and nicknamed Mrs Ples. Later Dr Broom reclassified Mrs Ples and other members of her genus as *Australopithecus africanus.* There are conducted tours of the caves every half hour. Next door, in the Robert Broom Museum, you can see a cast of Mrs Ples' skull and a bust of her discoverer, as well as displays of prehistoric animals and birdlife.

De Wildt Cheetah Breeding Station

Established in 1971 to protect and propagate the declining cheetah population in South Africa, this 75-ha sanctuary has successfully bred cheetah, king cheetah and other animals in captivity. On offer are Saturday tours, for which advance booking is essential, a nature trail for schoolchildren, and the chance to see wild dogs, brown hyaenas, caracal and Cape vultures. Children under six are not allowed to enter the sanctuary. Contact Satour for details, see *Tourist information,* p. 172.

Pilanesberg National Park

Pilanesberg is an exceptionally wild part of Africa, where large herds of game run free, just a few minutes' drive from the clatter of Sun City's slot machines and roulette wheels. It is the site of Operation Genesis, the largest game translocation operation ever undertaken, when 5 962 animals were released onto the rugged green plains, with their koppies (hillocks) of volcanic rock.

The park, covering 550 sq km in South Africa's North-West Province (formerly Bophuthatswana), is the fourth largest national park south of the Limpopo, and offers superb game-watching opportunities. The animal population includes 16 species of antelope, elephant, black rhino and the third largest population of white rhino in the world. There are also hippo, buffalo, giraffe, zebra, warthog, cheetah, leopard and hyaena.

Tranquil waterhole hides enable you to witness one of South Africa's great avian pageants as some 300 bird species, with multicoloured plumages, come down to the waterside to drink.

There are two luxury hotel and time-share developments in the park: Kwa Maritane Lodge, which has excellent accommodation, beautiful hides and game drives in open vehicles; and the recently opened Bakubung – "the place of the hippo" – on the western edge of the reserve. The chalets and hotel at Bakubung, on a ridge overlooking the volcanic valleys of the Pilanesberg, also overlook the Hippo Pool – a waterhole attracting a variety of game. Other attractions are a swimming pool, open-air boma and game walks and drives. Both lodges are just a few minutes' drive away from Sun City. To book at Kwa Maritane, tel. (01465) 21820; to book at Bakubung, contact Stocks Marketing, tel. (01465) 21861/2.

The Lost City

The Lost City, built at a cost of R730 million, is probably one of the most innovative and unusual resort complexes in the world. Opened in December 1992, it creates the mystery and marvels of an age-old mythical civilisation on 25 ha of exotic jungle, just 30 km from Rustenburg.

At the heart of the Lost City is the Palace, a mind-boggling, luxury, 350-room hotel, surrounded by indigenous gardens and exotic forests, as well as rock and waterscapes.

The Palace's exterior architecture is dominated by soaring towers, decorated with elaborate carvings of wild animals. A dome, towering above the six-storey-high royal entrance chamber, and other ceilings in the hotel are hand painted in the manner of Michelangelo's work on the Sistine Chapel, and feature the unforgettable fauna and flora of the African jungle.

Inside, sculptured cranes with outstretched wings seem to fly from the tower walls; elephants stand proud at stairways and bridges, and a life-size bronze model of one of Africa's largest tuskers looms skyward at the end of the hotel's Elephant Walk.

Many of the Palace's luxurious rooms have private sitting rooms, elaborate bathrooms and custom-designed furniture.

Not far from the Palace is the Valley of the Ancients, where more than one and a half million plants, shrubs and trees have been planted. This is the location of an entertainment centre, carved out of rock, where visitors will find gaming (in the Hall of Treasures), restaurants and bars, and dazzling live entertainment in the Crazy Monkey.

Other attractions in the valley include five thrilling rides down water flumes, a wave pool supplying waves 1,8 m high, and a cruise called the Sacred River Ride.

Another attraction is an 18-hole championship golf course, the first in southern Africa to be modelled on an Arizona-style course. Finally, there's the Royal Ballroom, which provides convention and banqueting facilities for up to 1 200 people. For more details on the Lost City and for reservations, telephone (011) 7807800.

Sun City

Another opulent complex is Sun City which, together with the Lost City, is probably South Africa's most popular hotel resort. It consists of three hotels, the Cascades, Sun City Hotel and the Cabanas, which overlook a fabulous landscape of subtropical gardens, sparkling swimming pools and undulating hills.

A casino complex – one of the largest in the world outside the United States – offers blackjack, roulette, Punto Banco and craps, while the massive foyer of the Sun City Hotel jingles with the constant sounds of slot machines in action.

There are live shows nightly, featuring bands, cabaret artists and other performers. Sun City is a paradise for sports lovers. Attractions include Waterworld, which offers just about every imaginable water sport, 12 tennis courts, three squash courts, a bowling green, ten-pin bowling, and a beautiful golf course – the Gary Player Country Club.

This course hosts the Sun City Million Dollar Golf Challenge annually, featuring some of the world's best players. For bookings and more details about Sun City, telephone (011) 7807800, or write to Sun International, Central Reservations, PO Box 784487, Sandton 2146.

GAUTENG AND THE NORTH-WEST PROVINCE AT A GLANCE

When to go: *Johannesburg:* Spring and summer (September – March) are preferred by visitors. *Pretoria:* October and November, when the jacarandas put on their spectacular flower show.

Getting around: There's an excellent freeway system around Johannesburg, comprising the M1 north and south, and the M2 east and west, which are linked to the main routes north to Pretoria and south to the Free State. Although well-signposted ring roads provide quick access to suburban destinations, travelling in the suburbs can be confusing, so take a map with you.

Traffic congestion and parking difficulties, and an abundance of one-way streets in central Johannesburg can be irritating and confusing, so try and avoid driving around during the peak traffic hours (07h00-09h00 and 16h00-18h00).

Johannesburg and Pretoria are both served by an efficient network of highways linking them to all the country's major towns and cities.

Car hire: All the reputable international car-hire firms are represented in Johannesburg (consult the telephone directory).

Taxis: Taxis do not cruise round Johannesburg, but wait at ranks. Use your local telephone directory, or contact your hotel reception, the Johannesburg Publicity Association, or the Pretoria Tourist Rendezvous Travel Centre for recommended taxis (see *Tourist information*, p. 172).

Buses: For information on municipal bus services, telephone (011) 3364961 (Johannesburg) or (012) 3137694 (Pretoria).

Main attractions: *Johannesburg:* Gold Reef City and the gold mines. Day trips or longer to the Eastern Transvaal, Kruger National Park, Sun City, the Lost City and the Magaliesberg. African tribal villages and African arts and crafts.

Pretoria: Historical monuments, Pretoria Zoo, parks, gardens and nature reserves. Sun City, the Lost City. Pilanesberg National Park.

Tours and excursions: *Aircraft:* Safariplan offers wing safaris to three unique game regions in the lowveld. Write PO Box 4245, Randburg 2125 or telephone (011) 8861810. *Helicopter:* Regular pleasure flights over Johannesburg and Soweto take place from the Heliport, Gold Reef City on weekends and public holidays, telephone (011) 4961600. *Balloon:* Airtrack Adventures offers champagne flights north of Johannesburg (contact Satour).

Train: The Blue Train, one of the most luxurious trains in the world, travels between Pretoria, Johannesburg and Cape Town, offering luxurious comfort and five-star cuisine and amenities, including baths, showers, a lounge bar and a cocktail bar. The Johannesburg-Cape Town trip takes 26 hours. Book at the main station concourse, telephone (011) 7735878/9.

The Union Limited runs steam safaris from Johannesburg on a daily basis, as well as a 15-day tour to Victoria Falls. Contact Satour, tel. (011) 3338082, or Transnet Museum, PO Box 3753, Johannesburg 2000, tel. (011) 7739118.

Soweto: Contact Tours of Soweto, tel. (011) 9320000 or Jimmy's Face-to-Face Tours, tel. (011) 3316109. Buses usually leave from the Carlton Hotel (enquire at the concierge's desk).

Coach: There are regular sightseeing tours of Johannesburg and Gold Reef City. The Greyhound Citiliner and Translux, following the most scenic routes in

South Africa, link Johannesburg and Pretoria with game reserves and all the major centres (including Sun City and the Lost City). Contact Satour (see *Tourist information* below) for details.

Crocodile River Arts and Crafts Ramble: A wonderful tour of an arts and crafts community on the first Sunday of every month; and the Antique Route of Johannesburg, Pretoria and Roodepoort. Contact the Johannesburg Publicity Association, tel. (011) 3364961/3376650.

Pretoria: There are full-day coach tours of Pretoria, the Premier Diamond Mine, the Magaliesberg, Heia Safari Ranch, the De Wildt Cheetah Breeding Station and Sun City. Two driving tours of Pretoria, the Culture Route and the Jacaranda Route, are musts. For details contact the Pretoria Tourist Rondezvous Travel Centre (see below). For tours to Pretoria from Johannesburg, contact Pretoria Tours, tel. (012) 3301400.

Tourist information: *Johannesburg:* South African Tourism Board (Satour), Ground Floor, North State Building, corner Kruis and Market streets, Johannesburg 2001, tel. (011) 3338082. Johannesburg Publicity Association, corner Market and Kruis Streets, Johannesburg 2001, tel. (011) 3364961/3376650). *Pretoria:* Pretoria Tourist Rendezvous Travel Centre, Sammy Marks Complex, corner Prinsloo and Vermeulen streets, Pretoria 0001, tel. (012) 3231222. *The Lost City and Sun City:* Sun International, 3 Sandown Valley Crescent, Sandown 2031, Sandton, tel. (011) 7807800.

Shopping: *Johannesburg:* Major shopping complexes are the Carlton Centre (Commissioner Street); Sandton City (Sandton), Rosebank Mall and the Firs (Cradock Avenue, Rosebank); Eastgate Centre (Broadway Extension) and Hyde Park Corner (Jan Smuts Avenue). *Pretoria:* Boutiques, speciality shops, restaurants and trading stores in the centre of Pretoria include Sunnypark (with three cinemas), Sanlam Centre, Arcadia Centre, Standard Bank Centre and The Tramshed. Three curio shops are JR Ivy, Tribal Gifts and Curio King.

Festivals and annual events: *Johannesburg:* Rand Easter Show (March-April); Dogmor Dog of the Year Show (August); Carols by Candlelight (December). *Pretoria:* Cars in the Park Show (August), Pretoria Show (August), Pretoria Wine and Food Festival (September), German Beer Fest (September), Jacaranda Carnival (October).

ACCOMMODATION GUIDE
JOHANNESBURG
Carlton Hotel and Carlton Court***** Luxury at its best in the heart of Johannesburg's business and financial district; all-weather roof garden with pool; gym, hairdressing salon. 3 restaurants, 2 cocktail bars. 663 rooms (including suites with fax machines). Conference facilities for 1 200. PO Box 7709, Johannesburg 2000, tel. (011) 3318911.
Braamfontein Protea**** Within walking distance of air and rail terminals. Minutes from

town. Pool, fine-food restaurants; car hire on premises. 308 suites. Conference facilities for 300. PO Box 32278, Braamfontein 2017, tel. (011) 4035740.

Down Town Inn**** Comfortable, close to all amenities. 270 rooms. Conference facilities. 88 Plein Street, Johannesburg 2001, tel. (011) 281770.

Gold Reef City**** Luxury hotel in reconstructed gold-boom town. Several cocktail bars, à la carte and table d'hôte cuisine. 39 rooms, 6 suites. Conference facilities for 230. PO Box 61, Gold Reef City 2159, tel. (011) 4961626.

Rosebank Hotel**** Rosebank. Luxury in suburbs, 15 minutes from town. À la carte restaurants, swimming pool. 193 rooms. 19 suites. Conference facilities for 400. PO Box 52025, Saxonwold 2132, tel. (011) 7881820.

Sunnyside Park**** Stately suburban hotel set among trees and terraced lawns. Swimming pool, restaurants, hairdressing salon. 93 rooms, 3 suites. Conference facilities for 650. 2 York Road, Parktown 2193, tel. (011) 6437226.

Devonshire*** Luxury hotel on Braamfontein ridge. Restaurants. Ladies' bar. 64 rooms, 2 de luxe suites. Conference facilities. PO Box 31197, Braamfontein 2017, tel. (011) 3395611.

Holiday Inn Garden Court – Johannesburg*** Two separate hotels linked by common access. Indoor pool, health centre, hairdressing salon. Several restaurants, shops and bars. 672 rooms. Conference facilities for 900. PO Box 535, Johannesburg 2000, tel. (011) 297011.

Karos Johannesburger*** Comfortable. Central. 371 rooms. Conference facilities for 250. Swimming pool, bar with live entertainment, à la carte restaurant, carvery. PO Box 23566, Joubert Park 2044, tel. (011) 7253753.

AROUND JOHANNESBURG

Mount Grace Country House**** In the Magaliesberg, one hour from Johannesburg. Luxury hotel in indigenous and English country gardens. Swimming, tennis, bowling and birdwatching. 65 rooms, some with private patios overlooking valley. Conference facilities. PO Box 251, Magaliesberg 2805, tel. (0142) 771350.

Aloe Ridge*** Near Krugersdorp. Quick access to authentic Zulu village, Phumangena Zulu Umuzi, and Heia Safari Ranch. 69 en-suite rooms; 4 suites. Conference facilities for 125. PO Box 3040, Krugersdorp 2040, tel. (011) 9572070.

PRETORIA AND VICINITY

Burger's Park Hotel**** Luxury, central hotel offering 2 restaurants, 2 bars, swimming pool, sauna and hairdressing salon. Excellent service. 232 rooms, 6 suites. Conference facilities for 350. PO Box 2301, Pretoria 0001, tel. (012) 3227500.

Karos Manhattan*** Five minutes from city centre. Swimming pool, squash court, sauna. Carvery buffet and à la carte menu. 255 rooms; 4 suites. 247 Scheiding Street, Arcadia 0007, tel. (012) 3227635.

Valley Lodge On bank of Magalies River (one hour from Johannesburg and Pretoria). Cosy ambience and Oregon furniture. Walks and trails along river valley, swimming pool, tennis courts, golf centre. 55 rooms. Conference facilities. PO Box 13, Magaliesberg 2805, tel. (0142) 771301/5.

PILANESBERG AREA

Sun City Hotel***** At South Africa's top resort complex. Excellent service, access to casino, sporting amenities (including swimming pools and championship golf course) and Pilanesberg National Park. 300 en-suite rooms, 40 suites. Conference facilities, tel. (01465) 21000.

Kwa Maritane Lodge*** Luxury hotel and game lodge in Pilanesberg National Park close to Sun City. Beautiful hides, game drives. Excellent cuisine. Conference facilities. PO Box 39, Sun City 0316, tel. (01465) 21820.

The Palace (Lost City) 30 km from Rustenburg. One of the world's most unusual, luxurious hotels, set in elaborate, indigenous and exotic gardens. Huge entertainment complex, includes water features, gaming hall, wave pool and fabulous restaurants. 223 luxury rooms; 100 premier luxury rooms; 11 suites; 3 luxury suites; 1 royal suite. Many suites have private sitting rooms, custom-designed furniture. Conference facilities. Sun International, 3 Sandown Valley Crescent, Sandown 2031, Sandton, tel. (011) 7807444.

THE EASTERN AND NORTHERN TRANSVAAL

The interior plateau of South Africa stretches eastward from Gauteng – a seemingly endless plain of grassland and undulating hills that rises in the northeast to the mighty peaks of the Northern and Eastern Transvaal Drakensberg. These mountains, which form the eastern rim of southern Africa's Great Escarpment, plunge almost precipitously to a low-lying, subtropical savannah woodland known as the lowveld – the very heart of the old Africa of adventure and romance.

The transition between the plains and the lowveld is one of South Africa's most breathtaking vistas. In this region, described by the author H Rider Haggard as "the inspiration for King Solomon's Mines", massive ramparts of sandstone, sculpted through millenia by the action of wind and rain surge out of deep green valleys, traversed by some great rivers. These include the Crocodile, the Olifants and the Blyde, whose canyon ranks as one of the scenic wonders of Africa.

The first Europeans to brave the wilds of the Eastern Transvaal were Portuguese explorers and traders, who were followed, in the mid-1830s, by a hardy band of Afrikaans pioneers called the Voortrekkers.

But it was the discovery of gold in the 1870s that made a real impact on the region. Pick-and-shovel prospectors poured into the area, leading to the establishment of gold-mining settlements, where gold nuggets or alluvial deposits fell prey to the persistent swarms of panners and diggers.

Hunters, safari traders and adventurers joined the rush. Some died of malaria; others were killed by lions. None, however, managed to subdue the enchantment that makes the Eastern Transvaal one of the world's most beautiful places.

The lowveld offers plenty of opportunity for exploration and enjoyment, but the real drawcards of the region are South Africa's largest game park, the Kruger National Park, and several smaller, luxury game parks, protecting the richest concentration of game in the world. Luxury game lodges throughout Eastern and Northern Transvaal offer five-star accommodation, game drives and all the amenities of modern hotels.

Other major attractions are the country walks, beautiful lakes and dams, bird sanctuaries, huge tracts of forest, mountain passes that plummet to the lowveld, and old gold rush towns, such as Pilgrim's Rest, Sabie and Barberton, which serve as excellent starting points for the traveller's journey into the heart of South Africa's wild.

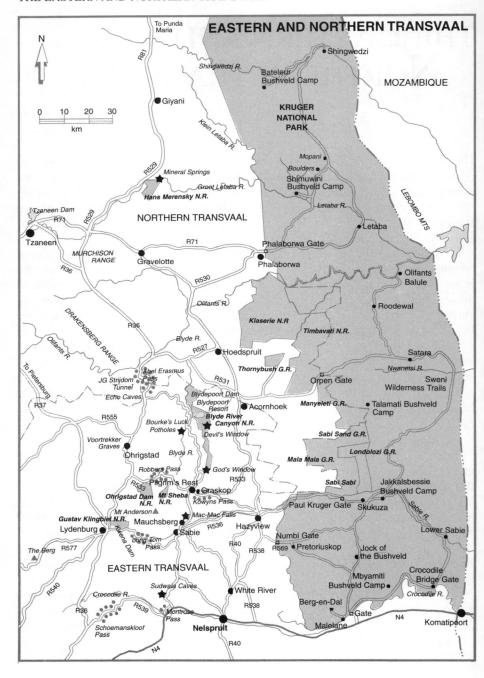

CLIMATE

The Eastern Transvaal's climate is subtropical, with hot summers and mild, dry winters. In summer the daytime average temperature is 30 °C, but on particularly hot days this can reach 40 °C, so take along some sun protection cream and a hat, especially if you're visiting the Kruger National Park. The summer nights average a warm 20 °C, so take light clothing for days and nights. While winter days are mild to warm, it cools down rapidly in the evening, sometimes to below 0 °C. Towards November, great banks of cumulus clouds gather over the region, unleashing torrential downpours that soak the land, filling up the rivers, dams and the Kruger Park's waterholes. The Northern Transvaal's summers are hot, but drier than the Eastern Transvaal, and the winters are mild.

WHAT TO SEE

■■■ EASTERN TRANSVAAL

The Kruger National Park

With a length of 350 km, from the Limpopo River in the north to the Crocodile River in the south, and a width of 50 km, from Phalaborwa in the west to the feet of the Lebombo Mountains in the east, the Kruger National Park is one of the world's most exciting natural sanctuaries.

The park was born on 26 March 1898, when the president of the South African Republic, Paul Kruger, signed a proclamation giving the go-ahead for a government game park in the Eastern Transvaal.

The wildlife

More than 250 000 mammals, representing 137 species, roam the reserve's tangled bushveld and sun-soaked savannah plains. They include the Big Five – lion, elephant, buffalo, hippopotamus and rhino; all the major southern African species of cats; all the larger southern African antelope; hyaenas, wild dogs, giraffe, zebra, kudu, wildebeest and a host of other smaller species. More than 120 000 impala live in the park, and there are 114 reptile species including 50 of snake. There are also 33 species of amphibian, and 49 fish species.

The diversity is not confined to animals. There are 507 species of bird, including ostrich, secretarybird, bateleur, buzzard, a variety of eagles and vultures, falcons, francolins, hornbills, rollers, loeries and korhaans.

In addition, there are some 300 species of tree in the park's five main botanical divisions, including mopane, marula, acacia and bushwillow, sycamore fig and flowering white pear.

The camps

The Kruger Park hosts about 3 000 people per day in 24 different rest camps (including four wilderness trail camps), all designed to be as unobtrusive as possible, and to project the essence of the African wild at its pristine best. The camps lie in the shade of trees in beautiful surroundings, some overlooking rivers such as the Sabie and Letaba, where you can watch hippo and crocodile. All are within easy range of waterholes, which attract a large variety of animals, particularly in winter. In spite of the size of some of the camps, they only occupy three per cent of the total area of the park.

The largest camp is Skukuza, a village-like complex, which is the administrative centre of the park, and is connected by air to Phalaborwa and Johannesburg. It has several shops, a post office, bank, restaurants and even a football field. There's also a doctor at Skukuza.

Four of the camps have swimming pools, and you'll find a wide variety of accommodation, ranging from large family cottages, to smaller, two- and three-bed huts. Most of the cottages are equipped with kitchen, bathroom, refrigerator and airconditioning. Communal cooking facilities are available for visitors in chalets without kitchens. Special accommodation for handicapped people is provided at nine of the rest camps. All rest camps have attractive caravan parks; there are also furnished tents at Letaba rest camp.

The major camps are airconditioned and have a laundromat and first-aid station, as well as a shop selling curios, food, liquor and a complete range of tourist needs. The Automobile Association of South Africa has emergency breakdown services and workshops at Skukuza, Satara, and Letaba rest camps.

The bushveld camps are less sophisticated and smaller than the main camps, but offer comfortable accommodation in family cottages.

An alternative is to book accommodation in a private camp. These camps are small and secluded, and may only be booked *en bloc* (the largest accommodates 19 people). Wherever you book, be sure to study a detailed map of the park and its camps, and to plot your journey accordingly.

Wilderness trails

If you have an adventurous spirit, you can join a wilderness trail, on which a game ranger escorts you on foot through the park. Groups spend the nights at a rustic base camp, where you eat round the camp fire and listen to stories of the African bush under the stars.

The private game reserves

A mecca for game-lovers in South Africa are the privately owned game reserves which flank the western boundary of the Kruger National Park. Apart from the luxury accommodation and pampering service they offer, most of these parks have highly trained game rangers to escort you on foot or in open-air vehicles on a daily basis.

Sabi Sand Private Nature Reserve

One of the largest of the private reserves is the Sabi Sand Nature Reserve, 500 km

---

TIPS FOR TRAVELLERS

When planning a visit to the Kruger National Park, there are some very important points to bear in mind: the park is full most of the time, so you must book ahead. You can book up to a year in advance. If the park is fully booked, reserve accommodation at one of several game lodges outside the park's entrance, such as Thornybush Game Lodge or Karos Lodge (see *Accommodation guide,* p. 191), but remember to book your day-visitor's entrance permit in advance – you won't be admitted without it (for details contact the National Parks Board, see *Tourist information,* p. 191).

There is an excellent, 2 000 km network of roads leading to viewsites throughout the park. Visitors may explore the park at leisure during the day, and experience the uniqueness of a picnic in the African bush (there are 12 picnic sites in the park).

Main roads are tarred, and smaller roads are gravelled. Two cardinal rules in the park are: stay in your car at all times, with the exception of designated picnic spots; and don't exceed the speed limit, which is between 40-50 km/h.

Petrol is available at the larger rest camps, and at many of the entrances.

The gates generally open at sunrise and close at sunset, but as these change throughout the year, check with the National Parks Board before you go (see *Tourist information,* p. 191).

The Kruger Park is in a malaria zone, so take anti-malaria tablets before you go.

For access to the park see *Getting around* under *Eastern Transvaal at a glance,* p. 190.

---

from Johannesburg, a network of professionally run game lodges offering access to all the big game of Africa.

Mala Mala

The best known of Sabi Sand's reserves is Mala Mala. Nestling in a tree-covered wilderness of 30 000 ha, Mala Mala has luxurious, thatched chalets, with double bathrooms and airconditioning. The spacious bush lodge accommodates about 50 people at a time, and includes a five-star, well-appointed complex called the Sable Lodge, which caters for groups of up to 16.

Ten rangers are allocated to look after their guest's needs. They offer, among other things, daily game-viewing drives to see black and white rhino, elephant, lion, cheetah, leopard, hippo, crocodile, buffalo, numerous antelope and fireside meals in a boma – a circular bush restaurant made of reeds.

Sabi Sabi

For a truly African flavour, there's little to beat this popular luxury reserve, about 480 km from Johannesburg. Sabi Sabi has 45 delightful two-bed chalets at its two camps, Bush Lodge and River Lodge. Here the game is as abundant as at Mala Mala, the food is excellent (venison is a speciality) and the service is outstanding.

Meal times are announced by the sound of a kudu horn and the beating of African drums. The rangers join you during your meals and often present slide shows or educational talks about the ways of the wild.

Shangaan women perform ritual tribal dances at night, then serve food to guests assembled in the boma. The atmosphere is relaxed and merry, and quite unlike anything you've experienced in the city.

Guests rise at dawn and prepare for an excursion into the bush in a safari vehicle directed by a ranger and tracker (who tries to pick up the spoor of lion, cheetah or leopard for the benefit of the guests). You may stop off at strategically positioned hides and watch game coming to the waterholes to drink. Guests return towards midday for refreshments and a rest, before setting out on another drive later in the day. A word of warning: the lodges are not fenced in, and it is unwise to wander around outside during the night.

Other camps in the Sabi Sand Nature Reserve are Londolozi (luxury chalets and rondavels); Inyati Game Lodge (luxury chalets); Kirkman's Camp (one- and two-bed cottages sharing a swimming pool and boma); Harry's Camp (seven double rooms with bathroom) and Trekker Trails (a bush camp for six).

Timbavati Private Nature Reserve
Another of the magnificent Eastern Transvaal reserves, Timbavati is famous for its white lions, which roam the reserve's 22 000 ha in the company of elephant, leopard, giraffe, hyaena, cheetah, white rhino, buffalo, blue wildebeest, zebra, kudu, waterbuck and impala. Be sure to take along a pair of binoculars – there are more than 240 species of bird here.

Like Mala Mala and Londolozi, Timbavati has a special appeal for foreigners and local tourists who enjoy personalised service.

On offer are morning and evening game-viewing drives in an open 4x4 with armed rangers, three-day hiking trails and escorted walking trails through the bush.

Nelspruit
Lying in the Crocodile River Valley, Nelspruit is a major stopover for travellers en route to the Kruger National Park, and offers good, comfortable hotels and fine restaurants. It is the second largest producer of citrus fruits in South Africa, and also grows an abundance of subtropical fruits such as mangoes, litchis, bananas, pawpaws and avocados, and nuts and tobacco.

A glorious botanical adventure awaits you in the 159-ha Lowveld Botanical Garden in Nelspruit, where bushveld trees, lawns, orchids and a profusion of lovely ferns, mosses and flowers abound. This garden, a branch of the National Botanical Gardens in Kirstenbosch, has 1 500 species of plant, including a cycad collection that is world famous. The garden is also home to a number of small mammals, and more than 245 species of bird. There are two attractive walks: the Falls, where the Crocodile River plummets into a narrow gorge, and the River

Walk, where you will see kiaat, combretum, marula and wild fig trees. For more information contact the curator of the garden at telephone (01311) 25531.

Recommended walks in and around Nelspruit are from the Trimpark in Piet Retief Street to the Botanical Gardens (5 km), and trails in the Kaapsehoop Nature Reserve, 40 km from Nelspruit (where there are overnight huts). For details contact the PRO, Nelspruit Town Council, tel. (01311) 599111.

At nearby White River, drop into Mama Tembu's Curios, an innovative and unusual craft village, which offers tribal dancing, traditional African theatre and a tea garden. For details see *African arts and crafts* under *Eastern Transvaal at a glance*, p. 190.

Makobulaan Nature Reserve

For a real piece of wilderness off the beaten track, the Makobulaan Nature Reserve, halfway between Lydenburg and Nelspruit, is highly recommended. Established in 1992, the reserve is a wonderland of mountain, valley and forest that affords spectacular views of the Drakensberg Escarpment.

Three trails pass through Makobulaan – the Uitsoek Trail, the two-day Houtbosloop Route (30 km) and the Bakkrans Route (11 km), which passes the scenic Bakkrans Waterfall. For a permit to walk one of the trails, contact the Director of the National Hiking Way Board, Private Bag X11201, Nelspruit 1200, tel. (01311) 52169.

Sudwala Caves

One of the really popular tourist attractions of South Africa, these gigantic underground caverns lie within a hill known as Mankelekele (crag on crag), whose abundance of aloes, wild pear and other flowering trees makes it a natural botanical garden of great beauty.

A magnificent dinosaur park, featuring life-size replicas of the bizarre creatures that once roamed southern Africa between 100 and 250 million years ago, is the highlight of the visit to the caves. On show are *Massospondylus*, a giant mammal-like reptile of the marshes, *Icthyostega* (the first fish to grow legs) and a mastodon, an early relative of the elephant.

Some 500 m of the caves are open to tourists, but they represent just a fraction of the huge subterranean complex that has not yet been fully explored. Within the caves a refreshing draught of air comes from some distant aperture not yet discovered.

Fascinating dripstone formations of stalagtites and stalagmites include the Screaming Monster. On the ceilings above the Screaming Monster are fossilised colonies of stromatolites – blue green algae, which are believed to be one of the earliest identifiable forms of life in southern Africa.

There are guided tours of the caves every half hour, and they last about one hour. A special six-hour tour of the caves – as far as the Crystal Room – is held on the first Saturday of every month. Book well in advance for this trail beyond the normal tourist route.

A five-minute drive away is the Sudwala Lodge, which has a swimming pool and an outdoor boma, where you can relax in convivial company and have a good meal. Also close by is Old Joe's Kaia, whose luxury log cabins, cosy rondavels or rooms offer the traditional warmth and hospitality of a typical lowveld home.

Lydenburg

This charming town, established by Voortrekkers moving in from the malaria-infested town of Ohrigstad in 1849, is the gateway to the lowveld and lies in a region of abundant water features, historic viewsites and scenic day drives.

A walk through the town should include a visit to the Lydenburg Museum in the Gustav Klingbiel Reserve, which has a fascinating display of African ceramic masks (replicas of the originals which date back to 500 BC), and a gallery of bearded Voortrekkers. The oldest school in the Transvaal, built by the Voortrekkers in 1851, is on the corner of Church and Kantoor streets. Also worth visiting are the NG Kerk (1894), the Voortrekker Church (1852), the Kruithuis (1890) and a variety of beautiful Victorian houses.

Several rivers and dams around Lydenburg offer excellent troutfishing or picnicking. They include the Dorps River in Lydenburg, the Kwena Dam, and the Du Plessis Dam on the De Kuilen Road. The beautiful, 244-m triple Lydenburg Waterfall should be on your itinerary if you're in the vicinity.

Set aside a morning for a drive to the Gustav Klingbiel Nature Reserve, where you can see a variety of game, birds, indigenous plants, as well as two archaeological sites – Iron Age ruins and trenches dug during the South African War. There are various hiking trails in the park: the three-day Sterkspruit Trail (33 km), from October to May; the 20 km Ribbok Trail and shorter nature walks. For more details of tourist attractions in Lydenburg contact the Tourist Bureau, Lydenburg Municipality, tel. (0135) 2121.

Scenic drives

The Eastern Transvaal has dozens of beautiful country drives, of which the most popular is the Summit Route, a drive that takes you from Lydenburg through the Long Tom Pass to Sabie, Graskop, the Blyde River Canyon Nature Reserve and the Abel Erasmus Pass, as far as the JG Strijdom Tunnel. Here you can turn around and head south back to Lydenburg, making short detours on the way to visit Echo Caves, Mount Sheba Nature Reserve and the Ohrigstad Dam.

This route incorporates the shorter 70-km Panorama Route from Graskop to the Blyde River Canyon and back via Pilgrim's Rest, and offers a variety of magnificent viewsites, waterfalls, gorges and tranquil picnic places along the way. Among the more spectacular stops are The Pinnacle and Driekop Gorge, the Lisbon Falls (a spectacular 95-m cascade tumbling into deep green pools), God's Window, with its breathtaking views across the lowveld to Mozambique, the Berlin Falls and Bourke's Luck Potholes.

Near God's Window is the Lowveld Panorama and Nature Reserve, which has some pleasant nature walks, and just past it is a turn-off which leads to swimming pools in the Blyde River. Further on is the turn-off to the Berlin Falls, which plummets 80 m into a deep pool. A pleasant spot for a picnic along the way is Watervalspruit, with its tree ferns and wild flowers.

Long Tom Pass

No trip to the Eastern Transvaal is complete without a journey through the Long Tom or Abel Erasmus passes, which take you to some of the finest mountain-top vantage points in the country.

The Long Tom Pass carries the tar road from Lydenburg over the crest of the Transvaal Drakensberg to Sabie, in a series of tortuous curves that seem to go on forever.

Don't rush this journey. The pass is 57 km long, and before it reaches its summit at 2 149 m above sea level, there are plenty of vantage points affording spectacular views of the green mountains tumbling to distant valleys. At the top of the pass are stunning views of the Sabie River's plateau and the lowveld in the distance.

This might be the time to reminisce about the early Voortrekkers who braved lions, malaria and a host of other dangers to build a wagon path in 1871 that would give their ox wagons free passage from Lydenburg to the lowveld and Mozambique. You can still see the old trail as it mounts four steep, successive summits known as the Devil's Knuckles, and the wagon tracks are visible in slate at a point in the pass known as the Staircase.

The pass was named after a 155 mm artillery gun used by the Boers to bombard the British during the South African War.

A sign marks the spot where Long Tom was once used, and craters where the shells fell so many years ago are still visible.

Abel Erasmus Pass

North of the Blyderivierspoort Resort the Abel Erasmus Pass takes you on a winding, 24-km-long journey to the lowveld, dropping 800 m as it does so. The Zederberg stage coaches used this pass on the journey to the lowveld, and you can still see the old track, which is clearly signposted. The pass includes the JG Strijdom Tunnel, which was opened in 1959 and named after a former South African prime minister. There are plenty of picnic spots and panoramic views of the Olifants River Valley and eastern lowveld.

Sabie

Born out of a gold boom that started in 1895, when the yellow metal was found on the farm Grootfontein, Sabie is a beautifully situated timber town, lying in a land of waterfalls and woods, forest-cloaked terraces of the Drakensberg and fern-lined streams.

The impetus for the town's timber industry was the need for pit props in the gold mines of the Eastern Transvaal and Witwatersrand. Today it is a centre for large-scale afforestation and sawmill enterprises. It has the biggest single tract of man-made forest in the country.

While you're in Sabie, its worth visiting the Cultural Historical Forestry Museum which houses some 373 exhibits, including petrified tree trunks, a talking tree and some antique working tools.

With the peaks of Mount Anderson and the Mauchsberg as a backdrop, the town is an important base for exploring the magnificent scenery of the Eastern Transvaal to the west of the escarpment.

Not only is Sabie near the junction roads leading to the major towns of the Eastern Transvaal, such as Pilgrim's Rest and White River, but it also offers some delightful day trips that take in no less than five waterfalls (Sabie Falls, which is just a stroll from the centre of town, Bridal Veil Falls, Lone Creek Falls, Horseshoe Falls and Mac-Mac Falls).

Mac-Mac Falls, just off the road on the way to Graskop, are spectacular twin cascades that plummet 56 m into a ravine. They used to be one waterfall, but the 1 000 or so early gold miners living in the area tried to divert the river's flow by blasting it. Instead of changing the river's course, they split it in two. A short way downstream are the lovely Mac-Mac Pools, where there are picnic sites, braai (barbecue) areas and access to the clear mountain waters.

A short drive from Sabie, on the road to Mount Anderson, there are roadside shops specialising in home crafts and curios.

Walks near Sabie

There are several scenic walks in and around Sabie, offering quiet picnic spots, panoramic views and tranquillity in a pure mountain environment. They include the Fanie Botha Hiking Trail and the Loerie Trail, both of which start from the Ceylon Forest Station on the way to Bridal Veil Falls (for details see *Tours and excursions*, p. 190).

Blyde River Canyon Nature Reserve

The beautiful Blyderivierspoort Nature Reserve is overlooked by the triple granite peaks known as the Three Rondavels, and the table-topped summit of Mariepskop, once the battleground of warring Swazi, Pedi and Pulana tribesmen. Waterfalls and cascades plunge down vertical rock faces to feed the Blyde River which cuts a 25-km-long path through the canyon below.

At its eastern end, the Blyde River runs into the Blydepoort Dam, a huge expanse of water held back by a 72-m-high wall.

The reserve offers numerous walks and trails that lead through creeper-clad undergrowth and forests of yellowwoods, black ironwood, proteas and heaths, to mountain-top vantage points swathed in mist. Particularly recommended is the Yellowwood Trail, a two-day circular hike from Bourke's Luck Potholes. Shorter walks take you around the Blydepoort resort and Swadini's visitor centre.

Animals you may encounter on the longer trails include chacma baboons, vervet and samango monkeys, reedbuck and klipspringers. There are leopards in the canyon, but you're unlikely to come near one. Also shy and furtive are the nocturnal servals, civets, caracals and genets found in the reserve. The 227 species of bird include a breeding colony of the rare bald ibis.

Recommended viewsites in the canyon are Lowveld Lookout, Wonder View and World's End, which are easily accessible from the main tarmac road (the R532).

The two resorts within the reserve are Aventura Swadini, on the northern side of the river, and Aventura Blydepoort on the southwestern side, which offer fully equipped bungalows in a small village setting.

Aventura Blydepoort has an à la carte restaurant, supermarket, library, petrol station and airstrip.

The Swadini Reptile Park near the Blydepoort resort is worth a visit.

Bourke's Luck Potholes

Within the Blyde River Canyon Nature Reserve, near the confluence of the Blyde and Treur Rivers, are a series of spectacular formations in the rock, known as Bourke's Luck Potholes.

Small grains of sand, rocks and pebbles, spun round like clothes in a tumble dryer for thousands of years, have eroded holes in the bedrock to create these fantastic hollows. Although they began as mere depressions in the rock surface, they now range between two and six metres in depth.

The potholes were named after an early prospector, Thomas Bourke, who correctly predicted that there was gold in the area, but never found any. His farm was called Bourke's Luck.

A visitors' centre here provides a fascinating insight into the history of the area, and the physical process that formed these potholes.

Echo Caves

These caves, in dolomite rock at the head of the Molapong Valley, get their name from the echo created when you tap the stalagtites and stalagmites within the caverns.

Artefacts found in the caves show that they were inhabited by humans during the Middle and Later Stone Age. The Bushmen (San) have left their mark with several rock paintings in some of the shelters.

There are two entrances, one of which is open to the public and has a tea room and curio shop. The other entrance on the southwestern side is known as Cannibal Cave, and leads down to a network of passages that eventually link up with the first cave. The largest chamber within the caves is 100 m long and 49 m high.

There are regular guided tours of the caves. Added attractions are an open-air museum and art gallery on the way to the caves.

Pilgrim's Rest

A reclusive gold prospector called Alec Patterson – known to his friends as Wheelbarrow Alec, because he carted his possessions round in a wheelbarrow – sparked off a gold rush in 1873 when he found gold in a small tributary of the Blyde River.

Hordes of prospectors converged on the area, set up their tents and huts around the river, and called the place Pilgrim's Rest. The name came from their belief that, after years of disappointment in their search for gold, they had finally found wealth – and the opportunity to rest.

The river yielded rich alluvial deposits, including the Reward Nugget, weighing over 6 kg. In 1875, 200 000 pounds worth of gold was brought out.

Pilgrim's Rest flourished as a busy, prosperous frontier town, steeped in the eccentricity of the gold diggers who came there, accompanied by a retinue of bankers, shopkeepers, hoteliers and even a journalist.

Eventually – in 1971 – after more than 20 million pounds worth of gold had been taken out by the Transvaal Gold Exploration Company, the deposits dried up, and Pilgrim's Rest faced becoming a ghost town. Fortunately, however, the then Transvaal provincial authorities bought the whole town and turned it into a living national monument.

You can now take a step back into the heady days of the gold rush by visiting the old wattle-and-daub cottages of the miners, the Miner's House, the old Masonic Church, the premises of the Pilgrim's and Sabie News and the old Bank House.

The Royal Hotel offers accommodation of a different kind: brass bedsteads, as used a century ago, quilted covers and other period furniture grace the old rooms; and the pub is fitted out with furniture imported from Lourenço Marques (now Maputo) in 1893.

Guided tours of the village take in the Diggings Museum and a mine manager's office.

Mount Sheba Nature Reserve

More than 1 000 plant species, including 100 different species of tree such as yellowwood, white stinkwood, Cape chestnut, ironwood and mountain cedar, flourish in this beautiful 1 500-ha reserve on the slopes of Mount Sheba – one of the few remaining pockets of indigenous forest left in the Eastern Transvaal.

The Mount Sheba Hotel offers luxury suites and time-share cottages, and the proprietors will recommend nature walks where you may see red duiker, bushbuck, samango monkeys and a variety of birds. Other facilities include tennis, squash, trout fishing and mountain bike rides.

Barberton

You may not strike gold in Barberton, but you'll certainly get the feeling of what life was like in the heady days of the gold rush. With attractions like the Fortuna Mine Trail, the Gold Nugget Hiking Trail, the relatively new Pioneer Trail, and a visit to creeks with names such as Eureka, Sheba and El Dorado, there's a pervasive atmosphere of gold dust in the air.

Nestling on the slopes of the Makohonjwa Mountains, Barberton is known as the Gem of the Lowveld. Once the home of Sir Percy Fitzpatrick, author of the best-selling book, *Jock of the Bushveld,* its reputation rests on forestry and the discovery of gold. The yellow metal was found here in 1883 by a man known as "French Bob", and the discovery sparked off a stampede of hopeful prospectors to the area, including Graham, Fred and Harry Barber, after whom the town is named.

Relics of the early mining days are on view in the Barberton Museum. The Belhaven House Museum is a grand old turn-of-the-century building worth a visit.

Other attractions include the Fortuna Mine Trail, a 2-km walk which takes you through an old mine tunnel; the Gold Nugget Hiking Trail, a three-day, 44-km hike; a 20,36-km aerial cableway linking Barberton to the Havelock Mine in Swaziland and a statue of Fitzpatrick's dog, Jock.

There are other interesting walks and hiking trails around Barberton, and two nature reserves, the Barberton Nature Reserve and the Songimvelo Nature Reserve. The Barberton Publicity Bureau will supply details of walks in the area (see *Tourist information,* p. 191).

■■■ NORTHERN TRANSVAAL

The N2 highway north of Pretoria is known as the Great North Road, and bypasses such country towns as Warmbaths, Nylstroom, Potgietersrus and Pietersburg, where an arterial road (the R71) leads to one of the most picturesque parts of the northeastern Transvaal – the Tzaneen and Magoebaskloof area.

Further north, between Pietersburg and Messina, there are three nature reserves worth visiting: the Ben Lavin, Honnet and Messina nature reserves.

Tzaneen

Timber forests, tea plantations and farmlands of subtropical fruits surround the Northern Transvaal town of Tzaneen, one-time headquarters of an anti-malaria campaign that virtually eradicated the disease in the 1930s. Today the town provides ready access to the Kruger National Park and the scenic treasures of the Drakensberg escarpment.

There are two hotels, one in town and one outside, and two caravan and camping sites. Colourful roadside stalls offer a tantalising array of subtropical fruits and plants in season.

Magoebaskloof

The evocative, tranquil names of hillside farms describe Magoebaskloof better than any formal prose can – Whispering Winds, Cloudlands, Clear Waters and Grey Mists. But still, they don't do justice to the luxuriant, subtropical beauty of one of the finest country drives in South Africa. The drive starts just west of Tzaneen, and takes you on a magical trip through the lush green valleys, forests, waterfalls and wild flowers of the Magoebaskloof.

The area is named after Makgoba, the late-19th century chief of the Tlou tribe, who, with 500 followers, fled to these forests to evade a band of white tax collectors. Eventually however, the lush subtropical camouflage of Makgoba's refuge in the highlands was penetrated by an impi of Swazi warriors, who caught and beheaded him.

The drive up Magoebaskloof gives you access to tall forests of pine and tranquil lakes, and takes you past private farms, which explode into colour in spring with the flowering of azalea and cherry trees.

There's a beautiful picnic spot in the Magoebaskloof at Debegeni ("place of the big pot"), named from the pool made by the Debegeni Falls. Attractions here include a swimming pool, cascade and natural slide. Further east is the Tzaneen Dam and Nature Reserve, home to about 150 bird species.

At the top of Magoebaskloof there is an 11,5-km drive along the edge of the escarpment that takes you to the Woodbush Forestry Station through a countryside of forests and flowers. If you continue on this road you'll get to Ebenezer Dam, a really tranquil hideaway where you can picnic and relax in natural surroundings.

The proper way to see the Magoebaskloof, however, is on foot. Two trails, the Grootbosch (50 km) and Dokolewa (36 km), offer three days of hiking through the De Hoek and Woodbush State Forests. There are overnight huts, but you must bring your own food and sleeping bags. For details of these and other hikes, contact the Regional Director of the Northern Transvaal Forest Region, Louis Trichardt, tel. (01315) 41051.

Modjadji – Land of the Rain Queen

Northeast of Tzaneen, beyond the Duiwelskloof Valley, is the land of the Rain Queen, Modjadji, site of a nature reserve of the same name. Legend has it that a princess Modjadji fled here from Zimbabwe in the 16th century with a secret formula for making rain. The name Modjadji has been handed down through a female lineage, and a 20th century rainmaker lives in seclusion in a forest of extraordinary cycads (*Encephalartos transvenosus*), a species said to be about 50 to 60 million years old. The Modjadji Nature Reserve protects several thousand of these cycads, and picnic and braai (barbecue) facilities have been provided for visitors on the top of the reserve's hill. There's also a curio shop, a kiosk and an information centre, where you can get directions for nature trails in the area.

The Ben Lavin Nature Reserve

Just south of the Soutpansberg, and 420 km north of Johannesburg, this 2 500-ha reserve was donated to the Wildlife Society of Southern Africa so that people could get close to nature. To fulfill this ideal, the society has laid out four marked walking trails, varying from 3 to 8 km, and established a 40 km network of game-viewing drives.

There's a wide cross-section of animals here – from the African rock python to blue wildebeest, tsessebe, giraffe, Burchell's zebra, nyala, eland, waterbuck, impala and sable. Smaller animals include dassies, banded and dwarf mongooses, bushbuck and reedbuck. There are also more than 250 species of bird.

Accommodation includes two fully-equipped, four-bed lodges with bathrooms; five-bed huts and large tents, which you can hire at a nominal fee. A secluded bush camp 6 km from the main camp has two rustic huts, a kitchen and ablution facilities. There's also a camping site with ablution facilities, in the vicinity of which you may see vervet monkeys.

The reserve is open from 06h00 to 19h00. For more details, contact Satour, see *Tourist information,* p. 191.

Honnet Nature Reserve

This 2 200-ha reserve on the northern slopes of the Soutpansberg is near the Aventura Tshipise resort, where there's a hotel and self-catering accommodation in 102 rondavels. The reserve offers hiking and nature trails where you can spot such game as giraffe, sable, tsessebe, blue wildebeest and Burchell's zebra. It's very hot here in summer, and precautions should be taken against malaria and bilharzia.

Not far from the Honnet Reserve is Greater Kuduland Safaris, a private reserve offering luxury accommodation with all the amenities, and two bush camps. Attractions here are guided game trails, game-viewing drives, swimming and canoeing. The large wildlife population includes cheetah, leopard, blue wildebeest, gemsbok, eland, kudu and impala (for more details contact the Tourist Rendezvous Travel Centre in Pretoria, tel. (012) 3231222).

Messina Nature Reserve

If you're heading up to Beit Bridge and Zimbabwe, stop first and visit this beautiful reserve 6 km south of Messina.

The 5 000-ha reserve is a natural sanctuary to about 12 000 baobab trees, about 350 other species of tree and shrub and about 143 species of bird. It is also the birthplace of the world's oldest rock formations, the Sand River Gneiss, which date back about 3 800 million years. There's an attractive circular drive that brings you into touching distance of the grand, patriarchal baobabs, and an array of small and large mammals, including giraffe, blue wildebeest, sable antelope, grysbok, kudu and African wild cat. For more details, contact the Department of Nature and Environmental Conservation in Pietersburg, tel. (01521) 2959300.

THE EASTERN AND NORTHERN TRANSVAAL AT A GLANCE

When to go: Winter, the dry season between May and September, is the best time to see animals in the game parks of the Northern and Eastern Transvaal, because they tend to congregate at waterholes in greater numbers at this time. However, although you can see them more easily from the road because the vegetation is sparse, the countryside tends to be brown, dusty and drab. Summer, by contrast, offers less game-viewing opportunities, but the rains revitalise the bushveld, bringing luxuriant mantles of green to the grasslands and trees.

Getting around: *Air:* There are regular scheduled flights from Johannesburg to Nelspruit, Phalaborwa and the Kruger National Park (some will take you there and back the same day) as well as flights to Pietersburg and Tzaneen. Comair offers flights to several private game parks in the lowveld, and group flights to Kruger Park from Durban. Contact Satour in Pietersburg or Johannesburg for details (see *Tourist information*, p. 191). *Road:* Excellent tarred roads connect Johannesburg with the towns of the lowveld, the Kruger Park and the Northern Transvaal. There are Avis cars for hire at Skukuza and Phalaborwa. All access roads to Kruger Park's eight entrance gates are tarred, while tourist roads in the park are tarred or good gravel.

Main attractions: Wildlife and game reserves. Scenic drives, particularly along the Drakensberg Escarpment (the Summit and Panorama routes) and in the Magoebaskloof. Waterfalls, lakes, rivers and dams. Historic gold prospecting towns. Swimming, boating and trout fishing. Walks and trails. Game drives, bird-watching and photography in private reserves.

African arts and crafts: *Kruger National Park:* Many of the larger camps, such as Skukuza, offer African crafts or curios for sale. *Nelspruit:* Tarentaal Trading Post, corner Kaapsehoop and Pretoria Road, Nelspruit, tel. (01311) 44241. *White River:* Mama Tembu's Curios, write PO Box 1700, White River 1240 or tel. (01311) 33562.

Tours and excursions: *Air:* Safariplan offers wing safaris from Johannesburg to three unique game regions in the lowveld. Write PO Box 4245, Randburg 2125, or tel. (011) 8861810. *Road:* Major tour operators offer luxury coach tours or minibus safaris of the Eastern Transvaal from Johannesburg and Pretoria. Springbok Atlas Safaris offers three to 17-day tours from Johannesburg covering scenic highlights of the Eastern Transvaal and the Kruger National Park (one tour extends as far as Durban). Swann Travel Promotions offers tours of the Northern and Eastern Transvaal (including the Kruger National Park) in luxury minibuses, leaving from Johannesburg, Germiston and Pretoria. For details of these and other tours, contact Satour (see *Tourist information*, p. 191).

Sabie: Sabie Camper Hire hires out fully-equipped explorer motor homes for touring the Eastern Transvaal. Write to PO Box 575, Sabie 1260 or tel. (01315) 43319.

Nelspruit: For luxury minibus tours of the Eastern Transvaal and other regions, contact Lawson's Tours, PO Box 507, Nelspruit 1200, tel. (01311) 552417 or Lowveld Tours (01311) 25134.

Walks and trails: Numerous walks and trails in the area include the five-day, 79-km Fanie Botha Hiking Trail (you can choose a shorter option), the Blyderivierspoort Hiking Trail from God's Window (65 km), Tzaneen's beautiful Rooikat Trail (11 km), and the Loerie Trail (15,5 km) near Sabie. Satour, or the National Parks Board (see *Tourist information* below) will supply details of these and other lovely walks in the region.

Festivals and annual events: Lydenburg: Easter Craft Fair (April); Lydenburg Show (April/May); Nelspruit: Lowveld Agricultural Show (August); Lowveld Lion Festival (biennial); Sabie: Forest Fair (every second year, April-May); Tzaneen: Agricultural and Industrial Show (August); Harvest Festival (September); Haenertsburg: Cherry Blossom and Azalea Festival (springtime).

Tourist information: South African Tourism Board (Satour), Ground Floor, North State Building, corner Kruis and Market streets, Johannesburg 2001, tel. (011) 3338082. Johannesburg Publicity Association, corner Market and Kruis streets, Johannesburg 2001, tel. (011) 3364961/3376650. Satour – Eastern and Northern Transvaal: corner Vorster and Landdros Mare streets, PO Box 2184, Pietersburg 0700, tel. (0152) 3025. National Parks Board, PO Box 787, Pretoria 0001, tel. (012) 3431991, or National Parks Board, PO Box 7400, Roggebaai 8012, tel. (021) 222810. Waterval Boven and Waterval Onder: contact the Town Council, Waterval Boven 1195, tel. (01325) 70058. Pilgrim's Rest: contact the Pilgrim's Rest Nature Conservation Office, tel. (01315) 81215. Barberton Publicity Bureau, PO Box 33, Barberton 1300, tel. (01314) 22121.

ACCOMMODATION GUIDE
EASTERN TRANSVAAL

Karos Lodge**** Hotel, time-share resort 100 m from Kruger Gate. 96 en-suite bedrooms. Game drives, swimming pool, tennis, mini-golf, lapa, excellent cuisine; PO Box 54, Skukuza 1350, tel. (01311) 65671 or (011) 6438052.

Malelane Sun Lodge**** On Crocodile River near Kruger Park. Luxury resort hotel. Game viewing, swimming pool, golf course. 100 rooms, 2 suites. Conference facilities for 150. PO Box 392, Malelane 1320, tel. (01313) 30331.

Mount Sheba Hotel**** West of Pilgrim's Rest. Spectacular forest setting and mountain scenery. Walks through indigenous yellowwood forests. 25 rooms. Conference facilities. PO Box 100, Pilgrim's Rest 1290, tel. (01315) 81241.

Casa do Sol*** Heart of Sabie Valley. Mediterranean atmosphere, with spacious villas, casas and suites. Cordoba tiled roofs. 500-ha game reserve. Magnificent gardens, walking trails. Conference facilities. Central reservations: PO Box 52890, Saxonwold 2132, tel. (011) 8802000.

Malaga Hotel*** In Elands Valley near Waterval Onder. Spanish-style hotel with panoramic country views. Floodlit tennis court, swimming pool, health centre, trout fishing, horseriding. 52 en-suite bedrooms. 2 suites. Conference facilities. PO Box 136 Waterval Boven, 1195, tel. (013262) 431 or (011) 8804032.

Ngwane Valley Inn*** Near Kruger Park. Comfortable, friendly, well-appointed. 42 en-suite rooms, 1 suite. Conference facilities. PO Box 162, Nelspruit 1200, tel. (013164) 5213.

Sabi River Sun*** Southern Sun resort near Kruger Park. Luxury hotel in subtropical sur-roundings. Hippo pool, 18-hole golf course. 60 en-suite rooms. Conference facilities. PO Box 13, Hazyview 1242, tel. (01317) 67311.

Hotel The Winkler*** Between White River and Hazyview. Unique architecture in beauti-ful setting close to Blyde River Canyon. 57 refurbished, spacious bedrooms. Conference facilities. Table d'hôte and à la carte cuisine. PO Box 12, White River 1240, tel. (01311) 32317.

Bongani Mountain Lodge In Mthethomusha Game Reserve (near southern Kruger Park). 20 chalets, 9 suites with double bathrooms. Game drives, swimming pool, curio shop, bush boma. PO Box 782553, Sandton 2146, tel. (011) 4823500.

Exeter Safaris Luxurious private game lodge in Sabi-Sand Game Reserve. 6 rondavels with en-suite bathrooms, accommodating 12 people maximum. Swimming pool, game-viewing, dinner around the campfire. PO Box 2060, Nelspruit 1200, tel. (01311) 27572.

Ngala Game Reserve Private reserve in Kruger National Park. Swimming pool, walking trails, game drives. 20 luxurious thatched chalets under trees. Conference facilities. PO Box 1211, Sunninghill 2157, tel. (011) 8038421.

Old Joe's Kaia Schoemanskloof Valley. Cosy log cabins in subtropical, country surround-ings. Swimming pool, birdwatching and nature trails. 13 rooms. Conference facilities. PO Box 108, Schagen 1207, tel. (01311) 63045/6.

Tanda Tula Timbavati, west of Kruger Park. Lodge and 8 exclusive, thatched rondavels in the bush, each with en-suite bathroom. Conference facilities. PO Box 32, Constantia 7848, tel. (021) 7946500.

Thornybush Game Lodge Bordering Timbavati, near Orpen Gate. 16 luxury, twin-bedded thatched rooms. Excellent cuisine. Game drives and walks. PO Box 798, Northlands 2116, tel. (011) 8837918/9.

NORTHERN TRANSVAAL

The Coach House***** Near Tzaneen. South Africa's best country hotel four years in succession. Exclusive, excellent service, five-star cuisine. Mountain and forest environ-ment. 38 rooms; 3 suites. Conference facilities. PO Box 544, Tzaneen 0850, tel. (0152) 3073641.

Magoebaskloof Hotel*** Family haven in forest surroundings between Tzaneen and Haenertsburg. Top class service and cuisine. Trout and black bass fishing, boating, walk-ing. 58 en-suite rooms. Conference facilities. PO Magoebaskloof 0731, tel. (015276) 4276.

Mabula Bush Lodge Beautiful private reserve, two hours from Johannesburg. Home of the Big Five. 41 twin-bedded, en-suite chalets. Swimming pool, tennis courts, game drives, walking trails, horse trails. Private Bag X22, Bryanston 2021, tel. (011) 4634217.

A-Z SUMMARY OF USEFUL HINTS AND PRACTICAL INFORMATION

Accommodation: There is an abundance of top-class hotels, motels, game lodges, country inns, mountain holiday resorts, guesthouses, private accommodation and camping and caravan sites throughout the country. The South African Tourism Board (Satour) produces an excellent guide to the options available in a publication called *South Africa – where to stay,* available at 12 Satour offices nationwide (see *Tourist information* in the *At a glance* sections of each chapter for Satour addresses and telephone numbers).

Hotels are graded by the South African Hotel Board, according to the quality of accommodation and amenities offered. Top of the range (and usually most expensive) is five star, while bottom of the range is one star.

Airports: South Africa has three international airports, serviced by some of the world's major airlines: Johannesburg International Airport, 30 km from Johannesburg and 60 km from Pretoria, the country's principal airport; Durban International Airport and Cape Town International Airport. There are domestic flights daily between Johannesburg and Durban, Cape Town, Bloemfontein, Kimberley, East London, Port Elizabeth, Upington and George.

There's coach transport to Johannesburg's main rail terminal every half hour between 06h15 and 23h00, and a reciprocal service from town from 05h30 to 22h00. There's also a coach service to Pretoria. Alternatively, you can hire a car or taxi from the airport. At Johannesburg International you'll find a 24-hour currency exchange service, duty-free shops, banks, cocktail bars, restaurants and a Holiday Inn, five minutes' drive from the airport.

Camping and caravanning: South Africa's wide open spaces and magnificent scenery have contributed to the popularity of camping and caravanning. More than 650 caravan parks offer clean, secure, well-kept surroundings, with facilities ranging from excellent to adequate. Most parks offer hot and cold showers, laundry and ironing facilities, ablution blocks and braai (barbecue) areas. Others, which also have hutted accommodation, offer restaurants, shops and swimming pools. Many parks, especially on the coast, are fully booked in December and January, so try to book in advance. You can rent a caravan and a car to tow it (contact the SA Vehicle Rental Association, see below), but the caravan will have to be returned to the point of hiring.

Car hire: Many international and local car-hire firms are represented at the larger airports, major cities and some game reserves in South Africa. Firms include reputable names such as Avis, Budget and Imperial (incorporating Hertz). You can hire anything from a campmobile, fully equipped with kitchen, stove, fridge, cooking utensils and linen, to a four-wheel drive vehicle. A wide range of sedans (mainly Japanese and German) is available, and rentals vary from about R83 a day for a 1300 cc sedan to about R300 a day for a large, luxury vehicle. Charges per kilometre travelled are added. A minimum age is usually stipulated for driving a hire car – either 23 or 25 – and a cash deposit may be required.

Details of rental facilities can be obtained from the SA Vehicle Rental Association, PO Box 2940, Randburg 2125, tel. (011) 7892591, or from the nearest Satour office (see *Tourist information* in the *At a glance* section of each chapter). Satour's administrative headquarters are at 442 Rigel Avenue, Erasmusrand, Pretoria 0002, tel. (012) 3470600; and its national information headquarters is: The Tourist Rendezvous Travel Centre, Sammy Marks Complex, corner Prinsloo and Vermeulen streets, Pretoria 0002, tel. (012) 3231222.

Climate and clothing: The climate varies considerably throughout South Africa, but as a rule of thumb, dress lightly in summer, particularly in the central, northern, eastern and western parts of the country, and keep a jersey at hand in winter wherever you are. You'll need an umbrella for the Cape winters and the Transvaal and Natal summers. For a detailed report on climate see p. 11. Although some upmarket hotels prefer patrons to wear jacket and tie to cocktail bars and dining rooms, there is a more informal approach to dress along the coast and in the game parks. Trousers and an open-necked shirt are quite acceptable at hotels after dark, but this formality doesn't apply at the game reserves.

Communications: South Africa's postal and telecommunications services are run by two public companies: the South African Post Office Ltd (postal services), and Telkom Ltd (telecommunication services). Post offices are open from 08h30 to 16h30 Monday to Friday (most are closed between 13h00 and 14h00), and from 08h00 to midday on Saturdays. They supply all the basic postal services: telegrams, stamps, money orders, postal orders and facilities for saving or transferring money. If you intend travelling to the game reserves, get a good supply of stamps from a post office before you leave, as they may not be available in remoter areas. Service in South African post offices can be slow, and you may have to queue. Bright red, oval-shaped post boxes are positioned at post offices and throughout town and city suburbs. *Telephones:* Modern pay telephones have been installed recently at local post offices, and require a minimum deposit of 30c. These phones accept 10c, 20c, 50c or R1 coins, the amount dependent on the distance and length of your call. Card-operated pay phones are an innovation in South Africa. For details, contact the Telkom Information Centre, tel. 08000 12255, toll free. International calls can be made from most post offices, with direct dialling to many foreign countries. Telephone charges at hotels are up to three times the post office rate. *Telegrams:* All post office counters accept telegrams. A 24-hour cable service operates from the main Johannesburg and Cape Town post offices. *Facsimile:* Most of the larger hotels offer telex and facsimile facilities.

Consulates and embassies: Most Western nations, including Britain, the United States, Canada, Australia, Germany, Austria, France, Italy, Ireland, Holland, Norway, Denmark and Sweden have consular representation in South Africa in Pretoria, Cape Town and Durban. You can get their telephone numbers in the Yellow Pages, from your nearest travel agent, or the South African Tourism Board, 442 Rigel Avenue, Erasmusrand, Pretoria 0002, tel. (012) 3470600.

Crime and theft: South Africa has one of the highest per capita crime rates in the world. Crime in the urban areas, particularly in Johannesburg and the rest of Gauteng, has increased dramatically since 1990. Generally, it is unsafe to walk around the central business districts or suburbs of the big cities (Johannesburg, Pretoria, Cape Town, Durban, Port Elizabeth and East London) after sunset. And many areas are positively unsafe to drive into at any time. There has been an alarming increase in car hijackings (particularly in Gauteng; more than 700 cars were hijacked in January 1995 in Johannesburg), some of them in the middle of town. As a rule of thumb, keep your car doors locked at all times while driving, don't venture into poorer shopping or residential areas without prior advice, and speak to your concierge or local tourist office before embarking on city tours. In hotels make sure your valuables are kept in the hotel safe, and don't leave anything of value lying around. Try and secure under-cover parking for your vehicle (except in the game reserves).

Customs and entry regulations: Most foreign visitors need a valid passport to enter South Africa, but holiday-makers from the European Union, the United States, Canada, Australia, New Zealand, Singapore, Switzerland, Austria, Japan, the Republic of Ireland, Namibia, Brazil and Botswana do not need a visa. For convenience's sake it is best to apply for a multiple entry visa, which will enable you to re-enter South Africa from neighbouring countries such as Lesotho, Swaziland, Botswana and Zimbabwe, without reapplying for a visa.

Your nearest South African consular office will organise a visa for you, or write to the Director General, Home Affairs, Private Bag X114, Pretoria 0001, South

Africa (tel. (012) 3148891). On arrival in South Africa visitors are subject to clearance by customs officials. Those with nothing to declare are given quick clearance, subject to random checks. What you may bring in: unlimited amounts of foreign currency (preferably traveller's cheques), provided it is declared on arrival; R500 in local currency; new or used goods up to R500 in value; 2 litres of wine, 1 litre of spirits, 50 ml of perfume, 250 ml eau de toilette, 400 cigarettes, 50 cigars or 250 g of tobacco. Items you are going to use such as cameras, tape recorders, binoculars, sports equipment, clothes and jewellery are duty free.

You will be given a temporary residence permit on arrival in South Africa, which you will have to renew at the Department of Home Affairs if you intend staying longer than three months.

Driving in South Africa: *Licence:* A foreign driving licence will be accepted if it carries a photograph and signature of the holder and is printed in English (or accompanied by a letter of authentication, written in English by an embassy or other authority). Alternatively, you can take out an international driving licence before your departure.

The law: South African law requires motorists to drive on the left-hand side of the road, and to wear a seat belt at all times. The speed limit on highways (expressways) is 120 km/h, and in the urban areas 60 km/h. An excellent network of more than 200 000 km of roads (85 000 km tarred) covers South Africa. Most of the roads are well signposted in English and Afrikaans, serviced by top-quality petrol stations and offer resting or "pullover" points in the rural areas, where you can picnic in the shade of a tree and stretch your legs. If you are driving through remote country areas, particularly in the Eastern Cape, be on the lookout for domestic animals such as horses, donkeys, sheep and goats crossing the road, especially at night. If you intend travelling in what was known as the Transkei, check first on the condition of the roads – some may be unnavigable because of potholes or heavy rain.

Maps and books: The South African Tourism Board (Satour), or your local publicity association or visitors' information bureau (see *Tourist information* in the *At a glance* sections) will supply detailed maps and touring guides for most parts of South Africa.

Motoring problems: The Automobile Association (AA) of South Africa is a large motoring club that offers a variety of services to members – on the road and off. If you belong to an organisation affiliated to the AA of SA, such as the AIT (Alliance Internationale de Tourisme) or the FIA (Federation de l'Automobile) you qualify for help if you run into any sort of problems on the road, mechanical or otherwise. If you are not an affiliate member, you can take out local membership of the AA (minimum of one year) by telephoning Johannesburg (011) 4071000.

Emergencies: Need the police in a hurry? Phone 10111 – the national emergency number for the Flying Squad. The national emergency number for an ambulance is

10177. Emergency hospital, fire brigade, poison unit and sea rescue numbers appear in the front of your local telephone directory. Emergency toll-free phone booths have been erected alongside expressways on the fringes of the major urban areas.

First-aid kits: If you intend hiking, camping, caravanning or visiting one of the reserves in South Africa, a first-aid kit should be an indispensable part of your baggage. The kit should include: anti-malarial tablets, disinfectant (such as Savlon, mercurochrome or calamine lotion), an anti-diarrhoeal, such as Immodium, or an anti-dysentery treatment such as Flagyl, oral rehydration sachets, cotton wool roll, gauze roll, sterile dressings, bandages of different sizes, an effective antihistamine, a broad-spectrum antibiotic, an anti-spasmodic for stomach cramps and anti-snakebite serum.

When assembling your first-aid kit, bear in mind that stings and bites (from bees, wasps, bluebottles, ticks, spiders, scorpions and even snakes) are always possible.

Food and wine: South Africa's vast mix of cultures has resulted in a variety of traditional dishes from the different ethnic groups. Typical of the ethnic dishes are the excellent curries of Natal's Indian community, the bredies and boboties of the Cape's Malay community and the old Cape Dutch fare of meat-based dishes which includes lamb, beef, venison and even springbok. Chinese and Japanese restaurants provide an oriental culinary flavour to the major cities. A culinary institution in South Africa is the braai or barbecue, where various meats are cooked on a grill above hot coals, and served typically with the lovely white or red wines of the Cape. The South African braai is more than just a cooking process – it is an outdoor social event enjoyed by tens of thousands on summer weekends.

Game reserves and national parks: There are 17 national parks in South Africa, 11 of which are fully geared to provide tourists with most of the facilities for a comfortable stay. They are: the Kruger National Park, Kalahari Gemsbok National Park, Augrabies Falls National Park, West Coast National Park, Karoo National Park, Wilderness National Park, Tsitsikamma National Park, Addo Elephant National Park, Mountain Zebra National Park, Golden Gate Highlands National Park and the Bontebok National Park. All these national parks are open throughout the year, and you should book accommodation in advance.

To reserve accommodation in any of the national parks, contact the National Parks Board, PO Box 787, Pretoria 0001, tel. (012) 3431991, or PO Box 7400, Roggebaai 8012 (Cape Town), tel. (021) 222810.

The other major conservation body is the Natal Parks Board, which is responsible for 74 sanctuaries totalling 627 240 ha in KwaZulu/Natal. There are 23 rest camps in its reserves, providing 2 500 beds a night. There are a further 31 camping sites, capable of accommodating 10 000 people.

If you want any information on the Natal Parks Board, contact their Pietermaritzburg headquarters, PO Box 1750, Pietermaritzburg 3200, tel. (0331) 471981. Alternatively, contact any of the South African Tourism Board offices, see the relevant *At a glance* sections of the book.

The standard of the National Parks Board and Natal Parks Board reserves is exceptionally high, both in the accommodation facilities provided and in the amount of game to be seen. In recent years many of the camps have been upgraded or renovated, and new lodges and bush camps have been built to cater for the ever-increasing needs of tourists visiting the reserves.

Health care: Malaria poses a threat in some parts of South Africa (particularly in the Eastern Transvaal and northern KwaZulu/Natal), so if you intend visiting them you must take a course of anti-malaria pills. Start the course on the day of departure and continue taking the pills for 15 days after your return. Bilharzia is prevalent in some rivers and dams, so before you venture into the water check with your hotel, tour guide or visitors' information bureau to see if the area is bilharzia-free. If you're arriving from a yellow-fever zone, you will need a valid international yellow fever vaccination certificate. Sunburn is common in South Africa. Take preventive measures such as an effective sunscreen, a hat and vitamin A tablets if you intend being out in the sun for more than an hour in summer.

Hiking: South Africa has literally thousands of beautiful walks and hikes, ranging from half-hour strolls to two-week trails through rugged, mountainous regions. For your own safety – and security – do not hike alone. Before setting out on a hike, establish what the likely weather conditions will be, make sure you have a reliable map of the area, and let someone know where you are going, and when you will be returning.

Hitchhiking: The South African police often warn against hitchhiking and picking up hitchhikers. If you have to hitchhike, don't do it alone. If you're driving alone, don't pick up hitchhikers.

Languages: There are 11 official languages in South Africa: English, Afrikaans, Zulu, Xhosa, Venda, Swazi, North Sotho, South Sotho, Tswana, Sindebele and Shangaan. English is the one language common to most language groups, and most South Africans will understand you if you converse with them in English. The principal black languages are Zulu and Xhosa, which are very similar. There are six Asian languages. Afrikaans is spoken by about 60 per cent of the white population, and the majority of the 3,25 million people of mixed descent. English is the first language of just under 40 per cent of the whites and an increasing number of Asians.

If you're travelling by car through South Africa, useful Xhosa phrases are: hello

– molo; how are you – kunjani; I need petrol – ndifuna ipetroli; where is the nearest hotel? – iphi ihotele?; thank you – enkosi; goodbye – sala kakuhle. Common Afrikaans words and phrases are: good morning – goeiemore; good afternoon – goeiemiddag; good night – goeienag; please – asseblief; thank you – dankie; what is the time? – hoe laat is dit?; how much is it? – hoeveel kos dit? If you're on the road watch for these Afrikaans signs: gevaar – danger; stadig – slow; verminder spoed – reduce speed.

Liquor and licensing laws: Most liquor retailers are open between 08h00 and 20h00 on weekdays, and between 08h00 and 17h00 on Saturdays. They are closed on Sundays, but may open on public holidays that are not religious holidays. Bars open at 10h00 and usually close at 23h00, although some nightclubs and bars in the larger cities stay open until 02h00.

Some restaurants are fully licensed, enabling them to sell spirits, wine and beer; others are licenced to sell only wine and beer; others are not licenced at all. If your intended restaurant is unlicenced you may take along your own drinks. Some licenced restaurants allow you to bring your own wine, but charge a corkage fee. Check beforehand.

Money matters: *Currency:* The official unit of currency is the rand (symbol: R), divided into 100 cents (symbol: c). Coins are available in 1c, 2c, 5c, 10c, 20c, 50c, R1, R2 and R5 denominations; notes are available in denominations of R5 (being phased out), R10, R20, R50, R100 and R200. Watch out for the similarity between the new R2,00 coin and the old 20c piece, the old 50c piece and the R5,00 coin. *Banking hours:* Most banks are open between 09h00 and 15h30 on weekdays, and between 08h30 and 11h00 on Saturday mornings. Some banks in the smaller towns close between 12h45 and 14h00 during the week. *Credit cards and traveller's cheques:* Some, but not all, credit cards are accepted locally, so check before you intend using one. All commercial banks, most hotels and many shops will accept traveller's cheques, provided they are in a currency accepted in South Africa. *Taxes:* From 7 April 1993, the rate of Value Added Tax was raised from 10 to 14 per cent on most commodities, with the exception of some basic foodstuffs, such as brown bread, maize-meal and samp. The advertised or labelled price of a commodity is the price you pay.

Newspapers, periodicals and magazines: The most widely read Sunday newspaper is the *Sunday Times,* with more than half a million readers. The Afrikaans Sunday equivalent is *Rapport.* The top daily newspapers in South Africa are: Johannesburg – *The Sowetan, City Press* (both African), *The Star, Beeld* (Afrikaans) and *The Citizen;* Durban – *The Daily News* and *The Natal Mercury;* Port Elizabeth – *The Eastern Province Herald, Evening Post* and

Oosterlig (Afrikaans); Cape Town – *The Cape Times, Die Burger* (Afrikaans) and *The Argus*.

Public holidays: New Year's Day (1 January); Human Rights Day (21 March); Good Friday (March or April); Family Day (the Monday following Good Friday); Constitution Day (27 April); Workers' Day (1 May); Youth Day (16 June); National Women's Day (9 August); Heritage Day (24 September); Day of Reconciliation (16 December); Christmas Day (25 December); Day of Goodwill (26 December). In the Western Cape 2 January is regarded as a holiday. When a public holiday falls on a Sunday, the Monday following is taken as a holiday.

Road signs: South Africa's road signs are explained in an excellent booklet called *Pass Your Learner's Easily,* available at most bookshops.

Shopping: Normal trading hours for most shops are between 08h30 and 17h00 (weekdays) and between 08h30 and 13h00 on Saturdays. However, many super-markets and speciality shops in the larger shopping centres are open till late during the week, and stay open on Saturdays and Sundays as well. The central business districts and the suburbs of the major cities offer modern, secure shopping complexes on a par with others in the Western world. Top names in South Africa's retail world are Woolworths, Stuttafords, Garlicks, Edgars, Pick 'n Pay, OK Bazaars, Checkers and CNA (Central News Agency).

Telephones: South Africa's largely automatic telephone network is efficient and reliable, and numbers in most cities and towns here and abroad can be dialled direct. The front sections of local telephone directories carry numbers to dial for international and local enquiries, emergencies and the time. To obtain a number anywhere in the country, dial the telephone enquiry service on 1023. For details of costs see *Communications* above.

Time differences: South Africa is two hours ahead of Greenwich Mean Time.

Tipping: South Africans are not as generous in their tipping habits as their European, British or American counterparts. The following is a guide: waiters, bar-men, tour guides, taxi drivers 10 per cent; petrol pump attendants R2 per fill-up and oil check; porters R2 per bag.

Toilets: City centres, parks, beaches, cinemas, theatres and amusement centres all have well-signposted public toilets, sometimes manned by an overseer. For hygien-ic reasons, however, it is probably better to use the toilet facilities of hotels or restaurants.

Tourist information offices: The South African Tourism Board (Satour) has 12 offices in South Africa that will put you in touch with just about anything you want to know about touring the country. For addresses and telephone numbers of your nearest Satour office, look under *Tourist information* in the *At a glance* sections of each chapter. Alternatively, contact Satour's information headquarters in Pretoria at the Tourist Rendezvous Travel Centre, Sammy Marks Complex, corner Prinsloo and Vermeulen streets, Pretoria 0002, tel. (012) 3231222. Alternatively contact the nearest publicity association or visitors' information bureau (there are more than 50 such associations in South Africa) through your local telephone directory. Most of these bureaux display the internationally recognised symbol for information – a green-and-white "i". The telephone numbers of the other major tourism information centres are: Johannesburg Publicity Association, (011) 3364961/3376650; Durban Unlimited, (031) 3044934; Cape Tourism Authority (Captour – Cape Town), (021) 4185214.

Transport: *Buses:* During the week daytime bus services in most cities are regular and punctual, but don't rely on a regular service at night or on weekends. *Taxis:* Unlike New York and London, taxis or "cabs" in most South African cities do not cruise the streets, but wait at ranks to be called (consult the Yellow Pages for the telephone numbers of registered operators, or ask your porter or concierge to call one for you). The cheaper option is to travel by minibus taxi, but they're often packed to capacity, cramped and sometimes quite hair-raising to travel in.

Water: In general, the quality of water in South Africa is good, but if you're really off the beaten track and the water is suspect, take along your own bottled water as a precaution against diarrhoea (see *First-aid kit* above).

INDEX

Photograph credits

Anthony Bannister, ABPL: 132
Duncan Butchart, African Images: 6, 8, 48, 50, 68, 80, 108, 111, 121, 122, 129, 131, 134, 137, 141, 142, 143
Sarah Coronaios, ABPL: 120
Roger de la Harpe, ABPL: 86, 99, 101
Nigel Dennis, ABPL: 94
Richard du Toit, ABPL: 59, 130
Robert Frost, Johannesburg City Council: 112
Dave Hamman, ABPL: 133
Eric Hosten, Landmarks: 4, 75
Beverly Joubert, ABPL: front cover
Doug Larsson, Landmarks: 73, 79
Jay Matthews, Landmarks: 62, 74, 78
Ivor Migdoll: 5, 9, 24, 26, 27, 35, 43, 44, 51, 52, 87, 88, 89, 91, 104, 146
Tim O'Hagan: 3, 21, 31, 81
Beth Peterson, African Images: 22, 49, 53, 65, 67, 82, 92, 93, 97, 136, back cover
Peter Ribton: 7, 15, 28, 47, 55, 60
Brendan Ryan, ABPL: 119, 144, 147
Lorna Stanton, ABPL: 110
Guy Stubbs, ABPL: 115
Sun International: 76, 83, 123, 124, 125, 126, 127
Mark Tennant, African Images: 90, 95, 96, 105
Lisa Trocchi, ABPL: 117
Mark van Aardt, Photographic Enterprises: 1, 2, 10, 11, 12, 13, 14, 16, 17, 18, 19, 20, 23, 25, 29, 30, 33, 34, 36, 37, 39, 40, 42, 45, 46, 54, 56, 57, 61, 63, 64, 66, 69, 71, 72, 77, 84, 85, 98, 100, 102, 103, 106, 107, 116, 118, 128, 135, 138, 139, 140, 145
Hein van Horsten, ABPL: 32, 38, 41, 58, 109,
Solly van Staden, Johannesburg City Council: 113, 114
Tris Wooldridge, Landmarks: 70